"Ada Ferrer's remarkable *Keeper of My Kin* is one of those memoirs you don't just read, but one that you feel in your bones. It's both a fearless excavation of the past and a bold, compassionate attempt to understand the difficult choices embedded, sometimes buried, within every immigration story. I loved this book."

—Daniel Alarcón, executive producer of Radio Ambulante and author of *The King Is Always Above the People*

"A gripping family memoir, *Keeper of My Kin* explores fraught relationships and secret pasts against the backdrop of big history. Here, Ada Ferrer, the 'historian daughter' and descendant of an enslaved Black maternal ancestor, tells the truths of her kin with an aching tenderness, revealing the traumas that come with the package of racism, war, revolution, and migration. In an intimate story lovingly told, memory, history, and emotional honesty combine in a beautiful act of retrieval."

—Tiya Miles, author of *All That She Carried: The Journey of Ashley's Sack, a Black Family Keepsake*

"The Ferrer family will forever stay with you for theirs is the story of all Cubans in the last seven decades. If you read this tender and brilliant book as I did—drying tears and holding my breath—it'll be yours to cherish as well. A triumphant memoir of love and loss."

—Mirta Ojito, author of *Finding Mañana: A Memoir of a Cuban Exodus*

"'What country, friends, is this?' asks Viola, washed ashore in Illyria at the beginning of *Twelfth Night*. Here, another island, Cuba, and the shores of America; another wine-dark, enclosed, estranging sea; other odysseys. Ferrer has written a history that is also myth: of those left behind, lost brothers, found families, old and new lives. *Keeper of My Kin* is exhilarating to read; I loved it; I loved knowing more about all the departures and returns, the losses and reparations, that have made the modern world."

—Carolyn Steedman, author of *Landscape for a Good Woman*

# Keeper of My Kin

## Memoir of an Immigrant Daughter

**Ada Ferrer**

SCRIBNER

New York   Amsterdam/Antwerp   London
Toronto   Sydney/Melbourne   New Delhi

Scribner
An Imprint of Simon & Schuster, LLC
1230 Avenue of the Americas
New York, NY 10020



First Scribner hardcover edition May 2026

SCRIBNER and design are registered trademarks of Simon & Schuster, LLC

Simon & Schuster strongly believes in freedom of expression and stands against censorship in all its forms. For more information, visit BooksBelong.com.

For information about special discounts for bulk purchases, please contact Simon & Schuster Special Sales at 1-866-506-1949 or business@simonandschuster.com.

The Simon & Schuster Speakers Bureau can bring authors to your live event. For more information or to book an event, contact the Simon & Schuster Speakers Bureau at 1-866-248-3049 or visit our website at www.simonspeakers.com.

INTERIOR DESIGN BY KARLA SCHWEER

Manufactured in the United States of America

10 9 8 7 6 5 4 3 2 1

Library of Congress Control Number: 2026934743

ISBN 978-1-6680-2565-9
ISBN 978-1-6680-2567-3 (ebook)

Scan here to get book recommendations, exclusive offers, and more delivered to your inbox.

For my daughters, Alina and Lucía,
with a love beyond measure

# Contents

Contents

Contents

# Three Notes to the Reader

In deference to the privacy of others, I have changed some names that appear in this book.

As a historian, I have used archival and other primary sources to help me reconstruct the worlds that my family inhabited. For many events in my lifetime, I have also relied on my own memory. But memory is a strange and fallible thing. I realize that other family members may remember events or people differently. When I am aware of such a difference, I point it out, trying to be as faithful and responsible to our family story as possible. Any remaining errors are, of course, my own.

It is important for me to comment on the question of language and translation. I have written this book in English, which though not my first language chronologically has long been my first language in a more practical sense. A lot of what appears here, however, did not unfold in English, or only in English. Most of the people portrayed in this book—my parents, my brothers, my grandparents, my aunts and uncles, and many other relatives—did not speak, write, or think in English but in Spanish. Their words appear here in English only because I have translated them. Occasionally, I retain short phrases and words in the original Spanish. While this book cannot convey exactly the bilingual rhythm in which it was lived, I think it is appropriate to give the reader a small taste of the linguistic shifting back and forth that is often the soundtrack to immigrant life. The consequences of migration are many. One is that people often have to live the intimacy of family across multiple languages, the burden (and privilege) of translation falling usually to the children.

# In My Mother's Arms

**My mother always loved** to hold me in her arms. When I was a young girl, or decades later when I myself was already a mother, and even after that when I was in my fifties and helping to care for her as she lay dying, she used to put her arm around my shoulder to pull my head in close. Or she'd take my hand in hers and bring it to her lips. Then she'd look at me and say always the same thing. *Cómo pasamos trabajo tú y yo.* How we struggled, you and I.

I was only ten months old when it happened. So I can conjure our story here, to begin, only through my mother's eyes as she saw it all transpire, only through her voice as she remembered and narrated the events over the years and decades that followed.

The first scene unfolds in Havana's international airport in April 1963. By then, Fidel Castro had been in power for four years. He had already declared the revolution socialist; a US invasion against his government had failed; and the superpowers had recently brought the world to the brink of Armageddon during the Cuban Missile Crisis. The events are well known; they are the stuff of history.

But all that is background, not the story as my mother told and retold it.

We were leaving Cuba to join my father in the United States. He had been there for about a year, having left when my mother was seven months pregnant with me. My mother was so nervous at the airport, she always told me. She had never flown before, never left the island, never seen a city other than Havana, which was majestic. She wore a skirt (or maybe it was a dress?) and high heels. She always wore heels for important occasions. We had no stroller, so she carried me in her arms, which she always loved to do. She was leaving her country and her people, and she had no idea how long the separation would last.

The immigration line went smoothly. At customs, officials closely inspected everyone's bags. One could not leave the country with more than $5 and thirty pounds of luggage, but our things weighed even less than that. My mother watched officials confiscate items from other passengers, and she stiffened when a woman in uniform approached us. The officer had noticed my tiny gold post earrings, a gift from my grandmother at birth. The woman put her fingers to the soft skin of my earlobe. Everyone knows that the feel of a baby's earlobe is intoxicating. She was about to take the little studs from my ears, but at the last minute changed her mind and let them be.

That was how we left Cuba together: my mother almost in tears, her narrow feet wedged into stiletto heels, and me, wearing my grandmother's blessing on my ears, feeling heavier and heavier on my mother's hip as the irreversible journey unfolded.

There were no direct flights to the United States. Commercial travel between the two countries had been forbidden since the Missile Crisis. So we flew not to New York, where my father awaited, but to Mexico City. My parents expected that the US Consulate there would grant my mother and me visas to enter the United States, that other America that was not ours. Our flight landed in Mexico City early in the afternoon. By my mother's count, there were some sixty Soviet passengers on our flight, and Mexican authorities processed those arrivals first. We didn't make it through immigration and customs until about 5 p.m. The people who were supposed to pick us up—relatives of her sister's husband—had already left, tired of waiting. My mother was traveling with proof of a wire transfer from my father, which she was to take to a bank branch inside the airport. But because the hour was late, the office was closed. Penniless, hungry, and exhausted, she sat down with me on a bench and began to cry. A man approached and asked her what was wrong. I don't know if she hesitated before speaking, if she wondered at his accent, which before that moment she had only ever heard in the Mexican movies she always loved. But she told him her story, our story. He got her something to eat, gave her the cash amount of the transfer, and then traveled with us in a taxi to the home of the family that was supposed to pick us up.

That was one of the parts of the story my mother used to tell me when she'd take my hand, or put her arm around me, and say, *cómo pasamos trabajo tú y yo*. How we struggled, you and I. Painful heels, no money, alone with a baby, everything unfamiliar, forced to distinguish within seconds between strangers who posed threats and others who might help. In her telling, though, she always paused to wish that Mexican stranger at the airport all the health and happiness in the world.

In Mexico City, did my mother look around in awe, noting the limestone fountains, the diners at sidewalk cafés, the poplars in the golden light? Within days of arriving, she had me confirmed in the city's most important church, the famous Metropolitan Cathedral, some of it built centuries earlier on the site of an old Aztec temple demolished to make room for a new order. I don't know how my mother met the woman who served as my godmother, Concepción. For a time, we lived with her in the middle-class neighborhood called Roma. At 4:30 p.m. on my first birthday, my mother took me on a boat ride in the lake of beautiful Chapultepec Park. She saved the ticket and years later tucked it in my bible.

Every week my father sent money from New York to cover our room and board. He was also collecting paperwork for our visas. (Recently, because I love to document my parents' memories, I discovered that our visa applications included a letter from his employer in Brooklyn, the Stelber Cycle Corporation, then the largest bicycle manufacturer in the country, where he worked as a punch press operator earning $48 a week. A letter from Ros Sportswear, a garment factory in East—then called Spanish—Harlem, promised my mother a job as a machine operator for $60 weekly.) It worked; the US Consulate issued our visas on June 28, 1963, almost exactly two months after our arrival in Mexico. Then on July 1, my mother boarded an airplane for the second time in her life. I traveled in her arms. A few hours later we landed in Miami.

My father did not meet us there. Maybe he couldn't get off work;

maybe he didn't have the money for another ticket. From the Miami airport, we somehow made it to the downtown building now known as the Freedom Tower, the elegant 1920s Spanish-style structure where most Cuban refugees were processed on their arrival in the United States. There, my mother ran into an old acquaintance, Bebo Zamora. For Cubans who arrived in Miami with no place to stay—which was our case—the staff at the Refugee Center issued vouchers for local hotels. This was 1963. The US South was still segregated, and Miami was a southern city. That meant that newcomers were assigned to hotels by race. Someone, perhaps Bebo, assigned my mother—who in Cuba was widely considered *mulata*—to a white hotel. She later told me that all the Cubans, regardless of how they might have been perceived in Cuba, were assigned to white hotels, except for one very dark man traveling alone.

My mother and I stayed at the hotel for three nights. Because there was no refrigerator in the room, she had to wake up early and go out by herself to buy my morning milk before I woke up. She did so quickly, rushing back, worried that she'd find me already awake and crying. But when she returned with the milk, she always found me sleeping. My mother needed me to be good, and so I was.

We finally landed in New York City on July 4. My father picked us up at the airport. When I saw him, I opened my arms to him as if I already knew him, even though I had never met him before. When my mother told that part of the story, she always repeated the scene of my first meeting with my father, as if to make sure that the listener understood how momentous that was, how proud she was of me.

I can picture the scene of our arrival: my mother unable to contain her joy, her arm around my father's shoulders as he held me aloft seeking recognition in my eyes, both of them oblivious to the passengers streaming around either side of us, like water parting around an island. Had there been a large plateglass window there, had the light been just right, the three of us together might have cast a single shadow, shaped something like a heart. There we were: an immovable trio, my mother's little family.

In the most consequential event of her life, I was my mother's companion. And if I close my eyes, I can see her eyes on mine, feel her fingers curled around my arm squeezing, hear the lilting sound of her voice as she tells our story again and again.


In all that storytelling, however, my mother failed to mention perhaps the most important thing about our journey: that when we left Cuba, she left behind a son. We left behind my brother.

His name was Poly. He was her almost nine-and-a-half-year-old son from her first marriage. My mother didn't want to leave him; she didn't want to take one child and not the other. But Poly's father refused to grant permission for him to go with us. Everyone in the family begged him to relent before our departure, to no avail. My mother, her sisters, and her mother all believed that once we were gone Poly's father would relent and my brother would join us maybe in a matter of months, perhaps a year, two at the very most. Besides, like many people at the time, they did not expect Fidel Castro's government to survive much longer. In the midst of the Cold War, they assumed the United States would make sure that it didn't. None of it—not the revolution, not our migration, not Poly's abandonment—would ever be permanent, they trusted.

I am not sure why my mother left Poly out of the story she told and retold so many times. His existence was not a secret. There was never a time when I didn't know that I had a brother in Cuba. As a little girl, I posed for pictures to send him. My mother bought presents for him. In one of her drawers or high on a closet shelf, I could always see the stash of items she was saving to send him. Sometimes, she bought things for me in his name, as if they were gifts from him. One such present was a doll I named Caté, because that was my nickname for Poly.

I still have it somewhere, wearing a faded black-and-white-striped shirt, the red tie at the top mostly gone, the doll's bottom full of ink-edged pen holes from improvised injections when I played doctor as a little girl. Very occasionally, because calls between the two countries were difficult, I talked to Poly on the phone; I wrote him notes at the bottom of my mother's letters to him. When his letters arrived, my mother often read parts of them aloud to me and my younger sister, Aixa, born in Brooklyn. Sometimes I copied Poly's handwriting because I thought it looked cool. And almost all my life, atop my mother's dresser, no matter when and where we moved, was the framed eight-by-ten-inch portrait of Poly, taken in a studio and touched up so that it looked like he was wearing a little bit of makeup. I sometimes used to kiss it, my lips covering his whole face.

I cannot remember when I learned another part of the story of our departure from Cuba. I was older, possibly in high school, maybe in college. It might even have been later, when I was in graduate school and made my first trip back to Cuba. I think I learned it from my mother, but it might have been from my aunt, whose name is Ada, too, and who died in Cuba. It's funny how I've blocked it out. Whatever the details about how I came by the revelation, it was this: that when we left Cuba in 1963, my mother did not tell Poly we were going. We left behind his back. She never said goodbye. Learning that crushed me a little and confused me. It still haunts me. I never told that part of the story to my own daughters, who adored their grandmother. They learned it only when I published an essay about it after she had already died.

Not long before she turned ninety-three, my mother revealed another little piece of the story. She was in the hospital in Miami Beach then, recovering from surgery, one of two that year. Her room in the new wing of the hospital had a plateglass window the size of the wall overlooking the bay, the boats and bridges, the skyscrapers on the mainland. I was editing a chapter about Cuban migration to the United States for a book I was writing, working on the little couch that at night we turned into a bed so that my sister or I could stay with her. I rose to stretch, walked over to her, kissed her on the forehead, and sat down on the bed at her side. "Tell me something about when we left Cuba," I said. She was used to that kind of question from me. She was my beloved mother, and my favorite source.

Her speech was faint, raspy. The tube used for the surgery was out, but her voice had not yet recovered. *Salimos a las seis de la tarde*, she whispered. We left at six in the evening. I leaned in closer to hear her better. I could tell this was something she had never told me before. She repeated the statement: simple, direct, indicative mood. But I wasn't sure I understood. "Our flight left at six?" I asked.

"No," she clarified, "we left the house at six in the evening. Poly was outside playing with friends." We headed first to an aunt's house, then in the morning to the airport. She had to do it that way so that Poly wouldn't see us go, she explained.

I am not sure why these new details hit me like a gut punch. Maybe it was because they painted a scene for me: of my mother plotting the moment of our departure, of my grandmother and aunts colluding to make sure that Poly wouldn't find out until after we were gone, of my brother playing innocently, completely unaware of how that simple, ordinary moment concealed a cataclysm. I think my mother's new revelation shook me because I heard her words as if they were the opening lines of a book. "We left the house at six in the evening. Poly was outside playing with friends."

My mother was a storyteller, and those were a storyteller's lines. She was giving them to me before she died, because she knew by then, as I did, that I was always going to write this book.

My mother left me an archive from which to write. Some of it I knew was there all along, in the one-bedroom apartment in Miami Beach where she lived the last two decades of her life with my father. There were the dozen-plus photo albums; the short stacks of old immunization records; the boxes with years' worth of Mother's Day cards, the oldest made in school of construction paper, the newer ones purchased from the Spanish greeting card sections of CVS or Walgreens. Even my mother's bible was an archive, inked with her marginalia, stuffed with little pieces of paper: a handwritten love note from my father; a funeral card from the death of her sister Lucrecia, the only one of her eleven siblings to follow her to the United States; a list of prizes garnered by my second book; a pamphlet for the porcine valve a surgeon once placed in her heart.

After she died in 2020, and then after my father passed two years later at the age of 101, when I could rifle through their closets and drawers without agitating him, I discovered many other things: bags, boxes, and briefcases full of treasures and trifles. In a clear Sterilite storage box, six-quart capacity, high in my mother's closet, there were more than a hundred letters written across the gulf of our separation, all still in their original airmail envelopes, old stamps intact. I was alone in my parents' apartment when I first found them. I opened one right away and saw the date of May 4, 1963, just days after my mother and I left Cuba. The handwriting was that of a boy, my brother. I remember talking to myself as I realized what I had before me. I uttered involuntary no's, sighed, "Oh my God," then, finally, I looked up at the ceiling and like a prayer said, "Thank you, Mami." For this story that I always knew I would need to write, my mother bequeathed to me the primary sources. As with the lines she once gave me from a hospital bed, she was granting me permission to do what I do. That, anyway, is what I tell myself.

My father left me his own archive, as well. Stacks and stacks of papers written in his own firm and loopy hand, most of it on lined three-hole paper. He took to writing late in life, and as he aged through his seventies, his eighties, his nineties, and as we all saw the piles of paper get taller and messier, I would always tell him, my mother, and the caregivers we eventually had to hire not to get rid of any of it. "Those papers are mine," I would say, and no one threw them away. Their sheer volume surprised me. There weren't just the papers he kept out in the open, unruly in stacks behind his armchair. There was so much more, stuffed into a briefcase that wouldn't close and into plastic grocery bags hanging from hooks behind the clothes in his closet as if hidden. Among them were letters, not dozens as in my mother's case, but hundreds. And if my mother's letters documented a family rupture I had known about all my life, my father's letters revealed a story that was never part of my childhood. They materialized an absence I didn't know existed until I was a grown woman.

I moved my parents' papers to New York City, where I lived at the time. But it took me months and months to tackle this archive that I knew would be mine even before I realized it existed. My home study was in my daughter Alina's old room. I laid out and sorted the documents on her bed, the diamond-shaped panels on the quilt disappearing one by one under the multiplying piles of paper. I separated the letters from the envelopes, which I now regret. I ordered acid-free sleeves, folders, and archival boxes, and then labeled everything. Eventually, with nothing left to organize, I began to read—always in short spurts, because I didn't just read them, I inhaled them. And sometimes it was too much.

I went to other archives, too, more traditional ones. I pored over baptismal records from remote Cuban towns; I puzzled over conflicting court documents and requested police records; I scoured photographs and lists in national archives. I filed requests under the Freedom of Information Act to retrieve my family's immigration files.

Yet even as I did all that, I knew it would never be enough. Research will never answer all the questions I have. It will not let me live this story through my brother's eyes or through my mother's, which is what I most want. I cannot walk in my grandmother's favorite sandals, brown with white stitching, and see the scene of separation unfolding as she saw it. I cannot know what she felt as an old woman left to pick up the pieces, sleeping with Poly to help ease his pain, his head nestled on her shoulder, his hair grazing the bottom of her chin. I will never see what my parents saw when they first arrived in New York City, what they made of it all, what it felt like as they reinvented themselves amid an unfamiliar language on unknown land. Neither can I reconstruct everyone's rapidly accumulating, swiftly disappearing every-days: the fleeting thought, the recurring memory, the fear, the resentment, the longing, the guilt, and the love of a ruptured family. But I imagine that I can feel some of it, perhaps the love above all.

I write then with what I have—with my family's papers and other papers, with my own memories and all the many questions for which I will never have answers. I write as the girl whose mother loved to hold her in her arms, the girl who was brought to a new life while her brother was left behind. I write as the strange daughter who loves to document her parents' memories. But I write, above all, as the woman our story made. Because I know as sure as I know my mother's touch, as sure as my daughters know mine, that *this* story—in all it contains, in all it cannot—is the story that has made me.

For more than thirty-five years, I have devoted myself to studying Cuba's past. I have traveled to the island regularly to visit family and to visit archives and libraries. I teach Cuban history; I write books about it. I have even won prizes for them. Yet I recognize that the decision to focus my life's work on Cuba has always been a kind of penance for being the chosen one that long-ago spring day of 1963. I became who I am to redress the balance. I write to make amends.

Now, with almost everyone in our story gone, I find that I must tell this story, a chronicle of a family broken by history and made by it, too. Here, I nestle my kin together on the same pages. Here, I write because I can and they can't. I bear witness to something that would otherwise be completely forgotten: unnoticed, untold lives lived on the margins of history. Those lives belong to my family, yes. But I know that—whether in this place or elsewhere, in this moment or another—the story told here can belong to so many of us.

# PART I

# Origin Memories

# ONE

# Rita, Mother of Our Mother

**My mother always told** me that my grandmother adored me. She gave me the little gold studs that nurses pierced my ears with at birth, as was the custom. She buried my very first nail clippings under a rosebush so that I might be smart, creative, perhaps a good singer. After she learned that I would be leaving the island, she gave me little tastes of very sweet Cuban coffee on the tips of teaspoons so that I would remember where I was from. As a parting gift, she embroidered a white handkerchief for me that I still have. I look at it many times a day, framed over my writing desk like an altar. And after we left, she made something of an altar for me, saving my toys and even buying me new ones on important dates, so that

I would find them waiting on my return, she said. For decades, I have used her name as passwords and handles on extra social media accounts and the online card games I sometimes use to procrastinate. If I were a spy, Rita Blanco would be my code name.

Rita was almost seventy-six when she saw my mother and me leave Cuba without Poly. By then, she had long ago lost her own parents. She had raised eleven children, losing a twelfth when he was still a little boy. She had forty-five grandchildren and an exponentially greater number of great-grandchildren. When my mother entrusted Poly to her care in 1963, my grandmother had seen and felt enough to know in her bones that life could surprise in ways that wounded.

For decades, I searched for Rita in the archives where I did my research. But I didn't find her until after I began writing this book. The sources I encountered revealed things no one in my extended family knew. Armed with this new knowledge of the ancestors who made her, combining that with what I already knew about the family she brought into this world, I can see on a much more personal level what I already knew as a historian. In Cuba, as in other places forged in the crucible of slavery and colonialism, there were always families whose members might find themselves on either side of the color line. And that color line could shift as imperceptibly as the length gained by a ten-month-old baby day by day or as abruptly as disembarking from a plane just landed in a different country.

Today, the only record of my grandmother's birth survives in the sacramental books of a beautiful small-town church called San Joaquín. Built in 1835, it sits high on a hill overlooking the town of San Luis, in far western Cuba. During the Cuban War of Independence, Spanish soldiers used the church's tower to send signals by using mirrors to reflect the sun's light. In normal times, the steeple towered over some of the lushest tobacco country in the world. Known as Vuelta Abajo, the region boasted vast expanses of rich green tobacco leaf that dominated the landscape like "mantles of emerald," in the words of a book published the year of my grandmother's birth. To the north, the terrain was hillier, leading to the strange and steep flat-topped hills called *mogotes*, and beyond them to the mountains my grandmother might have pondered on the horizon as a young girl. About ten miles in the opposite direction was the Caribbean Sea.

Before civil authorities recorded births, deaths, and marriages, the sacramental books kept by churches were the principal means by which such events were documented. As was the norm in all Spanish colonies, church officials recorded the sacraments of their parishioners in books divided by race. Records of the baptisms, marriages, and deaths of white congregants were logged in books for whites. Parishioners of African descent, meanwhile, appear in the books for *pardos* and *morenos*. The word *pardo* literally means brown, like the brown of a bearskin, a dictionary tells me, or of soil, a brown hinting of red, like the land on which Cuban tobacco flourished. But in Cuba, as in many Spanish colonies, it was also the word used to designate someone of mixed African and European ancestry. People believed that it softened the label *mulato*, just as *moreno* served as a more polite version of *negro*, especially when the people in question were free rather than enslaved.

In the church of San Luis, my grandmother's baptism appears in Book 4 of Baptisms of Pardos and Morenos. The brief handwritten entry indicates that she was born Rita Blanco García, not on May 22, 1887, as my mother had always said, but instead at 4 a.m. on June 2, 1887. Archival records and family memory are both full of inconsistencies like that.

Rita's baptismal record identified her father as Juan Blanco, a skilled artisan who made shoes by hand from new leather, an occupation that people of the time distinguished from that of a cobbler, who merely repaired

Sacramental books in a Cuban church, photo by David LaFevor.

shoes. The priest who baptized Juan shortly after his own birth in 1868 did not identify Juan's father, writing only *padre desconocido* (father unknown) in the record. But he did identify Juan's mother as Secundina Blanco, a *parda ingenua*. The first word referred to her color—brown, mixed race. The second term—*ingenua*—refers to her status as a free person born to free parents. Thus in this family of color, my grandmother's paternal line, the connection to slavery had been severed at least two generations before my grandmother's birth.

Rita's mother was Isabel García. That is the name my mother always relayed when she told me that Isabel was as far back as she could trace her mother's family. The church books confirmed that Rita's mother was the *parda* Isabel García, but they also allowed me to reach further back in our family history. According to Rita's baptismal record, Isabel's mother was the free *parda* Inés García, native of San Luis. Soon after discovering that, I received an unexpected message from a match on 23andMe. This long-lost relative is, like me, a great-great-grandchild of Inés García, and he had information about the family going back even further than that. Inés's mother, he told me, was a woman named Encarnación. It rang a bell. I went back to my notes from the Cuban National Archives, and there they were, listed in the original returns from an 1886 census: a household in San Luis that included, among others, Isabel García (my grandmother's mother); Inés García, born around 1845; and Encarnación García, eighty years old and the matriarch of the clan.

Encarnación García, sometimes called Encarnación Carabalí in the sacramental records, was born in Africa probably sometime around 1800 or 1810. That in Cuba she was referred to as Carabalí meant that she was from the West Central coast of Africa, an area where frequent raids provided a steady stream of captives to the slave-trade forts on the coast. There is no way to know when the woman who in Cuba came to be called Encarnación was captured, taken to the coast, loaded onto a slaver, and shipped across the Atlantic. In Cuba, she gave birth to a boy she named Epifanio. He appears to be her first child born on the island, but whether she had children in Africa before her capture is impossible to know. Epifanio, by virtue of Encarnación's status, was born into slavery, the records confirm. More children followed: a daughter Matilde born in 1848, Lucía in 1849, María del Pilar in 1851, and Raimundo Enrique in 1852, all of them born into slavery. In 1851, Encarnación buried an enslaved son named José, for whom we have no birth record. Around 1845, Encarnación gave birth to a girl named Inés, my grandmother's grandmother, enslaved like her mother and siblings. Yet by 1861, Encarnación had managed to secure her own freedom and that of some of her children. In that year's census she appears as a free woman living with several of her daughters—Inés among them—also now free.

Encarnación died in 1887, just two months before my grandmother's birth. Had Encarnación lived a little longer, maybe my grandmother would have someday spoken of a great-grandmother whom she met but could not remember. The parish priest at the San Joaquín Church in San Luis recorded Encarnación's burial in the Book of Deaths for Pardos and Morenos, where he wrote that the *morena* Encarnación, single, ninety-five years old, of the Carabalí nation died on March 27, 1887, of heart failure. He probably exaggerated her age. On the margin of the entry, the priest added a single word: *Pobre*. Poor. So few lines to sum up a life on two sides of the Atlantic.

Encarnación. Secundina. Inés. These are ancestors whose names I am only now learning. And for now, and likely always, they will be nothing but names to me, barely legible in old books full of worm-eaten pages. But the history in which their lives unfolded has been an object of my inquiry for decades. Slavery in their region of Cuba was not the large-scale plantation slavery that readers envision when they think of cotton and sugar. A majority of enslaved workers lived on much smaller tobacco farms. It is impossible for me to know what work Encarnación or her children did in slavery and freedom. Maybe Encarnación or Inés or Isabel worked in the house as a cook, or wet nurse, or laundress. Maybe they helped harvest the tobacco, their fingers checking leaves for worms and ants.

Whatever work they might have done, by the time my own grandmother was born in the spring of 1887, slavery had ended less than a year earlier on October 7, 1886. My grandmother, then, came into that world at a moment of great promise. The more than four-hundred-year-old institution of slavery was dead, and people who had been enslaved struggled mightily to give meaning to their freedom. Couples formalized their unions in churches, and women withdrew their labor from the

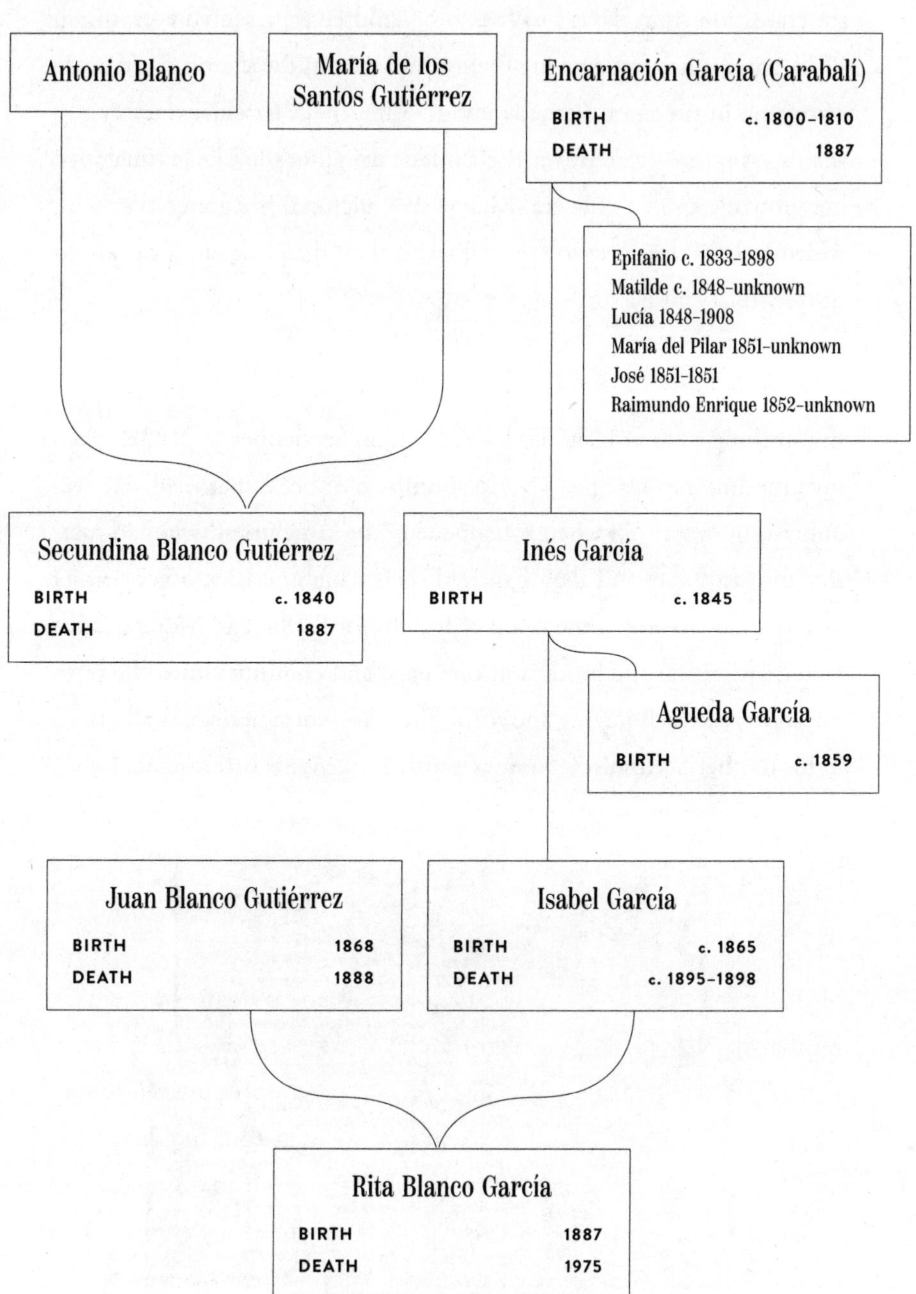

Antonio Blanco
María de los Santos Gutiérrez
Encarnación García (Carabalí)
BIRTH c. 1800–1810
DEATH 1887
Epifanio c. 1833–1898
Matilde c. 1848–unknown
Lucía 1848–1908
María del Pilar 1851–unknown
José 1851–1851
Raimundo Enrique 1852–unknown
Secundina Blanco Gutiérrez
BIRTH c. 1840
DEATH 1887
Inés García
BIRTH c. 1845
Agueda García
BIRTH c. 1859
Juan Blanco Gutiérrez
BIRTH 1868
DEATH 1888
Isabel García
BIRTH c. 1865
DEATH c. 1895–1898
Rita Blanco García
BIRTH 1887
DEATH 1975

marketplace to work in their own homes, with their own families. In the transition from slavery to freedom, children represented everything. Black parents imagined giving them a life without the shame of servitude anywhere in the land. Perhaps my grandmother's parents, watching as the priest poured water over their infant daughter's forehead, imagined her growing up in a new era. Maybe they pictured her going to school, wearing shoes, learning to read. She was their daughter, and she would be freedom's child.

But nothing went as it should have. First, on September 25, 1888, when my grandmother was just sixteen months old, her father died. He was only twenty years old when it happened. The same priest who had married him to Isabel and then baptized their daughter, Rita, a year earlier recorded his passing in the Book of Deaths for Pardos and Morenos. The record appears at the bottom of one page and continues onto the next, the corners of each fraying and torn. There are worm holes, as well. The *S* in his mother Secundina's name is a little broken; his wife's name, Isabel,

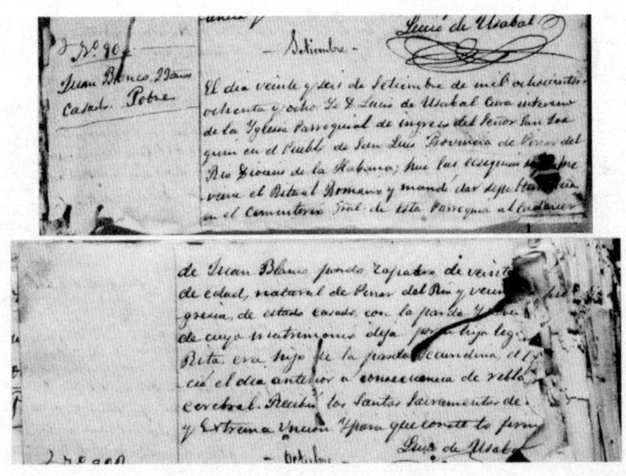

is more so. But four lines from the bottom, Rita's name, as Juan's legitimate daughter, is clearly legible, written in the neat hand of someone who imagined himself writing for posterity.

Though the record seems sparse at first glance, it suggests a story between the lines. The priest identified Juan as a cobbler rather than a skilled shoemaker, as he had just a year earlier. The cause of death appears as *reblandecimiento cerebral,* literally a softening of the brain. Any number of things can cause the softening or loss of brain tissue: stroke, head trauma, complications of a brain infection due to syphilis or tuberculosis. Whatever the cause in Juan's case, the priest notes having administered the last rites of penance and extreme unction. So Juan survived long enough for someone to summon the priest to administer the last sacraments. Whether Juan lingered for hours or days or weeks, it would have been with diminished capacity, his fate certain. Perhaps seeing Juan broken by circumstance is what explains the priest's decision—conscious or not—to downgrade his profession in the official record. Under Juan's name, he wrote the same single word used to record Encarnación's death: *Pobre.* Poor.

After Juan's death, his wife and daughter completely disappear from the record. I found no more traces of either of them in the San Luis church where Rita's birth, her parents' marriage, and her father's death were recorded.

My mother always mentioned the adjacent town of San Juan y Martínez as a place where my grandmother also lived. Unfortunately, the sacramental books of San Juan y Martínez perished over a century ago during Cuba's final war of independence from Spain, which began in 1895, the year my grandmother turned eight. General Antonio Maceo, nicknamed the "Bronze Titan" because he was Afro-Cuban, staged a monthslong fighting march from the eastern end of the island to its westernmost point, about forty-five miles beyond where my grandmother had been born. On January 19, 1896, Maceo's troops routed the Spanish and took control of San Juan y Martínez. But advantages in war are sometimes hard to sustain, and barely a month later, Spanish hostilities forced the rebels to cede control of the town. Before decamping, Maceo's forces burned it almost to the ground. Among the many things that went up in flames that day were the old books of the church.

Whether my grandmother witnessed those events, I can never know. But I do know that in addition to the loss of her father, which she could not have remembered, she suffered other tribulations that she would remember all her life. At some point, while Rita was still a child, her mother, Isabel García, died, too. That was what my mother always told me. She thought it happened during the war itself. No record of Isabel's death exists in San Luis, and in neighboring San Juan y Martínez there are no records in which to search. But finding Isabel's death record, should it exist, would not change the most important fact in the story: Rita became an orphan. More than that, she was an orphan in wartime.

In the fall of 1896, when my grandmother was nine years old, the Spanish governor of Cuba, nicknamed "the Butcher," ordered rural people to vacate their homes. He did not want them aiding the Cuban rebels with food, or lodging, or information, so he ordered them relocated to towns garrisoned by Spanish troops. With everyone forced to leave the countryside, food production plummeted, and hunger became widespread. Enacted across the island, this policy—reconcentration—was especially aggressive in my grandmother's province. There, the Spanish governor's order resulted in epidemics of smallpox and yellow fever. Across the province, more than fifteen thousand died in 1897 alone. So many people died that there was no space to bury the dead. Maybe my great-grandmother was among those many thousands of noncombatants dead from disease or hunger and lost to history.

If my grandmother was among the *reconcentrados*, she could have been one of the emaciated, unsmiling children that always appeared in the American press in this period. There were so many reconcentrated children left without parents that the Spanish provincial government decreed that children be picked up and distributed among local families with economic resources. Upward of five hundred children were relocated in this manner.

Many Cubans tried to evade the reconcentration order by fleeing to the woods and hiding, as Cuba's native population had done in the time of the Spanish conquest and as enslaved people had done for centuries after. According to one local historian, that is what many rural inhabitants of San Luis and San Juan y Martínez did. But surviving in the woods wasn't easy. People couldn't cultivate crops or keep animals, so they had to forage. Instead of sustenance, they faced death and deprivation.

Today, one of my cousins still living in Cuba remembers my grandmother talking about her experiences as an orphan during the war. Whenever he said he was hungry, she would harumph, "You don't know what hunger is!" Then she would tell him about her own hunger as a child during the war. She went for days without eating. She was so hungry that she had to catch rodents to cook and eat, she said. Whom would she have done that with? I wonder. I hope she was not alone.

At some point, while my grandmother was still a girl, she was taken in by her godfather, a prominent French carpenter who got his start constructing the carts used for the transport of tobacco and sugar cane. His partner was Águeda, who was the granddaughter of Encarnación, daughter of Inés, and aunt to Rita. With them, my grandmother learned to sing in French, and much later, after she had children of her own, she would sing those songs to them. Though my grandmother learned French songs, she never learned to read and write, and I am certain she never went to school.

I don't know how long Rita stayed with them, however. Águeda died young. According to family lore, one day she started vomiting and died. Perhaps Rita's move happened in the wake of that. My mother always told me that the family that had taken her in after the death of her parents later *gave* my grandmother to a wealthy landowner and his family. When I asked for clarification, she just repeated herself: they gave her away; they gifted her. *Se la dieron, se la regalaron.* If strange, the language was familiar to me. I had come across it during my own research on the years following the end of slavery, as the language of selling people disappeared, but occasional references to gifting people did not. In poor regions of Latin America, the practice of child circulation, of shifting children from one family to another in the context of poverty or death, was not uncommon. In some places, they were even referred to as *niños regalados*—children given as gifts. When I pressed my mother about it as part of our own family history, she confessed that she had never really asked my grandmother about it. Things were different back then, she said; children did not ask parents the kinds of questions I asked her. She hadn't wanted to embarrass her mother, out of respect, she said.

I wish I could have eavesdropped on one of their conversations. I imagine the moment when my grandmother says the very beginning of something potentially revealing. Does my mother think of pressing for more? I would have. I might have asked something like, "Were they actually giving you away? What gave them that right?" Maybe in one of my grandmother's pauses, I would have voiced another question, more direct. "Were your mother and grandmother slaves?" Suspended in the chasm between my query and her response, I imagine a cloud coming over my grandmother's eyes. And however much I want answers, I sense that my mother was right, that my questions might have felt like one more injury. In any case, I didn't know my grandmother long enough to ask. So I tell her story here with what I have, which will never be enough.

# TWO

# Children of Rita Blanco

**My grandmother was a literal gift.** The man to whom she was bequeathed in that manner was Agustín Sánchez, "a rich old man," *un viejo rico*, in my mother's words. He was a tobacco grower, owner of extensive lands east of where my grandmother was born, on the way to Havana. My grandmother worked for his family as a domestic servant, cooking and serving food, as my mother remembers.

The man's estate was named Chirigota, which was also the name of the modest settlement that grew up around it. In the first decade of the twentieth century, around the time my grandmother moved there, it had a population of a little over nine hundred people. Adjacent to the tiny village of Chirigota was the town of San Cristóbal. Residents there had to procure their water from wells; typhoid and intestinal diseases were endemic, and in many years deaths outnumbered births. The region was frequently punished by powerful hurricanes. Residents would come out of their houses after a storm passed and see bales of tobacco floating down the streets. But on its traditional saints' day, the town filled up with visitors, and the processions and cockfights lasted for days.

Perhaps it was there that my grandmother met her first partner, a man named Pedro Mazola, a white veteran of the wars of independence. He had joined the rebel army in January 1896, just as the troops of Antonio Maceo were sweeping across western Cuba. His unit took Maceo's name as its own: Infantry Regiment Maceo. When the United States intervened in that war, established a military government of occupation, and dismantled Cuba's Liberation Army, Mazola lined up with his fellow soldiers and turned in his gun in exchange for $75. A few years later, my grandmother bore him two children: Ricardo (whom everyone called Cuco) born in 1903, and Dolores (nicknamed Lola) born in 1906. But he refused to recognize the children or marry my grandmother "because she was Black," in the words of a cousin. I have not found baptismal records for either of those children, but I imagine that, like the ones for Rita's parents, the entries might have read *padre desconocido*, father unknown.

Sometime after the birth of Lola in 1906, with Pedro Mazola no longer in the picture, my grandmother moved once more. Again, the language my mother used to describe it was strange and off-putting. She explained that a man "took" Rita—"*se la llevó*"—to care for his father. They did not go too far, as he was already working on the lands of the wealthy Sánchez family and lived in a house on the large estate.

The man who took her, Lucas, would become my grandmother's life-long partner and my grandfather. She bore him ten children. The first, a girl whom everyone called La Nena, was born at three in the morning on Sunday, August 20, 1909. Their second child came three years later on August 12, 1912, at 9 p.m. They named him Cresencio, but he died at the age of seven of a heart condition. Valentín Adelino came next on December 15, 1915, at five in the afternoon. Seven more children followed.

I know the dates and hours of all their births because my mother recorded the information in a little notebook, one page for each of her siblings. My mother's handwriting in the book is a child's handwriting. As a young girl, she must have sat at her mother's knee or trailed behind her elbow as she prepared a meal, asking her for the details of each birth. Did my grandmother really remember the time of birth of each of her twelve children, or did she just give my mother a time simply to please her, so she had something to write down for everyone equally?

I found the little book of genealogy in 2017, tucked in a purse that hung looped around a sagging wire hanger in a closet in Havana, in the house where I had once lived with my grandmother and Poly. Finding it was like finding a treasure in an archive. I wrapped it up in a sheet or two

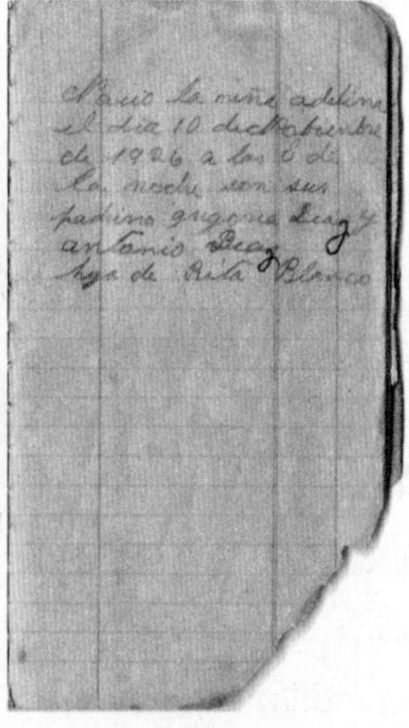

The cover of the little notebook where my mother recorded information about Rita's children. The page on the right is where my mother recorded her own birth.

of paper and tucked it in my bag to return to my mother, by then the last remaining child of Rita Blanco.

We sat at her dining table and pondered the book together. The cover was stained; the corners of all the interior pages were missing. At the bottom of every

The four youngest children of Rita Blanco and Lucas Fernández. *Clockwise from top:* Lucrecia, my mother, La Niña, and Tatá.

page for each of her brothers appears the line *hijo de Rita Blanco*, son of Rita Blanco, and for each sister, *hija de Rita Blanco*. Here was a record of my grandmother's life as a mother.

All my life, I had heard about my mother's siblings by their nicknames. Ada was La Niña; Isolina was Tatá. Those I knew. But many of the others, I knew only by names such as Cuco, Ñeñe, Lola, La Nena. They appeared in the book by their formal names, not always recognizable to me. My mother explained them all, and I took notes.

My mother miswrote her own name on the page dedicated to her birth, appearing there not by her real name Adelaida, or even the shortened form by which most people knew her (Adela), but instead as Adelina. I asked her why she had changed her own name in the book, but she said she couldn't remember. Maybe as a young girl she had just liked the sound of it better.

A couple of weeks before my mother's birth, a terrible hurricane struck western Cuba. The worst in living memory, the storm killed perhaps

650 people. My grandfather would have gone outside as the hurricane approached to shoot a gun at the clouds in the traditional, if vain, effort to break up the cyclone. There was always something about my mother that reminded me of a whirlwind. I see her in my mind's eye wearing a full skirt, spinning round and round, her shins so skinny it seems a miracle they can hold up all that energy.

According to her own record of her birth, my mother was born on November 10, 1926, at eight in the evening. When my mother was ten months old, her parents had her baptized at the church in San Cristóbal. By then, churches had done away with separate sacramental books for whites and people of color, but racial labels still sometimes made it into individual records. The priest designated my mother as white: *una niña blanca*. For centuries, the condition of slavery had followed the status of the mother. But decades later, in cases like that of my mother—a mixed-race child of legitimate birth born to a woman of color and a white man—official racial designations could well follow that of the white father. The priest might not even have thought to ask, presuming he was being polite and doing the father a favor.

Of my mother's childhood and that of her siblings, I know mostly the stories she told me. In the early 1930s, during Cuba's depression, times were hard and food was scarce. The older sons used to go with my grandfather to cut sugar cane on the north coast. They got paid daily and with their earnings immediately bought food at the company store. My grandmother could not cook dinner until they returned home late at night. When all the kids sat down to eat, my mother would sometimes spray spittle across her plate to keep her brothers, who ate much faster than she did, from stealing her food before she was done. My mother, like her siblings, was a country girl, a *guajira*, a colloquial term for a peasant or a person from the country. Growing up whenever I felt shy about something and told her, or when she saw me shrink away from attention, she would say to me, *no seas tan guajira.* Don't be like that. Don't be so country. She wasn't, even though her origins might have given her reason to be.

The kids grew up in the country, climbing trees, eating fresh plums and mangoes, stealing pineapples from a neighboring farm. Sometimes they would sit to hear the stories of another old neighbor, Genaro Lucumí. His last name referred to his birth in Africa's Yorubaland, corresponding today to the countries of Nigeria, Benin, and Togo. He told the children stories about fighting in the troops of the Afro-Cuban general Antonio Maceo in the final war of independence. Meanwhile, Genaro's wife, Irene, used to tell stories about acquiring her freedom in the waning days of slavery. I included their story in two of my books on the history of Cuba. Slavery was not that long ago; my grandmother could have told them that, too.

My mother was the first of Rita's children to attend school through the sixth grade. All the primary grades in her school were taught in the same classroom, and the teacher, Amparo Álvarez, knowing that my mother was smart and good, had her help teach the younger kids. A local charity that identified promising girls from the area and helped fund their education in Havana selected her for their program. They took her to a fancy girls' school in the capital, where they made her wash and iron the clothes of the other girls. She hated it, figured out how to get on a bus, and returned home.

Back in the countryside, she took formal sewing classes, with no inkling of how much sewing she'd end up doing later, on a factory floor in a different country. She also taught catechism classes for children preparing for their First Communions. Her godmother, who became a nun late in life, took my mother on missions to nearby country settlements, where they would marry couples who had not been married by the church (or at all), quickly prepare children for Holy Communion, and baptize scores of infants and others. One time, they baptized thirty-seven children in one go, my mother serving as godmother to all of them. For a time, she considered becoming a nun. She had the example of her godmother; she didn't have any suitors. Maybe if Poly's father hadn't come along, that might have happened.

As Rita's children grew older, their country outings changed. They would dress up a little, take a guitar and food for a picnic: my mother, Niña, Lucrecia, Tatá, some of their brothers, and their friends. Sometimes, the teacher's son took a camera to memorialize the outings. Among the group, courtships formed, but my mother never mentioned anyone courting her. They often took my grandfather's horse on these excursions.

My mother as a young woman among palm fronds during a country outing.

They called it Tranbú—*trans-bus* pronounced in Cuban, so without either *s*—because he was so long that six people could ride on his back at one time, my mother insisted. The horse was sometimes a nuisance. Every time he saw someone approaching on the path, he would stop. He had learned to do that with my grandfather, who always stopped to talk to people on the road, usually about politics.

My grandfather was a follower of Cuba's first mass political party, the Auténticos, created in the aftermath of a thwarted revolution in 1933. In its origins, it was a progressive political party that believed firmly in the necessity of social rights. Later, it was plagued by corruption scandals. My grandfather did not just vote for the Auténticos, he actively campaigned for them as well. Two of the party's principal figures—both future presidents of Cuba—were from parts of the province not far from my mother's family. One senator, Paco (Francisco) Socorrás, brother of a future president, used to come to my grandparents' house. As the seasoned politician said his goodbyes, he always tucked some bills in my grandfather's pocket, so that he might dispense favors in exchange for votes. In this small, unremarkable corner of the Cuban countryside, politics was patronage, and patronage was politics.

It was my grandfather who always left the house to conduct business, run errands, solicit votes for his party, and generally engage the small world outside their doors. My grandmother usually stayed behind, minding the house and the children. When his wealthy employer held a wedding banquet for his daughter, my grandfather went alone, arriving with a lovely framed painting as a gift. When his own children wanted to attend small country dances on the weekend, he was the one who took them. Someone always placed a rope on the dance floor to divide the room by race. What would that have meant for the children of a white man and a woman of visible African descent? Every time my mother told me that story, I'd ask what side of the room she danced on, and she always said the white. She always went to the dances with her father, she offered, and he was the fair-skinned, light-eyed son of a Spaniard. What if your mother had taken you? I always asked. She brushed me off: "Mamá would never have taken us; she hardly ever left the house." With so many children and so much work there, how could she have, she tried to explain. But even then, I suspected that there were other reasons as well.

At some point, my grandfather bought a little farm of his own, about ten miles west of San Cristóbal in a place called Aspiro, literally "I breathe," or "I aspire." Things took a turn for the worse there. He couldn't make a go of it and had to borrow money, using the farm as collateral. As soon as she began living on the new farm, my grandmother developed severe asthma. She soon grew so ill that the family decided that she should move to Havana, where she lived in a rented one-bedroom wooden house right next to the homes of her first two children, the Mazolas. Soon after, my grandfather lost the farm and moved to Havana as well.

Rita and Lucas saw a lot over their lifetimes, in their own home and in the world around them. They beheld the coming of independence and then two separate military occupations by the United States. They survived the Depression. They witnessed two revolutions; the most famous, of course, brought Fidel Castro to power. Shortly after that revolution, the land owned by the wealthy Sánchez family, on which my grandfather had labored and on which my grandmother had raised her children, was confiscated by the state in the agrarian reform. The brother of Fulgencio Batista, the strongman Castro had just defeated, had a "chalet" on the land. It was burned to the ground, as was the school.

But by then, much of our family was in Havana. My grandfather Lucas died in November 1959, the same year that Fidel Castro rose to power. My grandmother suffered the loss of the man she'd been with for half a century. The following year, she lost her oldest daughter, aged fifty-four. Lola was a midwife who sometimes gave her patients injections of adrenaline to speed up stalled labors; she sometimes used it on herself to alleviate severe bouts of asthma. It must have been a bad one that led her to take a double dose that day. She died of a heart attack.

Then in 1963, my grandmother saw her daughter—my mother— leave the country, the first in the family ever to do so. She watched as my mother wrapped me in her arms, not knowing when she might see us again. With us gone, she was left to love and raise Poly, to lie down with him at night, to lighten the load of his loneliness. Maybe on those nights, she remembered herself at Poly's age, having already lost so much. But she would have consoled herself, thinking perhaps that Poly was not hungry, that there was no war raging around them, that he was not an orphan as she had been, and that, anyway, Poly's loss—unlike her own—would only ever be temporary.

# THREE

# A Home Behind the Military Hospital

**I have never been to Rincón** on December 17. But every year, tens of thousands of Cubans make a pilgrimage to the village to venerate a saint named Lázarus on his feast day. One of Cuba's most beloved deities, San Lázaro is the patron saint of the poor and sick, an old man on crutches accompanied by two dogs who lick the wounds on his legs to ease his pain. People begin arriving in Rincón, about seventeen miles south of Havana, the night before. They travel by bus, car, horse-drawn buggy, or on foot. Many make part of the journey barefoot; some even crawl on bare knees or drag chains attached to heavy rocks. The pilgrims gather around the small church that houses the saint's effigy and around the leper hospital that sits adjacent to it. They sing, they dance, they talk. Some feel a presence descend on them: Babalú Ayé, the African *orisha* (deity) that in Cuba is fused with San Lázaro. In the morning, when church officials bring the saint out to his devotees, everyone rejoices and prays for humble miracles, or momentous ones.

December 17 is an important, fortuitous day even for Cubans who do not make the pilgrimage, sometimes even for nonbelievers. In 2014, when presidents Raúl Castro and Barack Obama announced that the two governments were embarking on a path less hostile than what had predominated already for almost sixty years, they happened to do so on December 17. Surely, that was an auspicious sign. Perhaps a different, more secular kind of miracle was in store.

I don't know what miracle my mother might have asked for on the day she made the pilgrimage to Rincón with my father. They walked together, my mother wearing flip-flops that left her feet bloody and swollen. Perhaps she prayed for the saint's blessing of their still young love; perhaps my father was praying for permission to enter the United States; maybe she was already pregnant, and they both prayed for me.

I can surmise with more confidence what my mother prayed for on an earlier visit to the shrine of San Lázaro. It was December 17, 1951, years before she met my father. Just twenty-five years old, she lived with her parents and other family in the countryside. On that day, she traveled with her mother, sixty-three years old and suffering from severe, debilitating asthma. The family was making the pilgrimage to pray for her health. So rather than walk, as so many others did, they hired a car.

The man who drove the car for a fee that day was Hipólito Cabrera. Cubans love nicknames, and everyone called him Polo. He flirted with my mother, immediately began courting her, and proposed matrimony soon after. Though she was only twenty-five, she already feared never getting married. A very skinny woman in a culture that valued curves more than angles, she had never considered herself attractive. While her sisters and her friends had regular suitors, she did not. Her father, a strict man, never let her do anything unaccompanied. She was dying to get out of her house, she recalled decades later, and marriage was the most acceptable way for a modest country girl to do that. She wed Polo in a civil ceremony on April 25, 1952, just four months after meeting him. They rented an apartment; she bought furniture, paying cash on installments, and before long she had set up her first home. I imagine her looking in the mirror behind their new dresser and seeing the reflection of a woman. Less than a year later, she was pregnant. And on December 6, 1953, she gave birth to her first child, a boy the couple named Hipólito after his father, but whom everyone in the family would call either by the diminutive Poly, or by the diminutive of the diminutive, Polito.

My mother began to lose faith in her new husband even before the birth of Poly. Just two months after their marriage, he fell behind on rent but insisted on staying put until the landlord kicked them out. As an old woman recounting the story to her granddaughter Nailah, she asked, still disbelieving and indignant, "What kind of person does that?" She refused to and left him. She went back to him soon after, then left again. The chronology is hard to decipher, but she told Nailah that she finally left Polo when Poly was around eight months old, in the summer of 1954.

Studio portrait of my mother and Poly, c. 1955.

My mother and Poly moved into a new family home in Havana, where her parents had recently relocated, part of a migratory wave that increased the population of the capital by 44 percent in one decade alone. The home was a modest three-bedroom house in a popular working-class neighborhood in Marianao, a growing municipality that was like a borough of Havana. With no interior hallways, the house was just a rectangle divided up into small rooms. Family members lived their lives within view of each other. And when they couldn't see each other, they could almost always hear each other. At some point after the house was built, the landlord added a second-floor row of small units that opened out to an exterior hallway, built on the roof of my grandparents' house. Everyone's walls were thin, and louvered windows that opened to all the sounds of the neighborhood made even the pretense of privacy impossible. In my grandparents' house, a small decorative window over the front door was the only concession to something other than functionality. Elaborate spirals looped around the name Zoila and the year 1948, both etched in glass to commemorate the house's first resident and the year of its construction at a time when my family was not yet in Havana. For all that, my grandparents paid 50 pesos a month, my mother in charge of taking the money to the landlord every first of the month. Like more than 75 percent of Havana's residents, we were a family of renters.

My family's home was always full of people. My grandparents, Rita and Lucas, had ten children together, and my grandmother another two before that with a different man. Now, in the little rental, my grandparents received scores of children and grandchildren. Their youngest child, Ada (La Niña), lived with them. Right before her was my mother. Then came Isolina—whom everyone called Tatá. For a brief time, Tatá worked as a live-in domestic for a wealthy family in a much nicer part of Havana called Vedado. When that family left the country after the revolution, she moved back into the family home. Often, however, Tatá was away at a place everyone called Mazorra, the country's main psychiatric hospital, where she was a residential patient with a diagnosis of schizophrenia. Whether she was home or away at work or the hospital, her son, Carlitos, lived in the house with the rest of the family.

Relatives who didn't live there visited often. Lucrecia, next in line before Tatá, was married with a daughter and living in Vedado, the same neighborhood where Tatá once worked as a maid. But Lucrecia was often at the family home, helping out, buying this or that for my grandparents. One of the brothers, Celedonio, lived nearby. With three different women, he had fathered seventeen children. The six from the last relationship—all boys—were often at the house, playing, getting into trouble, always eager for small indulgences from my grandmother. But no matter how crowded the house, when my mother and Poly moved in after her separation, everyone just made room.

The family ran a little restaurant out of the house, a *fonda*, as such establishments were called at the time. The front room—technically the living room—served as the dining room for clients. There were eighteen or twenty regular customers, many of whom had accounts and ate there every day. Some had their food delivered at home or work. My grandfather made the deliveries, my grandmother and a hired cook prepared the food. My mother helped them and also served the customers. No one could cut the *boliche* (Cuban pot roast) the way she could, so thin and even that she could get twenty-eight slices from one roast. The *picadillo* they stretched by adding little pieces of fried sweet plantains or potatoes, so that a little meat could make a large pot. It was hard to make a profit, though. There were always so many family members around, all of them eating. Celedonio's boys, Carlitos, Poly, and others were always there, opening and closing the refrigerator, sneaking bites as my mother readied the dishes for serving, often underfoot, shooed away and told to play outside.

The house with its restaurant sat very close to three important military establishments. Half a block away was the back fence of the Carlos Finlay Military Hospital named after the Cuban doctor who at the turn of the twentieth century discovered that yellow fever was spread by mosquitoes. About a half mile past the hospital sat Camp Columbia, the largest military installation on the island, the undisputed seat of military power and sometimes the seat of political power as well. Also nearby were the offices of the SIM, Cuba's Military Intelligence Services. The SIM was responsible for surveilling and repressing government opponents at a time when their ranks were growing significantly. Given the house's location, it made sense that many of the customers at my grandparents' little restaurant were men affiliated with the army.

It was in that restaurant that my mother met and fell in love with my father, an army stenographer. His first job in the military had been in the office of the Photographer of the Army. But not long before he met my mother, he had been moved to another office, still a stenographer but now working in the SIM. There, he typed up reports on investigations into potential subversive activity. In December 2023, looking for my father's service record in a Cuban archive, I found instead a report he had typed. Under the author's signature was my father's typist's mark: *ferrr*—the *ferr* for Ferrer, the third *r* for his name Ramón. I was relieved to find confirmation of what he had always told me, to know that he was a typist rather than something more sinister, as someone once implied and then denied when I asked directly.

One day, a brother-in-law, married to his sister Juana, picked him up at the SIM to take him for a meal at my family's *fonda*. The man thought that my father might like to meet my aunt Ada. Instead, my father noticed my mother and became a regular. It was either 1957 or 1958, on August 31, my father's saint's day, San Ramón, a twelfth-century Catalan monk who ransomed himself to liberate captives and whose name was traditionally invoked by women in labor. My father walked into the restaurant that day, noticed my mother, and with his eyes fixed on her, pulled out a chair at the first table, right next to the front door, just under the wooden louvered window. He wore crisp white pants and a blue-and-white-checked shirt, the checks neither too small nor too large. My mother noticed everything, and then thought to herself, "My God, he is just what the doctor ordered."

He came back the next day, then the day after that. For their first date, my father invited my mother to see a 3-D movie, then all the rage in Havana, which in the 1950s had more movie theaters than either New York or Paris. My grandfather would not let her go out alone with men, even though she was over thirty, had a child, and was separated. So she snuck out, pretending to do something else. They never made it to the theater that night. They stopped to talk at a park bench and just stayed there, sharing their first kiss. The next time, just a week after they had first laid eyes on each other, my father picked her up at the house. It was September 8, the feast day of Cuba's patron saint, La Caridad del Cobre, and they went to a party and danced. According to my grandfather's wishes, they went with a chaperone, her friend Estela, a woman whom my grandmother had raised with her own children in the countryside. On their third date, they walked with Esther to the corner and ditched her. From then on, they lost their chaperones every time. Poly, four or five years old, always had a fit as my mother was leaving the house, crying because he did not like being left behind.

When my mother was an old woman living in Miami, someone asked her to share the most memorable pickup line she'd ever heard from a man.

She didn't hesitate. It was my father's, from one of his first visits to the restaurant. As she was serving him dessert, he looked up at her intently and asked, "Can you please add a little of your sweetness to my dessert?" She smiled, and he thanked her. The year she turned eighty, she told him it was the sweetest pickup line she'd ever heard. She always knew he was *un sato del carajo*. A damn flirt. "But he was so beautiful," she mused, still with stars in her eyes.

Back in Havana, the two of them much younger, my father only had to meet her gaze to see what she was thinking. He knew she would fall in love with him. A woman fell in love with him wherever he went, he would often tell us later. It was the story of his life, or one of them anyway.

# FOUR

# This Love
# of a Man

**My father narrated his birth** at least twice in writing, once for my girls and once for my sister's daughter, Nailah. He was born, he wrote, on the clear and beautiful morning of May 2, 1921, at 11:23 a.m. (His birth certificate put the hour at six p.m.) His family lived in the center of the island, in the province today called Villa Clara, far from my mother's people. The nearest town was the small and beautiful colonial city of Remedios, founded in 1515, as the eighth European settlement on the island. Just five miles as the crow flies from Cuba's north-central coast, pirates and smugglers made regular calls. A century after its founding, a Spanish priest claimed that the town was overrun with demons and that Lucifer himself had taken up residence in the bodies and souls of its *vecinos*. The priest convinced some of his parishioners to follow him and found a different town, abandoning in Remedios those who put no stock in demons or who had no resources to run away from them.

My father was born in the vast countryside that surrounded Remedios. As was the custom, his mother gave birth at home. Her name was María Adolfina Correa Fabelo, but I grew up thinking her name was Zoila, which was what everyone around me used to call her. She was not yet fifteen when she married my grandfather, Jesús Ferrer Guevara, born in 1879 and some twenty-five years her senior. She gave birth to my father, the couple's second of seven children, when she was seventeen, I think.

I have no idea how my father's parents met. He was from the area; she was originally from rural Havana Province. After they married, they moved to La Rosa, a sugar farm, or *colonia*, that my grandfather purchased. *Colonias* were farms that specialized in growing sugar cane but that had no capacity to grind the cane or make sugar. Their owners (*colonos*) sold the cane harvested on their farms to larger, industrialized *centrales*, which then ground the cane and produced sugar, mostly for export. Historians have sometimes regarded *colonos* as a kind of homegrown rural middle class, high in patriotic spirit and skeptical of US dominance in the industry. My grandparents' *colonia*, La Rosa, used to sell its cane to a *central* named Adela, which was also my mother's name.

When my father was born during the sugar harvest of 1921, everyone came to wish the family well—neighbors, relatives, the seasonal laborers my grandfather hired for the harvest. My grandfather organized a party to celebrate not one, but two happy events: the birth of my father and the purchase of a second *colonia* adjacent to La Rosa.

The harvest season before my father's birth had been dizzying. At its start, the price for sugar on the world market was 7.28 cents a pound, a price already higher than normal. By the end of the harvest, just six months later, the price had skyrocketed to 22.51 cents a pound. It was the biggest boom in all Cuban history—"dream-like," said observers, more like a movie than real life. People called it the era of the fat cows or, more elegantly, the dance of the millions. Given the promise of so much profit, it made sense that my grandfather chose to buy another cane farm.

Using sugar's exceedingly high price to make their calculations, people like him—and many who were richer—borrowed, bought, and speculated. Then, the bottom fell out. Those who had borrowed against the price of sugar months earlier suddenly found themselves bankrupt. One quarter of Cuban sugar mills passed to National City Bank of New York, and by 1922, fully two-thirds of the island's sugar harvest was produced by US-owned companies. My grandfather was but one of many victims of the crash. He lost both farms: La Rosa and the second mill he had bought at the time of my father's birth. The sugar mill that he had sold cane to, Adela, also went bankrupt, ending up as property of the Bank of Canada.

When my father was about five, the family purchased and moved to a new farm about twenty miles away, outside the village of Jarahueca, barely on the map. My grandfather called the farm *Jayún*, an indigenous Taíno word for a marsh reed. The farmhouse sat at the top of a gentle hill, and on the land around it the family grew all manner of crops: tobacco, rice, corn, beans, yuca, tomatoes, cucumbers, melons, even a little sugar cane. The northern route of the national rail line crossed through their farmland.

When Fidel Castro's government enacted the first agrarian reform in 1959, seizing all private landholdings over a certain size, my grandfather retained the farm. When Castro enacted a second, more radical agrarian reform in 1963, the family once more was able to keep the farm. In both cases, the farm was too small for the government to confiscate. Still, it had been large enough to sustain an extended family. When my father was young, his maternal grandparents lived on the farm, as did two paternal uncles and their respective families. Cuban cousins of my own generation still own and work the farm today.

My father loved that farm. As a little boy, he often accompanied his father on horseback, doing rounds around the property. He used to love climbing the roof of the farmhouse to watch the yoke of oxen drink from the water tank, which he regarded as a "beautiful spectacle." He liked that his father used to love the sound of the bells on the oxen's necks, and that my grandmother used to tease her husband about it. My father often told another story about one of the first times he used a machete and caught the top of his thumb with it. For the rest of his life, the nail on his left thumb had a sharp ridge protruding vertically over the length of the nail like a tent.

It was at Jayún that my father grew into a man. So did his three brothers. Gregorio, the oldest, was a stern, exacting man. A younger brother Jesús would eventually join us with his family in the United States, and the very heavy-set José Manuel (Joseíto), the youngest boy, was an excellent baseball catcher. There were also three sis-ters: Orelia, the youngest; Nena (María), who later moved to the United

The house on my father's family's farm, Jayún, photo by author, 1990.

States, and Juana, born soon after my father and married to the man who first took my father to my mother's restaurant.

Whatever my father wrote about his childhood on the farm, he penned much more about the day in 1945 when he left it forever. In fact, he wrote about that day over and over: in short autobiographical sketches that he drafted many times; in letters started and never finished, in others finished and never sent. I have over a dozen of his attempts to narrate that day.

This is the story those scraps of writing tell.

One day, when he was away from the farm, two or three men showed up at the house, armed, furious, and looking for my father. They were the brothers of a woman named Elia, whom my father had made pregnant. If he refused to make things right by her, they vowed to kill him. When my father returned home later that day, my grandfather addressed him firmly: "Ramón, what are your intentions regarding this problem you've brought on yourself and on your family." My father equivocated; maybe he could not meet his father's eyes; maybe he passed the ball of his index finger over the sharp ridge that was his thumbnail, as he looked down at his feet. He begged the night to think it over. In the morning, he spoke more clearly: He would not marry Elia. I don't know if he explained his reasons then, but he did not mention them in his writing. "Then you have to leave," said my grandfather. If he stayed without consenting to the marriage, he would be in danger, and maybe the farm and the family would be as well. My father left the next morning and never lived on the farm again.

He traveled with his maternal grandfather on a train headed east to the province of Camagüey. Their destination was a large estate owned by a family friend named Manuel Triana. My father recalled the trip vividly.

"That train, which as it rolled along the rails that guided it, cared only about respecting the distance it needed to cover in its appointed time, without considering those it drove mad with its dull whistle and the clanging of its bell," he wrote. When he arrived with his grandfather at their destination—he couldn't remember the name of the place—a young man waited with two elegantly saddled horses. "Are you the guests of Manuel Triana?" They were, they said, and the three men journeyed on a muddy path to the *hacienda* to meet the man who would be my father's host and, he hoped, his savior.

His grandfather made the introductions, embraced my father, and quickly left. Almost immediately, Triana introduced my father to his daughter, Micaela, sitting in the living room at a little bit of a distance, reading a book, perhaps by a window, like a character in a Regency novel. In all my father's drafts of the episode, she is beautiful, refined, enchanting. And she was immediately taken with him. Rather than house him in the workers' barracks, she ensconced him in what he described as a little apartment set apart from the others, even though he was there, like them, to work on the farm, which specialized in the cultivation of bananas. My father felt so at ease with Micaela and her father, he later wrote, that he didn't even miss his parents or the farm at all.

Micaela's mother had been in Havana tending to family matters when my father arrived. When she returned, however, she noticed the attentions her daughter was lavishing on him. Everything changed after that. The mother made his life impossible; "Leave right now. I don't want you here," she told him, and he had no choice but to comply. Micaela was so crushed by his departure that she traveled to his family farm. But he wasn't there. At some point, I'm not sure when, they met again in Havana. Only once. I don't know what happened. My father would mention her sometimes

My father in an army uniform in 1946, soon after moving to Havana.

as an old man, and my mother would roll her eyes.

When Micaela's mother evicted him from the farm, my father traveled to a nearby town, Florencia, where his sister Juana and her husband were then living. He stayed with them for a bit, working as a sugar cane cutter nearby. But on the road that he traveled to and from work every day, he noticed another beautiful young woman always standing outside her house, always meeting his eye. She fell in love with him, too, he ventured at the age of ninety-one. So, he left, went to Havana, and started a new phase of his life, joining the army, learning stenography, becoming a different kind of man.

In Havana, my father met the one woman whom he would never leave, and that was my mother. But my mother sometimes worried that he might. She always noticed other women noticing him. He was so handsome that he could easily have his pick among them. And, well, men always did what men were wont to do. All that, she believed almost as steadfastly as she believed in God. She sensed something else, too: the disapproval of some of my father's family, all so light-skinned, light-eyed, so very white. His oldest brother, Gregorio, whom everyone looked up to, opposed the union and made it known to other members of the family. My mother, as many

Cubans who looked like her, did not consider herself Black. But neither did she think of herself as white. And for some of my father's relatives, if not for my father, that was a problem. Might their disapproval turn into a reason for him to leave her, she might have wondered. But my mother could be a very stubborn woman. As she told me many years later, "I did not *let* him leave me." He was her catch, and she would make sure that nothing changed that.

# FIVE

# A Revolution Story

**When my parents met,** Fidel Castro was in the mountains of eastern Cuba waging a guerrilla war against the army and seeking to topple the government of Fulgencio Batista. My mother's father listened furtively to the radio programs broadcast from the mountain hideout of Castro's rebels, rooting for their victory, playing with the controls to make out the telltale words, *Desde un punto secreto del territorio libre de Cuba*—"from a secret location in the liberated territory of Cuba." But he listened very discreetly, not wanting to alert any of the army men who frequented his restaurant.

Across the country, students, workers, and women who had lost sons and lovers to state violence were all mobilizing against Batista's government. It was the accumulation of all those efforts—not just those of one leader—that forced Batista to flee the island in defeat in the middle of the night on New Year's Eve, 1958. My mother remembered hearing the news from a regular customer at the restaurant who stopped by early in the morning of January 1, 1959, to share word of what had happened.

Cubans poured into the streets to celebrate; some danced even without music; cars blasted their horns; churches rang their bells. Dissidents took over government buildings, and in some neighborhoods the Boy Scouts came out to direct traffic. Worried that disorder might follow, that this band or that one might start erecting roadblocks, my mother took Poly and went to pick up Tía Tatá's son, Carlitos, from school.

A week later, Fidel Castro arrived in Havana to thunderous cheers. People donned emblems of their approval on their own bodies—stubble on the chins of young men starting to emulate the bearded, green-fatigued heroes before them; red-and-black bands on forearms of all sizes. Red and black were the colors of Fidel Castro's revolutionary group, called the 26th of July Movement, after the date of his initial attack against Batista's government in 1953. In my parents' immediate neighborhood, there were no armbands. But some residents distributed red T-shirts as a sign of support and enthusiasm for change.

Castro's first stop in Havana was the stately Presidential Palace. He stepped out onto the balcony to address the large, jubilant crowd. It was his first time in the palace, he told them, and he didn't like it—it was not the people's house. He preferred to address the public at Camp Columbia, the large military installation about a half mile from my mother's house. "I want the people to go to Columbia," he said, "because Columbia now belongs to the people. Let the tanks, which now belong to the people, go in the vanguard of the people, opening up a path. No one will be there to stop their entry now. And we will meet there." The caravan of tanks and jeeps, followed by a massive procession of people, arrived well after sunset, and no one impeded their entrance. My parents did not attend, but people would have spilled out into the surrounding streets late into the night. Castro began his speech at about 8 p.m. At 1:30 a.m., he was still talking. At one point, as he talked about peace, the sun long gone, a white dove circled above him and landed on his shoulder. It was, said one witness, as if the dove was the Holy Ghost descending on Jesus Christ, as if the Father himself had come to Havana to announce, "This is my beloved Son." It was a remarkable scene in every way, made even more so by virtue of its setting in Camp Columbia, seat of the nation's military power, which was now all his. It was at that point, my mother always told me, that my grandfather, devoted enthusiast of the revolutionary movement, first expressed doubts. It was too strange, too much like hero worship, maybe even a portent of communism, he told her.

The new government, aware that many military men ate at the family's restaurant, closed it down briefly to search for hidden weapons but found none. On January 13, 1959, less than a week after Fidel's speech at Camp Columbia, the new government issued its thirteenth law, which dissolved the Cuban army of which my father was a member. I'm not sure my father lasted even that long. He used to tell me that very soon after the revolutionaries arrived in Havana, he was walking out of one of the buildings at Camp Columbia one day when a green-uniformed

Fidel Castro entering Havana, January 1959.

man stopped him midstep. The man looked at my father, pointed a long index finger at him, and said, "I know you." My father denied it and quickly left. He never went back. In my father's telling, the man who recognized him was sometimes Fidel himself; other times, it was one of his officers.

Without a job or a uniform, my father began to sell sandals in Fraternity Park, not far from Havana's Capitol Building, partnering with the brother-in-law who had first taken him to my mother's house. Then, after my mother's father died late in 1959, he moved in with her family—my parents in the front bedroom; Tía Tatá (when she was home from the the psychiatric hospital) with her son, Carlitos, and Poly in the middle room; my grandmother and Tía Niña in the last room. Every night when he came back from selling sandals, my father would count out his earnings in front of Poly and give him a few coins.

My father didn't like selling sandals in the park. Maybe he missed the status and uniform that had come with being a stenographer in the army or the privilege of working indoors in an office. Most of all, he did not like the new government and its leader. In Cuba, before the ascent of Fidel Castro, anticommunism had more adherents than did communism. Indeed, many of those engaged in the struggle against Batista had been avowed anticommunists, members of anticommunist student groups and Catholic youth groups, for example. My father, once a country boy educated only to the sixth grade, came from a different world than those students, but, like them, he was stridently anticommunist. Long before Fidel's triumphant march into Havana on January 8, 1959, my father believed that the bearded leader was a communist, and he disapproved with all his being.

My mother, initially, was of a different opinion. She cheered when Fidel entered Havana, eagerly distributing red T-shirts to neighbors. A few months later, when Castro's government issued a new Urban Reform Law cutting urban rents by half, she felt vindicated. Instead of taking the family's fifty pesos to the landlord, she now showed up with just twenty-five. More than that, the government designated her as the representative of the Urban Reform for her house and the units above it on the second floor. She liked the role; it suited her sense of competence and poise. Whatever her initial enthusiasm, however, as my father's grumbling got louder, as consumer items became scarcer, she wavered. The family had to shut down its restaurant. No matter how far my mother stretched the *picadillo* or *boliche*, beef had become almost impossible to come by. As Tía Niña would tell me many years after those events, my mother always liked nice things. She liked having her nails painted, being able to don a pillbox hat when the occasion called for it. She loved her New Look skirts, even though they had already started to fall out of fashion. She loved their fullness, their pleats, their pockets. She didn't buy them at a fancy department store like the Encanto in downtown Havana; she made them herself, and she ironed them to perfection. But more than a full, crisp skirt over high-heeled pumps, more than a nice round roast of beef, more even than paying less rent or having a minor post in the Urban Reform, my mother loved my father. And the more frustrated and angrier he became with the young government, the more she doubted as well. And as he increasingly mentioned the possibility of leaving, she listened and worried.

It wasn't an intimate family episode that sealed my father's resolve to leave, but the stuff of history with a big H, in the form of an invasion of Cuba orchestrated by the US government and carried out by Cuban exiles trained by the CIA. On April 15, 1961, in the lead-up to the landing, exile pilots, hoping to undermine the Cuban Air Force's ability to cripple the invasion from above, bombed Cuban airfields. The attacks injured fifty-three people and killed seven. It was at the funeral for those victims that Castro first referred to the Cuban Revolution as socialist—in public at least. "We have made a socialist revolution under the very noses of the United States," he declared. He called on Cubans to occupy their posts. The Committees for the Defense of the Revolution (CDRs)—created less than a year earlier to serve as the eyes and ears of the Cuban government in every neighborhood—rounded up people whom they suspected might support the US invasion once it came. According to one estimate, perhaps fifty thousand people were detained across the island. There were no jails large enough to hold them, so theaters and stadiums were turned into temporary detention centers.

Following Castro's speech, a neighbor denounced my father as a counterrevolutionary, and he was immediately detained. My father always told me that the reason for his arrest had nothing to do with the invasion, that it was only the retaliation of an acquaintance to whom he owed money. Even if the reason for my father's detention in that moment may have been spurious, I suspect that had the invasion ever reached Havana, he would have supported it, in sentiment if not in action.

When my father did not show up for dinner that night, my mother had cause for alarm. The political climate felt tense and perilous. Seven Cubans had just been killed during the bombing of the airfields. Two days before that, dynamite planted inside dolls in the toy section of the Encanto department store brought the store to the ground, killing one worker and injuring eighteen. The government had recently granted sugar workers the authority to arrest, punish, and execute saboteurs, with the workers themselves forming the revolutionary tribunals and firing squads.

With no idea of my father's whereabouts, assuming that he had been detained, trying frantically not to think about executions, my mother searched everywhere for him. Orelia, my father's youngest sister, arrived from the countryside fearing the worst. Together the two women went from detention center to detention center. At each, they grew more anxious. My mother found it harder and harder to smile at the officials she queried; her shoulders slumped in defeat as she navigated her way from one center to the next without an answer in sight. They found him on the sixth day at the Blanquita, then the largest movie theater in the world and later to be renamed the Karl Marx. The government held as many as five thousand people there. An FBI account about an American couple in their seventies detained in that same theater-cum-prison stated that those arrested were given no food or water. Prisoners were not allowed to use the bathrooms, and they were soon ankle-deep in urine. Several women miscarried pregnancies, and some detainees went out of their minds. "In order to keep the prisoners quiet, shots were fired over their heads. One couple was shot, typhoid broke out, bloodhounds were brought on the stage, and the prisoners were threatened with their unleashing unless they kept order," read the report.

I shared that description with my father when he was in his late nineties; he didn't recall anything like that. But he very much remembered being afraid. Even if they let him go this time, he had thought, they could arrest him again. He personally knew of people who had been executed, men he'd seen around Camp Columbia before Fidel Castro made it his, men like the ones he and his companions had typed for. Might he, too, become victim to a firing squad someday? He would wonder about it almost until the day he died.

On April 17, 1961, he was still in the Blanquita theater, one of thousands of detainees, as exile troops landed on Cuba's southern shore at the Bay of Pigs. The invasion failed spectacularly. A hundred and fourteen of the exiles were killed, and 1,189 were captured and imprisoned. My father always told me that it was those events—his arrest, the failure of the invasion, the fear of what his fate might be—that convinced him to leave Cuba. In that decision, he was far from alone. By the end of 1961, an astounding twelve hundred Cubans a day were applying for entry to the United States.

On April 24, 1962, when my mother was seven months pregnant with me, my father boarded Pan Am's daily flight from Havana to Miami. Every day, the plane traveled virtually empty from Florida to the Cuban capital; every day, it returned with its 109 seats occupied. On landing in Miami, people applauded in unison. Most of the passengers, my father among them, fully expected that they would return to Cuba in a matter of months, perhaps a year, two or three at most.

The day my father arrived in Miami, or maybe it was a day or two later, someone recruited him to work in a hotel in Upstate New York. For decades, Cuba had been famous as a tourist destination, so hoteliers looking to employ people for the summer season up north sent recruiters to Miami to find Cuban workers, presumably good (and inexpensive) prospects for the hospitality industry. A recruiter offered my father and another new arrival jobs at the Sagamore Hotel, a posh resort in Lake George, New York.

The three men drove north from Miami through the segregated South, my father seeing for the first time in his life the notorious signs that designated bathrooms, water fountains, entrances—most public spaces—into spaces for Blacks or whites and never both. Fair-skinned and light-eyed, he entered the white spaces. I never thought to ask him if he thought about my mother as he did that.

His expectation, and my mother's, was that she would join him in the United States soon after giving birth to me. Both of them began working toward that end almost immediately. On May 31, 1962, less than three weeks before I was born, my mother appeared before a judge to dissolve formally her marriage to Poly's father. The judge ruled that Poly would remain "definitively in the shelter and care of his mother." His father would not be denied the right to see and communicate with Poly, and he would pay a monthly allowance of twenty-five pesos for his son's upbringing. To both parents, the judge granted "full guardianship," or *patria potestad*.

While my mother was dealing with all that, she was getting ready to have me. When she went into labor on June 17, 1962, she hailed herself a taxi to Maternidad Obrera, Workers' Maternity Hospital—a beautiful 1941 art deco building crowned with a white ceramic sculpture of a mother and child. My mother looked up at it in prayer before entering. Maybe she also invoked my father's name, doubly appropriate since he was her lover and since San Ramón was also the patron saint of women in labor. My mother's contractions were so far along that she almost had me on a stretcher in the hallway, she always told me. The next day, a relative sent my father a telegram at the Sagamore Hotel to let him know that she had given birth to a girl and that we were both fine. On June 20, three days after my birth, my mother's divorce from Poly's father became final.

In addition to the divorce proceedings, my mother applied for passports for herself (issued in August 1962) and for me (issued in November 1962). She also began the application for Poly's passport. I recently found his passport picture in a photo album that my mother made for him much later. Poly, maybe eight years old, wears a dark suit jacket with a white shirt and a light tie. His ears protrude; his brows look tense; his expression is somber. On the album page itself, my mother wrote above the photo: "For the passport." Under the photo, she added, "Your father did not sign."

Poly's father was a member of the new revolutionary police, and he did not think that it would look good for his son to abandon the country for the United States. Maybe he was also a vindictive man and did not want my mother to be happy. Whatever his reasons, he refused

to authorize Poly's departure. My mother, my aunts, my grandmother begged him to reconsider. They were hopeful that he would, but by the time I was born that had not yet happened.

Maybe my mother felt a little down, a little anxious. Her new baby required a lot attention, and I wasn't always easy. In a letter to my father, Poly wrote, *Adita está acabando*. A literal translation might be that I was finishing, but what it really meant was that I was trying my mother's patience, exhausting her nerves. And Adita, of course, was (and is) my nickname in Spanish. According to Poly, I pulled my own hair and made myself cry. Poly was giving my mother a hard time, too. Maybe he was jealous of the new baby. "Today I got angry with Mamá because I wanted two pesos to buy a little present for [Adita] and she said no." Meanwhile, Poly's father was still being impossible about Poly's passport and permission for travel.

Perhaps above all, my mother missed my father. She missed him because she was in love, because she had just borne his child, and I think she missed him because she worried that a world away, she might lose him. Her favorite song at the time, one she sang over and over, was called "Tuya Soy"—I am yours. I can hear the lyrics in my head, because later she would sing it to me.

*Tuya soy*
*Porque tú me enseñaste a querer*
*Porque tú me enseñaste a sentir*

*Ven a mí que me siento muy sola sin ti*
*Que mi alma te espera otra vez*
*Yo no puedo vivir más sin ti.*

. . .

I am yours
Because you taught me to love
Because you taught me to feel.

Come to me, because I feel so lonely without you
because my soul waits for you once more
I can no longer live without you.

My parents wrote each other letters all the time. She wrote him a little every day, sharing details of her life without him, professing her love, reporting on my progress in my first months of life. Then every Saturday, she would add a million kisses by way of closing, put the long letter in an envelope, and walk to the post office to mail it. (Living in the United States, my mother saved their letters high on a closet shelf, in a brown velvet box that had once held a Fabergé perfume gift set.) But as much as she wanted to join my father, she worried deeply about leaving Cuba and her family. Everything was uncertain. What would it be like to leave her aging mother with whom she was so close? Would her ex-husband allow Poly to leave with her? If not then, when? Would my father wait for us? If she left, when would she be able to return? In those tumultuous times, would some international event intervene?

. . .

My mother had her passport in hand, was waiting for mine, and negotiating with her ex-husband about Poly's when the Cuban Missile Crisis wrested the world's attention from everything else. On October 14, 1962, an American reconnaissance plane flying south to north over a little town, just six miles west of where my mother had grown up, caught sight of Soviet missiles on the ground. A nuclear warhead on each could pack seventy-five times more power than the US atomic bomb detonated over Hiroshima, and their range enabled them to strike Miami, Washington, and New York. On October 22, 1962, President John F. Kennedy addressed the nation: The US government had incontrovertible proof that the Soviet Union had established missile sites in Cuba. Lest anyone wonder what that meant, he elaborated: "The purpose of these bases can be none other than to provide a nuclear strike capability against the Western Hemisphere."

I don't know if my father, alone in the United States, worried about the end of the world as much as he worried about what would happen to my mother and me. Commercial flights between the two countries were suspended. All my father could think was that my mother and I were, in his words, "trapped in Cuba."

When the news broke, he had just moved to New York City, having finished working the tourist season in Lake George. He was sitting alone in a restaurant on Broadway in Manhattan, having dinner at around 8:30 p.m., wondering what he should do about us, when he noticed two men watching him, not bothering to hide the fact that they were talking about him. They approached his table and sat down without asking his permission. My father felt uneasy. Was his anxiety so clearly written on his face? he wondered. Were these men trying to take advantage of him? Did he look as vulnerable as he felt?

One of the men opened the conversation, and then the other joined in to explain their purpose. By the sound of their Spanish, maybe by their looks, my father could tell they were Cuban. They were driving to Miami that night and were wondering if my father wanted to join them and help pay for the gasoline. He hesitated, continued eating, still a little wary, but soon said yes. The three men left New York at 11:30 p.m. that night. More than once during the journey, my father wondered what he was doing with two strangers on a dark, empty highway in the middle of nowhere in a foreign country. But about thirty hours after their departure, the three men arrived safely in Miami.

I don't know if it was one of those two strangers or someone else he met in Miami who first told my father that it was possible to apply for US visas in Mexico. Still in Miami when he received word that my Cuban passport had been issued in Havana, he went immediately to the Mexican Consulate in Miami to see about getting our visas to Mexico. For the rest of his life, my father always believed that his impulsive decision to join two strangers on a road trip to Miami had been the key. It had helped get my mother and me to him. Absent that, he said, it might have been years before we'd been able to travel. By then,

The three of us celebrating Poly's ninth birthday, December 1962.

who knows what might have happened. Perhaps he would have met someone else, or my mother might have. The decision my father made in a New York restaurant that night epitomized "his style," he said. What was that style? Acting decisively, not overthinking things. He acted without delay, and the results had been good.

My mother soon had her own chance to act impulsively. One day when she was in the Old Havana neighborhood near the docks with Poly and me, she saw a crowd gathered around an American ship. I think now that it was around Christmas 1962, and that the vessel may have been the SS *African Pilot*, which had arrived in Havana with medicines and other supplies to be exchanged for prisoners from the Bay of Pigs invasion. In an arrangement apparently worked out on the spot, the American officials on the ship allowed relatives of the prisoners onto the US-bound ship. Suddenly everyone claimed kin among the prisoners; passersby were spontaneously seizing the opportunity to join them, and more than three thousand clamored for passage.

I have heard the story so many times that I can easily picture it in my head, unfolding like a video clip. In the crowd, I make out my mother wearing one of her full, pleated skirts, her narrow feet perched on heels, her shins impossibly skinny. She has my brother's small hand grasped in hers; on her other side, she carries me on her hip. She ponders all the people boarding the vessel and learns that it is bound for the United States. Uncertainty shows in her dark eyes, eyes that I can see without even trying. If she leaves now, she thinks to herself, she can be with my father in a matter of days. She can take Poly and get around her ex-husband's refusal to let the boy travel. Yes, she decides, and starts toward the line of people filing onto the ship. But she hesitates. She must steel her resolve to go through with this. She squares her shoulders and tries once more, a few steps forward, fast at first, then slow. She stops, stares up at the waiting ship, so heavy that it doesn't even seem to bob on the water. She looks back down at us, Poly and me. Her arms stiff from carrying me, her feet starting to ache, her eyes moist, she turns away from the scene, back to the little house behind the military hospital, her two children in tow, a boy just turned nine and an infant girl of six months.

My mother's version of the story always ends the same way, not with a scene but with an explanation. I heard it dozens of times. She hadn't been able to leave the country without saying goodbye to her mother.

Four months later, on April 29, 1963, she left Cuba without saying goodbye to her son.

# PART II

# Sad Geography

# SIX

# Letters to Our Mother

**When Poly said goodbye** to his friends and returned home for dinner that April evening of 1963, he found my mother and me gone. My grandmother and aunts told him that we had traveled to the countryside for a few days to help care for an ailing relative. So, in the beginning, he wouldn't have been too worried. Less than a week after our departure, however, they told him the truth. Every night, Poly clutched my mother's housedress and cried. He was one month shy of nine and a half.

A whole world mobilized to comfort Poly. People took turns taking him to school. Tía Lucrecia bought him clothes and took him to her place in Vedado for weekends. Sometimes, when he was playing with her daughter, Isabel, the television would be on in the background, Fidel Castro giving speeches, Lucrecia's husband watching skeptically. With Lucrecia's family, Poly went to the zoo, the beach, and carnival celebrations, places he would probably not have gone otherwise. My grandmother and Tía Tatá were not young or well enough to take him, and Tía Niña was, by her own admission, a little lazy about things like that. Sometimes my mother's brothers in the countryside took him for a few days and defeated his reluctance to eat by plying him with roast pork and sweets. Everyone made themselves present for Poly because we weren't.

Thirteen-year-old Carlitos, with his mother, Tatá, in and out of the psychiatric hospital, sometimes took him to the movies, which he loved. "I am the one who understands him," wrote Carlitos to my mother. "No one knows how to indulge him like I do." Still, he thought Poly had been acting spoiled (*malcriado*) since our departure. He misses you, he wrote, adding that sometimes Poly cried at night, and our grandmother let him sleep in her bed to make him feel a little less sad. No one told my mother that he developed a nervous tic; he kept shrugging one shoulder and jerking his head down to it.

On May 4, 1963, five days after we left Cuba, Poly sat down and wrote a letter to my mother, to our mother. I don't know if it was his idea to write, or if my grandmother and my aunt made him do it. "You know that without help, I can't write," he would explain a few months later. Maybe that was because Tía Niña assisted with spelling and such, or maybe it was that my grandmother's presence helped him with all those feelings he had now, things too daunting and new to put into words.

The first lines of Poly's first missive to his absent mother read: "I write this short letter so that you may know that I am well, that I go to school every day. I take good care of grandmother and I don't make trouble for her, and I run errands for her." It was the letter of a little boy—the cursive sometimes illegible, the spelling poor, the punctuation unreliable. But it was also the letter of a boy proud to behave, proud to be weathering the shock of his mother's abrupt and unannounced disappearance. I am good, he seemed to be saying; you don't need to worry about me. The only indication that anything was unusual was the third sentence: "I want to speak with my father so that he can give me permission to go with you, and *tía* will speak to him, too." Forgoing capitalization,

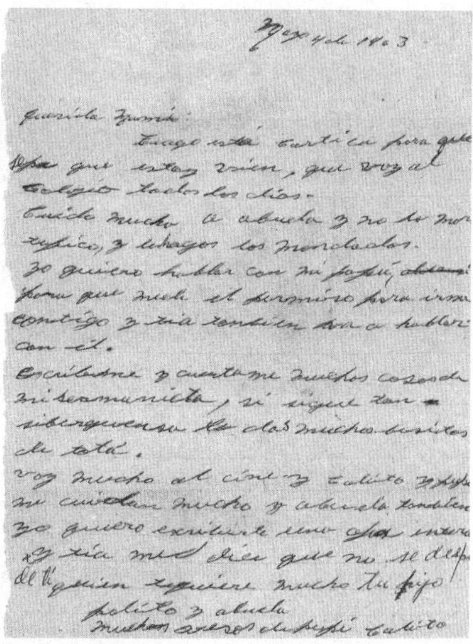

Poly's first letter to our mother.

my brother signed the letter *polito y abuela*, the first being the diminutive of the already diminutive Poly and the second Spanish for grandmother. Since my grandmother did not know how to write, he was doing it for both of them.

Very soon after he wrote that letter, Poly received his first letter from our mother. I don't have my mother's letter to him; I have only his response to her, only half the conversation. Poly replied to my mother's letter immediately, so his second-ever letter to her was dated May 6, just two days after his first. He opened with a standard formulation. Maybe Tía Niña taught it to him, or maybe he adapted it from the letter he had just received from my mother. "I pray to God that upon receipt of this letter you find yourself well, in the company of Adita and Ramoncito." My mother and I were in Mexico City, not yet in New York with my father, but maybe nobody had told him that. What did he feel as he wrote those words and pictured us together without him? "I imagine the snow and how cold it must be there," he wrote, even though it was May. He mentioned me, repeating something that my mother had shared with him in her letter: *Adita está acabando.* I was difficult, demanding. Then Poly added, "I beg you not to hit her." Occasional physical punishment for children in our family, and in others around us, was the norm. But he was my big brother, my protector, even though we were now apart.

Mother's Day, celebrated in Cuba as in the United States on the second Sunday of May, came just two weeks after my mother and I left Poly. This would be his first Mother's Day without his mother, my mother's first without him. In his third letter to my mother, a little over two weeks after we left, Poly explained that he gave our grandmother a little elephant figurine as a Mother's Day present "on behalf of both of us." He recalled the Mother's Day elephant again in another letter two months later. "It was going to be your present," he said to my mother, "but you left." He wrote something right after, but he (or maybe my aunt) crossed it out so heavily that it is illegible. Then he added, "and I couldn't give it to you."

Poly with our grandmother Rita.

That was the manner in which Poly revealed something of his feelings, in snippets that sometimes did not survive the editing, resolute scrawls inked over the inconvenient things that sometimes slipped out. Maybe he was scared to acknowledge his emotions; maybe they overwhelmed him, or perhaps my aunt dissuaded him. Instead, he tended to reassure my mother that everything was okay.

"I go to school every day . . . I eat well . . . I am getting a haircut on Sunday. . . . I am behaving well," he reported in another early letter. Sometimes, he wrote as if he was the one responsible for our mother. "Take good care of yourself, *mi flaquita* [my little skinny one]," he advised in one letter, "so that you can gain weight [and] . . . send me presents." In a single line, he assumed the role of parent urging a child to eat and of a little boy asking his mother for gifts.

When my mother and I arrived in New York City on July 4, 1963, she sent a telegram home with the news. Poly wrote soon after to tell her that he was "very happy that you are with Ramoncito and Adita." But the news that we were all together in New York maybe felt to him more definitive than our waiting in Mexico. He was still in Cuba, wanting to leave, not knowing when that might happen. Maybe that realization prodded him to put some feelings down on paper: "Mom,"—*Mima* was the word he used—"I so want to go there." But he couldn't quite bring himself to say that he missed her. So he merely wrote that he "wanted to leave to go on a trip."

Before Poly ever told my mother that he missed her, he told her that he missed me. "Mami, I really want to be with Adita," he wrote on July 27, 1963. On September 30, he used the word *sad* for the first time. "Mima, if you only knew how much I want you to send me something, because I am sad." And right after, "Mima, if you only knew how much I miss you all, especially my little sister." Then in February 1964, with us gone for a little over nine months, he wrote with a powerful and simple eloquence:

When a letter arrives from there, I get so happy that sometimes it makes me sad.

I found Poly's letters in December 2022, a few months after my father died and more than two years after my mother did. Clearing out their apartment, I came across the letters in a clear plastic container high on a closet shelf. My mother kept every letter she received from Poly in its original envelope and then tied them all together with gold curling ribbon, the same kind she always used for wrapping our Christmas presents. Maybe she saved them for Poly; maybe she saved them for me, her historian daughter who was always asking her questions. Whatever her intention, today I am the keeper of the letters. What a strange gift they are: the paper remains of something that should never have happened.

I began reading the letters for the first time in 2023, exactly sixty years after Poly began writing them. They are excruciating.

I can only read two or three in a day; I take mindless, distracting breaks between them. Sometimes Poly's words make my breath catch, and I have to stop and look away. I glance up from a letter, and see my large computer monitor, good for failing eyes and a bad neck. Floating an inch or two above the top is an old passport photo of mine, faded now from having sat too long in a bowl on a sunny windowsill. It is attached to a skinny brown stick that I've taped to the back of the monitor. An assortment of sticky notes in yellow, green, and orange dot the edges of the screen. They read, "look here," and thick Sharpie arrows point up to my picture hovering over the top. The whole setup was a reminder to look not at the live image on my screen but at the monitor's camera just under my photo. It dates back to July 2021, when protests erupted across Cuba, and I was interviewed about them on live television.

Having just read a particularly poignant phrase in one of Poly's letters—I can't now remember which one—I look up and start ripping everything off the monitor, frenetically, without thinking. The stick that was holding up my old photo, I toss into the trash bin. But then I remember that it wasn't just a stick; it was a porcupine quill that my cousin Papito had brought back from his time serving in Angola, during Cuba's long intervention there in the 1970s and 1980s. He had given it to me as a present on my first trip back to the island in 1990. According to one of Poly's first letters, Papito's daughter inherited my crib after my mother and I left in 1963. I retrieve the quill and tuck it safely in a desk drawer.

In that moment, the present recedes to background, and multiple pasts clamor for my attention: Poly as a lonely little boy against the backdrop of a revolution consolidating its power; my mother and I flying to Mexico, to Miami, to New York; my parents as young, scared immigrants; a cousin inheriting my crib; her father later deployed to war in Angola; me as a young woman returning to Cuba for the first time. And it is both too much and never enough. In an instant, I feel what I have always known: that this is the story that has made me. And through it I am connected to so many other people, to so many other worlds.

I return to the letters. Even if I must take breaks, I cannot resist them, really. I *need* to read them. I want to understand.

> . . . if you only knew how much I miss you all.

> . . . I want you to send me something, because I am sad.

> . . . because you left.

> I have been missing you a lot these days.

> When a letter arrives from there, I get so happy that
> sometimes it makes me sad.

I know the house. I can imagine the scene clearly. Poly comes home from school; he races to the kitchen in search of a snack. My grandmother tells him there's a letter from his mother. He's ecstatic. He reads it aloud to my grandmother, who cannot read. Maybe he takes it out to the porch, sits on the rocking chair, kisses my mother's signature at the bottom of the page. My grandmother interrupts him to deliver a snack. He reads the letter again, and then once more. Maybe this time, he pauses at the date, notices that the last digit on the year is no longer the same. Nineteen sixty-three has become 1964; too soon after, it will be 1965. The letter probably ends with a standard closing: a million kisses from your mother who loves you and never forgets you. But then that's all there is. There are no more words; there are no actual kisses. Now, there is only waiting for the next letter, which will also leave him wanting. He goes back inside, sets the letter on the dining room table, and goes out to play with friends before dinner.

It was on nights like that, when he was feeling especially sad and abandoned, that our grandmother let him crawl into bed with her. There, he could sleep nestled in the crook of her shoulder, feeling a little comfort before drifting off to sleep.

# SEVEN

# A World of Dusk and Iron

Growing up, I never saw photographs of my parents as children. I once found a grainy shot in which my mother stands on the edge of a large group of family members in her Cuban countryside. She is skinny as always, her long thin arms crossed in front of her, her elbows sharp and bony, her head cocked to the left with her hair in two long braids. She is maybe thirteen years old. That is the closest I ever came to a childhood image of either parent, and I think my mother was already dying when I found it.

In New York in 1963, my parents—he at forty-two, she almost thirty-seven—purchased the first camera they ever owned and began documenting the life of their Cuban daughter in America. They took many more pictures of me than of each other, as parents usually do. Two early ones are set in Riverside Park, a block away from the tiny brownstone apartment my father rented for the three of us. In the first, we sit together on a park bench. My mother stares directly into the camera, wearing a dress and heels. Next to her, I stand on the bench. But I don't stand alone. My father holds me up, looking down at me, enamored. In the other photograph, I am learning to walk. I took my first steps unassisted in Riverside Park, and my parents captured the moment on film.

It was my father who took the rolls to be developed. He did more of the errands and was learning to speak a little English. But it was my mother, usually home with me, who wrote short dedications on the backs of the photos and tucked them into the letters she mailed to Poly. She sent him pictures of us all the time. It is from his letters back to her that I can figure out which photographs she shared. In one of them, I stand atop a dining chair in a pale pink pleated shirt, holding a black phone to my ear, rolling the coiled cord around my finger, pretending to talk with my grandmother in Cuba. In another, I pretend to read an open newspaper on a coffee table, even though I was much too young to read. My mother

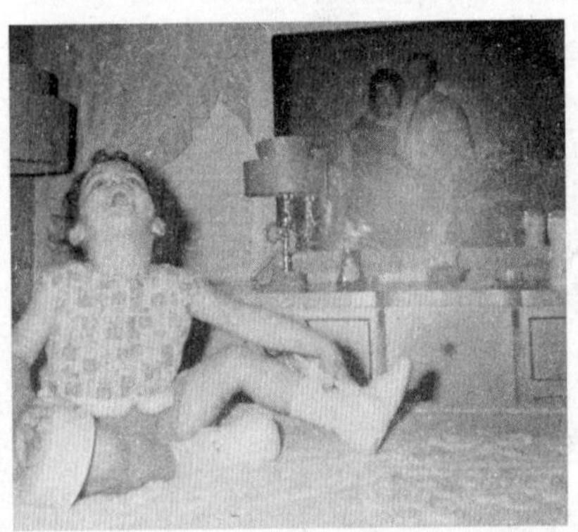

probably did not send Poly one of my favorite photos. I am sitting on my parents' bed laughing, my head thrown back, my mouth wide open, a perfect horseshoe of little white molars revealed for the camera. Behind me, a mirror reveals the flash of the camera's light bulb just below the reflection of my parents, my father's arms around my mother's shoulder, both of them smiling at their daughter's joy.

Less than six months after our arrival from Mexico, my mother became pregnant. At first, she hesitated to share the news with Poly, fearing he would grow jealous. But when she told him, about three months before her due date, he surprised her: I am not jealous at all, he reassured her, suggesting that it was me who would be envious instead. Poly was so excited about a new sibling that he even picked out baby names: Ramón, like my father, for a boy, and Katia if the baby was a girl. He preferred a girl and worried a little about competition from a new brother. "I think my new little brother will be prettier than me," he fretted, "even though I am not pretty, the only thing I have going for me is that I'm a boy." My grandmother, too, was hoping for a girl, and she felt pleased when in a dream she saw my mother sewing a pink *mosquitero*, not realizing that most New Yorkers did not use canopy nets over their beds.

Our family in Cuba was excited, and some thought that maybe with this new development, my mother's ex-husband might reconsider his refusal to let Poly leave. One of our aunts was working on convincing him. "I think he will let me go . . . and then we will be together and happy," Poly wrote in July 1964.

The baby, a girl, was born on August 13, 1964, and my parents named her Aixa. They wanted a name that started with *A* to match my mother's and mine. In the hospital waiting room where expectant fathers paced, my father happened to see the name in a baby name book sitting on a table, and that was that. Poly loved it, and he could not wait to meet her in person: "I will see her soon, God willing." He proudly showed off the photographs my mother sent. The baby's cheeks were round, her hair fair, her eyes bright blue. (They would soon turn hazel.) My grandmother cautioned my mother not to favor the newborn, not to ignore me.

Maybe Poly was right: Perhaps I was a little jealous. The name *Aixa* refused to form on my lips. I couldn't force the requisite air through my teeth to make the hissing sound that the *x* demanded. So I called her simply the baby, the definite article in Spanish, the noun in English. She became *La Baby*, not just to me, but to others in the family even to this day, both of us in our sixties.

For the first Mother's Day after Aixa's birth, Poly wrote my mother a letter from school. Mother's Day was never easy for Poly. "I will miss you because I always gave you something, and now I have to give it to Abuela. I have been missing you a lot these days." We had been gone for just over two years, and though Poly had confessed earlier to missing me, to missing all of us, this was the first time that Poly said outright to my mother, "I miss you." Then he complained about his father. "Since you've left, he's only given me twenty pesos." The judge's divorce ruling had stipulated that Poly's father would provide twenty-five pesos a month of support, but that was not enough to make him comply.

Poly's next mention of his father later that year was more matter of fact: "Pipo says that he will *not* sign to let me go be together with you." The sentence takes up three lines of his letter, and Poly's handwriting changes almost by the word, sometimes neat and vertical, sometimes slanted and sloppy. Some words appear dark and purposeful on the page, others rushed and faint, almost as if the boy who held the pencil thought that by not pressing hard, by getting through the statement quickly, it might become less true. He closed the letter as he usually did: *Bueno mima se despide tu hijo que tanto te quiere*. Well, Mom, your son who loves you very much says goodbye. Then he sent kisses for his two sisters, one of them unknown to him.


By the time Aixa was born, we were living in Brooklyn. I have no idea how my parents found or chose their new apartment or neighborhood, whether they scoured streets looking for rental signs in windows, whether they relied on an agent or classified ads in the paper, or whether they followed someone they already knew. But they ended up in the Brooklyn neighborhood of East New York. For decades, it had been a vibrant Jewish neighborhood, mostly working and lower middle class. Yiddish was the lingua franca of shopkeepers, and the flickering of Shabbat candles on Friday evenings reflected through sheer drapes on windows.

First, we lived at 601 Alabama Avenue, a three-story building just off New Lots Avenue, the main commercial thoroughfare in the neighborhood. I think my very first memory of anything was in that apartment. The image in my mind is gray and out of focus. It might have been any bitter winter day in January 1965, as New Yorkers huddled against temperatures below 10 degrees Fahrenheit and snowstorms every few days. Or perhaps it was January of the following year, or February of the one after, as blizzards howled through the city. New to winter, my mother was stunned by both its power and the minutiae of its effects. On the day I remember, my mother and I sat together at a window closed tight against the wind. If the glass pane had not been so cold, she might have leaned her forehead against it to look down at the ground outside. She noticed how it had changed color, how it was chalkier and paler than usual. I can picture it: concrete, ugly with a residue that is not snow. There is a particular way that New York sidewalks sometimes look on a cold winter day that stirs my memory of that day even now. However vague the recollection, I associate it with something very clear and familiar: the feeling of my mother and me, learning this new world and its winter.

In 1966, we moved around the corner to a larger place at 330 New Lots Avenue, two and a half blocks from the third-to-last stop on the 3 train, the elevated IRT Broadway-Seventh Avenue line. We paid $60 a month for six rooms. In this building, as in the prior one, our neighbors were all Jewish. A few buildings down stood the New Lots Talmud Torah synagogue, where neighborhood boys prepared for their bar mitzvahs with stern, ancient-seeming men who had survived the Holocaust and rapped the boys' knuckles with rulers in response to misdeeds real and perceived. In neighborhood stores, my mother bought items like kosher Manischewitz dry soup mixes, to which she added a bit of garlic, maybe some lemon juice, and pinches of staple Cuban spices such as cumin and oregano. Our landlord, super, and neighbor was a man whom my parents both called Mr. Fink. Long after we had left Brooklyn, whenever something happened at home that no one wanted to confess to, we would all say jokingly that Mr. Fink had done it.

The women who were our immediate neighbors in both buildings became my mother's first acquaintances in this country. With them, she tried to stave off a little of her isolation. When my sister and I were sick, she turned to them for advice. Maybe they were the ones who took some of our pictures, or maybe they came upstairs to watch my sister and me when my mother had to run an errand while my father was working. They taught my mother basic words in English and where on the Lower East Side of Manhattan to buy fabrics for the clothes she sewed for us.

It was from those neighbors that my mother learned to light candles every week. The women lit candles on Friday before sunset. But my mother saw them on Saturday, so that was when she lit hers. Early every Saturday morning for the rest of her life, she lit a candle and kept it lit all day. When she was old and bedbound, she would ask her daughters or caregivers to do it for her. Always eager to somehow locate my mother in history, I took the fact that she lit candles on Saturdays rather than Sundays as possible evidence that some of our ancestors must

Brooklyn with our neighbors, April 1965.

have come from an old *converso* family, those who after the expulsion of the Jews from Spain in 1492 continued to practice even after having to publicly profess Catholicism. I asked my mother about it when I was in college. No, she said, I just learned to do that from our neighbors in Brooklyn. A new immigrant, vulnerable and unsure, she thought she should pray every way possible.

None of it was easy. She had to learn so many new things: how to shop for food in American grocery stores, how to use public transit when necessary, how to get us immunized, how to enroll me in school, even how to mail a letter, because through all of it she never stopped writing home, nor waiting anxiously for Poly's letters to her.

Sometimes, pain and guilt can become transactional. When Poly wrote to our mother, he often asked her to send him things. "You promised that you were going to buy me a pair of shoes," he wrote to my mother a month after we left. Twice, Poly asked for a bicycle. My mother sent the money for someone to buy one for him. The new bike was Hungarian, blue, model number (as he wrote it) 24x1+3-8, with large tires, a basket for groceries, and a key holder. For a while, he slept with it parked next to his bed at night. Once, Poly asked my mother for a Beatles record. There was no record player in the house, but he said he could sell it for twenty pesos.

My mother did her best to comply with Poly's petitions. She likely thought it was the least she could do to make up for having left him. This, then, was my mother's world: taking care of two young daughters, buying clothes and trinkets for Poly to assuage her guilt and address his need, and all of it in a place she was not sure she'd ever be able to understand. But back then, she believed that everything would work out: Poly would join us soon, or, even better, we would return to Cuba, back to Poly, to her mother, to the place that had been her world.


I, meanwhile, was learning English without even realizing it. I remember my first day of kindergarten at P.S. 213. My new teacher asked me my name. *Ada*, I said, pronouncing it with both *A*'s short and a *D* that began at the tip of the top row of my teeth. That is the way you say it in Spanish, the way my parents said it at home, although usually they just called me Adita. The teacher looked at my eager face and responded, "Here"—or maybe she said in America—"we say Ada," pronouncing the name in English, with a long *A* at the beginning and a *D* formed near the roof of her mouth. I started calling myself Ada in English that kindergarten day. I think I might have taken it as a sign that I was learning, growing up. I was too young to think that maybe an American name might propel me to a world separate from my parents. A lot of people I knew had both Cuban and American names. Rodolfo was also Rudy; his son Rodolfito became Ralph. One friend was Francisca, also Panchita, also Franny, later Fran. The list goes on. Still, I wonder what my parents thought when I announced that I had a new name. I think my father would not have been surprised, because he, too, had multiple names in two languages. In Spanish, people called him Ramón, or Ramoncito, or sometimes Mongo. At work, in English, he was Raymond or Ray.

Since 1963 my father had been working at the Americana Hotel in Manhattan, first as a "kitchen helper," then starting in 1966 as a short-order cook at the hotel restaurant called simply The Coffee Shop. He worked the breakfast and lunch shifts and learned to make American pancakes and French toast, the two things he sometimes cooked for us on his days off. My mother did almost all the other cooking and feeding in our household, though my father always took care of our before-bed snack. Every night, she would bring him three apples, a knife, a large bowl, and two little ones. In Cuba, my family had eaten apples mostly at Christmas. He peeled each apple, sliced it, and put the slices in a little bowl for my sister and another for me. He shared his own apple with my mother, handing her the slices on the knife. When I finished my apple, I ate everyone else's peels from my father's bowl. It was a nightly ritual—maybe they thought of it as an American one—the thing that every night preceded our changing into pajamas and going to bed.

My mother was always a bad sleeper. She would lie in bed awake, ruminating, worrying, imagining things she kept at bay in the daylight. She dreamt that Poly was turning into skin and bones, that he had no shoes, that he got into a fight. One time, when she told him about a dream in which he was late to school, Poly was offended. He was never late to school, he asserted. "Don't dream [that] again . . . it hurts my feelings." Later, when she dreamt that he got lost on his way back from school, he was even more indignant: "I don't get lost." And to prove it, he showed off his command of the city's bus system: I take the 43 and transfer to either the 22, which takes me to the military hospital, or the 34, which drops me off at Bar Reyna.

Bar Reyna disappeared about a year later, when the Cuban government, in a campaign dubbed the Revolutionary Offensive, transferred some fifty-eight thousand businesses from private hands to the state—everything from bars and restaurants, to retail stores and street vendors' carts. The idea was to eradicate even more private property and thereby hasten the nation's transition to communism. As he played on the streets, walked to school, looked out a bus window, Poly noticed the changes. "Mami," he wrote, "you should see how this is getting," before listing all the places just nationalized in the immediate neighborhood: Divina's bodega, Simón's bar, Modesto's bar, Estevita's bodega, Estrella's kiosk, the barbershop, Bar Reyna. He listed them by name knowing that my mother would remember them easily. Her memory was always formidable.

Our own lives in Brooklyn were changing as well. A few years after arriving in the United States, my parents began serving as sponsors for other family members seeking to leave Cuba. Many stayed with us in the beginning. Suddenly, we had Cuban kin at our side. We could speak Spanish beyond our little circle of four. It was a momentous change for us, and it was a direct reflection of an important change in Poly's life. People suddenly disappeared from his domain, and then, just as abruptly, they appeared in mine.

Among the very first to arrive in New York was Gladys, my mother's niece, whom we called aunt because she was so much older than us. Some of my father's family arrived shortly after: my father's sister María—whom everyone called Nena—with her husband and two children, Miriam and Angel, named after his father. They arrived in February 1967. On the ride from the airport to Brooklyn, looking out at the colorless winter landscape, my aunt wondered why Americans didn't just cut down all the dead trees. We have pictures of my cousins on their first full day in New York, wearing clothes that would never ward off the cold and the snow. When buds appeared on the trees in springtime, it felt like a miracle to them. Nena had traveled to Brooklyn carrying a symbol of summer in her bag: a red tissue-paper rose that Poly had asked her to give to my mother. (Today, it sits on my desk, faded but still red, in a little jar in which my mother also placed a tiny folded note that reads, "The rose, a gift from Poly when Nena came, '67.")

The next to arrive after Nena was my mother's sister, Lucrecia, with her family. She had been a regular fixture in Poly's life after we left. She bought him things and helped him write letters; he went on outings with her family; he spent time on weekends and vacations at their house. Now they were in New York with us. I remember Lucrecia's husband, Pablo, knocking on our door one day. I was the one who opened it. The front of his shirt was covered in blood, and his hand was bandaged. He had lost part of a finger that day at his new job working as a machinist in a toy factory. My sister, Aixa, was baptized after their arrival. It was a late christening; she was close to four years old and stood almost as tall as I did then at six. The christening had been delayed by years, because the godfather was meant to be Poly and the godmother Lucrecia's daughter, Isabel. My mother hadn't wanted to baptize Aixa with both godparents missing. Now they did it with just Poly absent.

So, there we were: an extended family—together minus the still many of its members who remained in Cuba—making new immigrant lives in the place so often called the greatest city in the world. How strange, my parents might have thought, that this is now where we are, that this is now who we are. What went through my mother's mind as she dressed me for school in all those layers, pushing my hat down to my eyebrows, wrapping scarves around my mouth to protect me from the cold? She used to tell me that once during a particularly frigid day, she tried to keep me home, thinking the walk to school would surely make me sick. I cried and cried until she finally decided she had no choice but to take me, depositing me at the door to a world that conducted itself in English.

As they saw our own family change in a new country, did my parents sense that their immediate world was changing, too? As outsiders, would they have had the tools to understand the transformations unfolding all around them, and to understand that they themselves were a part of that change?

In 1960, a few years before our move there, the population of East New York was 80 percent white, most of it Jewish, with some Italians and Irish, as well. By the end of the decade, it was 80 percent Black and Puerto Rican. *The New York Times* referred to the neighborhood as a "pocket of poverty and racial tension." In the summer of 1966, that tension exploded. On July 14, a group of young white men assaulted a Black grocer; a few days later a woman was shot in the hip. Then on July 21—the very day that the mayor of New York City visited the neighborhood—a Black eleven-year-old boy named Eric Dean was shot and killed by a sniper. Later that night, three-year-old Russell Givens, also Black, was critically wounded, again by a sniper. The streets became "total chaos," reported one city official. White gangs chanted slurs at Black residents. Meanwhile, "tire jacks, bottles, Molotov cocktails, and bricks rained down from rooftops at the police," who numbered almost a thousand.

The unrest, like the worst of the tensions that preceded it, was concentrated on New Lots Avenue. My parents would have heard the sirens. By then, they had a television and might have seen something on the news. My father would have insisted on closing the windows and curtains. (Reading about these events, I think now of my father as a very old man in Miami Beach, always insisting that the blinds be shut after dark. It wasn't about privacy, he told me, but because someone might shoot into the apartment from the building across the street. I always wondered if he was thinking about 1950s Cuba; now I wonder if he was remembering the snipers in Brooklyn.)

One day, while we were all out, someone climbed up our fire escape and broke into our apartment through the kitchen window. I can't remember if anything was stolen. Soon after, we were all home one night sleeping when a burglar broke in through the front door and stole our television. My sister and I shared a room with windowed French doors facing the living room. I heard something, woke up, and saw the outline of a man. I assumed it was my father and went back to sleep. For years after that, I would sometimes lie awake, trembling in my bed, assuming a burglar was watching me to make sure that I was really asleep. It was after this break-in that my parents decided to leave Brooklyn, "that world of dusk, of rust, of iron . . . [that] fork in the road where all American lives cross," as Alfred Kazin once wrote.

My parents waited until the end of the school year to move to Miami, a place of palm trees and flamboyants, and already by then the capital of Cuban America. But things did not go particularly well for my parents there. My father developed back problems and couldn't work at all for a while. My mother, for the first time in the United States, had to get a job. She made $977 that year working as a factory seamstress at a place called Gilma's Fashions. From bed, my father taught my sister and me snatches of songs to welcome her home at the end of the day, but he'd change the lyrics as a joke. She'd return home by bus, tired both from the work and the commute. We didn't yet have a car, and she never learned to drive, anyway. My sister developed asthma, like our grandmother and our midwife aunt who had died a few years before. One memory I have from that time in Miami was my mother telling me that the pronoun *I* in English is always capitalized even when it appears in the middle of a sentence. Six-year-old-me told her she was wrong.

My parents couldn't make a go of it in Miami and decided to head back north. But ever the conscientious parents, they once more waited for summer so that I would not miss any school. We made the trip in a white Chevy sedan that my father purchased used for the journey. We didn't take much with us, only what we could fit in the trunk of the car. Arriving at our final destination in New Jersey, where my father's sister Nena lived, my parents took only a few things upstairs. Pajamas to sleep in, toothbrushes, maybe some clothes for the morning. Everything else could wait, said my father, tired from the long drive. But my mother hesitated. She reached back into the trunk and grabbed a small box. Poly's letters.

I write this book the way I do now, because she did that then, because that night she refused to part with the more than sixty letters that Poly had written to her since we left Cuba. Someone stole our car that night, with almost everything we owned packed tightly into the trunk.

# EIGHT

# Across the Skyline

**If my parents discovered America** in Brooklyn's East New York, it was in a town called West New York that I discovered Cuba. I couldn't help it. Cuba was everywhere there.

As its name implied, West New York was located west of New York City, across the Hudson River and in New Jersey. My parents chose it because some of our relatives were already living there. On my father's side, his sister Nena and her family had moved there from Brooklyn shortly before we came from Miami. So, too, had my mother's niece Gladys. She babysat us that first summer, after my parents started working and before we started school. One afternoon, as my mother was walking up the stairs to pick us up, she heard the radio on inside and a man's voice announcing that Fidel Castro's government had fallen. It was over, she thought. She would see Poly again; she would see her mother. She ran upstairs faster and faster, out of breath, desperate to hear more. But when she rushed inside, already fantasizing about her long-awaited return, she realized that what she had overheard was not news on the radio, but a skit by Cuban humorist Álvarez Guedes. She broke down in tears. I think that may be the only time I ever saw my mother really cry.

We arrived in West New York in the summer of 1969, when I was seven and about to start second grade. I know that because I measured my American childhood in school years.

We moved into an apartment around the corner from my father's sister Nena. My parents took the back bedroom with windows opening to a fire escape. After the Brooklyn break-ins, they always took the room with the fire escape to spare Aixa and me that danger. Their room was where we kept our *World Book Encyclopedia*. The typewriter I asked for on my ninth birthday sat atop the cabinet of my mother's sewing machine. On my mother's dresser was the ever-present portrait of Poly. My sister and I shared the other bedroom, and that was where we kept our only television, a small one. My father used to sit on my bed to watch the Yankees. One summer afternoon, we were watching a game side by side when he received word that there was a telegram for him at the Western Union. I kept watching the game, more attentively than usual—walks, errors, bases stolen, runs scored, all remembered in precise order so that I could narrate it for him on his return. But he came back with a telegram bearing news that his sister Juana had died in a train accident traveling from their hometown to Havana. The train had derailed on a bridge, and all the passengers were killed. My father wasn't interested in the game anymore.

The first time I ever wrote in Spanish was in that apartment. I was maybe nine years old and already a good reader and writer in English. I won spelling bees sometimes, though my mother used to feed me half a Xanax beforehand to calm my nerves, or maybe hers. But as my English expanded, I didn't often read or write in Spanish. Chronologically speaking, it was my first language, my mother tongue. Yet it was slowly becoming something of a second language to me. One night, a rare one in which my parents were out for some reason, I took it upon myself to write something in Spanish, as a challenge for myself and a surprise for them. The composition I wrote went something like this: I am Ada (pronounced in Spanish, because that was the language in which I was writing); I was born in Cuba; I live in West New York, New Jersey, with my parents and sister. My brother, Poly, is in Havana. I spelled *brother* incorrectly, writing *ermano* rather than *hermano*, and my mother had to explain the silent *h* to me. The short composition I penned that evening was probably the first time that I used writing to try to bridge the distance between my parents' world and mine.

I was eleven and in the middle of sixth grade when we moved to a nicer building, safer, too, with a locked door and an intercom at street level. We lived on the same floor as my father's brother, Jesús, who had just arrived from Cuba with his wife and two sons. Again, my parents took the bedroom with the fire escape, giving my sister and me the larger room with two windows facing south onto the street. Our room even had a walk-in closet with its own window. I learned how to make braids there, sitting cross-legged on the floor and practicing on the cloth belts that hung down from our dresses and blouses. My mother took pride in decorating the apartment. She bought pictures and vases to place just so, necessities like electric rice cookers, conveniences like a washing machine for our eat-in kitchen. My mother was making our apartment a home fit for the family she wanted us to be, for the family we already were: an entity that cohered, hopeful, its children a future.

. . .

I always thought that the only beautiful street in West New York was Boulevard East, lined with a strip of pretty park that had a glorious view across the Hudson River to the skyscrapers of Manhattan. The older I got, the more time I spent there, going for walks and reading books on a bench less than a mile from where Aaron Burr had killed Alexander Hamilton in a duel in 1804, and a block or two away from a bust to Cuban patriot leader José Martí. Martí faced in toward the town; I always sat facing out toward Manhattan.

Manhattan was where my father worked. On moving to New Jersey, he returned to the job he had held when we lived in Brooklyn, as a short-order cook at the Americana Hotel, which became the Sheraton in 1979. Every morning before 5 a.m., he took a bus to the Port Authority; then, no matter the weather, he walked the 1.3 miles to work. He always loved being a walker in the city. My mother's job, at a factory sewing collars onto coats and blazers, was just a few blocks away from our apartment.

My father always worked on weekends, so those days were my mother's days with us. She made my sister and me help her clean. Only when we finished could we watch cartoons. Often, she'd make us write letters to Cuba or add a note to one that she was writing so that we could send our love to Poly, to our grandmother, to Tía Niña. We did our hair on weekends, too. She straightened mine with an iron sometimes, then switched to a blow-dryer after those became popular. Sometimes, she sat on a chair in the middle of our bedroom room facing the mirror over our dresser, and my sister and I would pluck out her gray hairs one by one with our fingers. There weren't that many yet. I don't remember playing with friends and neighbors that much on weekends. We did that every day after school, after homework. Outside on the street in front of the building, mothers suddenly appeared at the windows above to call us to dinner when it was time, one *suban, ya está la comida*—come upstairs, dinner is ready—following another, till we all went up, and the street was quiet.

As we made these everyday memories, all of us—our own nuclear family, our extended one, many of our neighbors and classmates—were remaking the place where we lived. We turned West New York from a predominantly Italian and Irish working-class neighborhood into a new Cuban enclave, like Miami but smaller and colder. At the time, the United States was seeing the largest wave of Cuban migration since the beginning of the revolution. It was not a dramatic seaborne exodus like some of the ones that came later. This one was slower. Approximately three hundred thousand Cubans arrived on daily "freedom flights" between 1967 and 1973. The federal government had recently started a resettlement program to incentivize newcomers to move to places such as West New York. In the spring of 1968, town officials reported that every month some thirty new students enrolled in the public schools, the vast majority of them Cuban and many of them unable to speak the language. By 1970, the town of less than a square mile had a population of about forty-five thousand, over half of whom had been born in Cuba.

Political circumstance made our immigrant story deviate from the American norm. Unlike our occasional classmates from other Caribbean islands, my sister and I did not spend summer vacations back "home" with grandparents while our parents worked. Our parents could not do what immigrant parents from other countries did: They couldn't visit ailing relatives or attend their funerals after their passing.

Yet there were clear advantages to being a person from Cuba living in the belly of one of the world's two superpowers. US immigration policy was Cold War policy. That meant that Washington welcomed Cubans with open arms, because their arrival in the United States helped discredit the Cuban government. In 1966, the Cuban Adjustment Act fast-tracked Cubans to US citizenship. All those who had arrived after January 1, 1959, could now apply for legal residency after just two years in the country. (In 1976, that was shortened to a year and a day.) The expedited residency status meant that Cubans could become US citizens—and thus voters— faster than other immigrants. African Americans, meanwhile, did not have their voting rights enshrined in US law until 1965.

My parents became US citizens in 1971, my mother on November 8, two days before she turned forty-five, and my father on September 14. He had turned fifty a few months earlier. As was required at the time, he wore a jacket and tie to his swearing in. My mother, I know, would have worn a dress and pantyhose, her hair short and brushed back and up from her forehead, as she wore it most of my life. I didn't go through the swearing in until two years later. I have the originals of all three naturalization certificates, my mother's, father's, and mine, each with an attached photograph, each photograph with our respective signatures written vertically, first name on the left, last name to the right of our faces. My sister doesn't have one, because she was born in Brooklyn.

The certificates meant that we were US citizens. But asked what we were, none of us would have said American. Other people—seeming to belong without even trying—those were the Americans. The most impor-

tant Americans in our daily lives were our teachers. But the only Americans we ever observed in their own homes (or in ours) were all on television screens. They tended to live in houses with stairs on the inside. The parents went out on dates and gave their kids allowances. And everyone always spoke English. There was no one who remotely resembled us.

In high school in West New York in the late 1970s, I used to love a short story by Philip Roth titled, "The Conversion of the Jews." One part of the story that resonated with me was a paragraph about a mother and grandmother who always counted Jewish names on lists. Among the fifty-eight casualties of a plane crash at LaGuardia, for example, they found either eight or nine, depending on whether they treated Miller as a Jewish name.

I counted names, too, looking for people like me: Spanish-speaking, culturally other, and living in the United States. On the team rosters of the baseball games I watched with my father there were some (not nearly as many as later). Among the authors anthologized in our English textbooks in school, there were absolutely none. On the television shows we watched, I remember only two Latino characters, both of whom appeared in reruns from shows then decades old: Desi Arnaz in *I Love Lucy* and a gardener who went by the name of Frank in *Father Knows Best*. Not one woman, not one child. Whenever I went to the movies, I stayed for the credits, studying them for names like my own. Toward the very end, an occasional one might appear as a grip, say, or a prop assistant. Even today, put a *Playbill* in my hands, stand me in front of the Vietnam Veterans Memorial or even a rack of personalized key rings, and I will still count names. I do it reflexively, the same way I kiss stale bread before I throw it out, as my mother taught me to always do.

Rather than call ourselves American, we all called ourselves Cuban.

Perhaps it is no surprise that my parents and their generation did that. But I did the same. So did most of my friends. My sister was born in Brooklyn, and even she usually described herself and thought of herself as Cuban.

At home, we spoke Spanish, and we ate only Cuban food. My mother hung promotional calendars from our local stores, most of them with photographs of Havana's iconic Morro lighthouse, or the Cuban Capitol Building that looks just like the US one, or sometimes just a landscape with palm trees and a country *bohío* (hut). We had a small shrine to Cuba's patron saint, La Caridad del Cobre. My father had bought the little statue for my mother in 1969, while we were living in Miami, shortly before we moved to New Jersey. Today my sister has it, and on the bottom, written in my mother's handwriting on a piece of masking tape is the notation, *Miami 1969 Comprado por Papy.*

The neighborhood outside our doors was almost as Cuban as our home. At the corner bodegas and the dry cleaners and even the doctor's office, we all spoke Spanish. Our dentist, once licensed in Cuba but not yet in the United States, used to fill our cavities in his living room without anesthesia. We had two grocery stores on our corner, both Cuban-owned. My mother favored the one not owned by the woman named María, whom my mother suspected of flirting with my father and maybe vice versa. At the other one, the owner let regular customers like us buy things on installment. He kept track of our purchases and payments in a little book. At the end of their pay period, my parents settled their accounts. My sister and I went there all the time, to buy candy and snacks and to pick up whatever item my mother might be missing for dinner: garlic, lemon, plantains, salad stuff.

A block away was Bergenline Avenue, "a straight shot of Spanish for almost a hundred blocks," as Junot Díaz once described it. There, one Cuban establishment after another opened its doors: La Isla Bakery, La

Comercial Gift Shop, La Campana China Restaurant, and on and on. Cubans bought out existing businesses, sometimes left up the signs that said "Pharmacy" or "Funeral Home" and replaced Giovanni or Sugarman with Díaz or Alonso. Some of the new stores were resurrected versions of ones owned by the very same people in Cuba, businesses that had been confiscated during Fidel Castro's Revolutionary Offensive. In the same way that people around Poly had disappeared and then suddenly appeared in my world, so, too, did some stores, restaurants, and bars.

My mother took us to church services in Spanish, and every Sunday one of the petitions during the collective prayers was always a plea for the freedom of political prisoners in Cuba: *Te lo pedimos, señor.* One day at church, my mother ran into somebody she had baptized in one of those sacrament marathons she used to do with her godmother in the country-side when she was a young woman. Every year on the Sunday closest to the feast day of La Caridad del Cobre on September 8, my sister and I accompanied my mother on a procession in the saint's honor. We marched along Bergenline Avenue, past buildings sporting anti-Castro graffiti and the names of the militant anti-Castro groups Alpha 66 and Omega-7, the latter established in 1974 and considered by the FBI to be "the top domestic terrorist organization operating in the United States" at the time.

In addition to our prayers, my mother taught us all kinds of things to ward off bad luck and draw the good. A glass of water under the bed, on the headboard side; never putting a hat on top of the table (or was it the bed?); saying *bésame el culito* (kiss my little butt) under our breath whenever someone complimented us. And on and on: never leaving our shoes crossed on the floor at night; never letting anyone sweep over our feet with a broom; never placing a purse on the floor. I thought all those prescriptions were Cuban, but I know now that some of them also exist in other parts of Latin America and in the US South. Whenever one of us was sick, my mother would bless us with the traditional prayer to San Luis Beltrán, known as the Apostle to the Americas. She crossed herself at every designated place and then spit lightly on our foreheads before making the sign of the cross there, too.

That was the strange, hybrid world where my sister and I grew up. In one drawer were things my mother was saving to send to Cuba, in another my growing collection of books. It began with titles such as *Snowbound with Betsy* (which I read aloud to my sister), *The Brady Bunch in the Mystery of Treasure Island*, and *From the Mixed-Up Files of Mrs. Basil E. Frankweiler*, most of them purchased through the Scholastic Books program at school. Because I had so few books, I kept a tally on the back covers of how many times I'd read them. *Mixed-Up Files*, I think I read nine times, ⊩⊩ ‖‖. I went to school in English, watched TV in English, spoke to my sister and friends in English. But with my parents, it was always Spanish.

As my English soared, I became more and more a bridge between two worlds, or at least a bridge between two languages. My mother always called on me to translate and interpret. She also volunteered me to do it for neighbors, relatives, even strangers. Part of me liked the feeling of competence it gave me; part of me resented the responsibility, especially when I didn't understand the real substance of what I was translating, adult things about taxes, or unemployment benefits, or union pensions. The stakes felt higher than I could handle. I hated that sometimes, when we left West New York for places where English was the norm, the Americans in charge would look at me as much as my mother, because they knew that she needed me in order to understand what they were saying. One time when Aixa and I were shopping with my mother in Sears, she wanted us to ask the sales clerk something in English. We didn't want to; she couldn't make us do it. "Fine," she insisted, "I'll ask her myself." My sister and I hid inside a circular rack of clothes, because her English embarrassed us. Now, of course, I wish I could take it back. A therapist once told me that parents forcing their children to translate for them might be considered a kind of abuse. The therapist wasn't an immigrant.

In all the back-and-forth between English and Spanish, as we all made our way in a distinct corner of America populated largely by people like us, Cuba permeated everything. "An absent presence, a present absence," I would eventually call it in one of my books. But it wasn't just Cuba, the place. It was also the people. Most of our family was still on the island: Poly, all our surviving grandparents, eight out of nine of my mother's living siblings, four out of six of my father's, and the hundreds of souls who were their issue. Yet in many ways, they inhabited our world, too. They were on my parents' lips, sometimes a yearning in their eyes.

Poly, of course, was both never with us and with us all the time. I cannot remember a time when I was not aware of his existence and of his absence. I watched my mother miss him—write to him, buy him things, pray for him. I invoked his name to show her that I had not forgotten, even though I had no memory of him at all. When I looked at the letters he wrote, I noticed the way his *A*'s looked like triangles. I thought it meant he might be a born architect, like the father in *The Brady Brunch*. When I watched that show or read a novel like Beverly Cleary's *Fifteen*, I thought of Poly. Maybe someday soon, he would live with us. He would study architecture, and he would have handsome friends who might fall in love with me.

There was also my grandmother, Rita. I grew up on stories of her. Whenever my mother combed my hair—standing before me as I sat on the bed facing her, cheek against her belly, arms around her waist, her hand guiding the brush through my hair—she always said longingly that that was how her mother had combed her hair.

When I was difficult with my parents, they called me Gregorio, the name of my father's oldest brother, a man so picky and exacting that he did not marry his girlfriend until they'd been together for decades. When I scratched my mosquito bites incessantly and gave myself ugly scars, my mother tried to deter me with stories of her brothers Adelino and Celedonio, who had scratched so much and so hard that their wounds never healed, and both had to have legs amputated. (I didn't learn until later that they were diabetic.) When I rocked myself in chairs that were not rocking chairs, my mother would snap at me, "That was what Tatá always did," referring to her mentally ill sister. The thought that I might display some of Tatá's behaviors terrified my mother. I think my mother was also scared that she herself sometimes displayed them. She would mutter under her breath, "I'm getting like Tatá."

I didn't know any of these people; they were something like ghosts to me. But in that unusual form—as a refrain, a warning, a lament, even just a sigh—they made the journey with us from Cuba and kept us company in the United States.

My mother missed them so much. I imagine her reading details of their everyday lives in the letters she received, pausing to run her finger over the words on the page, leaving the latest letter by her bedside table to read again before turning off the light. Closing her eyes, she could see her mother, follow her footsteps around the old house, in the kitchen making tamales, on the porch sharing news with a neighbor. She worried when she noticed in a photograph that my grandmother's feet were swollen. She would have to send new sandals soon. "Adela never forgets my feet!" my grandmother always said. My mother smiled to herself as she pictured her mother—she could do it so easily—tucking a few coins into the handkerchief she rolled up and pinned to the inside of her housedress like a pocket. She was happy when she imagined her leaning her head as far back as she could, opening her eyes wide for Poly to put in eye drops, the Murine she had sent not long before. She teased her mother in her own mind when she saw her doting over the little chick someone had brought her as a gift, keeping it in a box, feeding it, laying out water, wrapping it up for warmth at night, and moving the box close to her own bed. All those scenes my mother read in the letters she received, and it ached.

One weekend afternoon, the sun pouring into my sister's and my bedroom, my mother sat us down on the bed to tell us about Cuba, and her people, and her past. But she didn't reveal too much. That was her way, hurrying ahead before too many thoughts and feelings caught up with her. Mostly, she sang. Her voice was beautiful, but without meaning to or even realizing that she was doing it, she often changed the melody of the original. Today, there are old Cuban songs that I sing the way she did, and when I hear the originals, I wonder at how different they sound from my mother's versions.

With a cassette recorder in front of her, my mother enacted for us a kind of soundtrack of her Cuban life. She performed the chants of street vendors, imitating the accent and cadence of each peddler, as she would have heard them from her window or porch. *Vaya, el billete entero, a San Cristóbal le toca ahora, vaya* went the cry of the man hawking lottery tickets. She sang the favorite songs of different members of the family: her oldest sister Lola's favorite about the landscape after heavy rains; a sad ballad her mother used to sing about the death of a child, one of her own sons having died at the age of seven in 1919; her father's favorite *punto guajiro* (peasant songs with improvised lyrics) about a country man pining for a woman's attentions. My mother sang us snippets of songs she would have heard in her house her whole life, until they faded away with her exile. She shared her own favorite songs, including the one she always sang after my father had left for the United States and she was yearning for him—"Tuya Soy." I am yours.

Toward the end of the tape, she recited patriotic poems she had memorized as a child, including the famous Bonifacio Byrne poem written shortly after the end of the Spanish-American War, narrating the poet's return to Havana and his pain on seeing an American flag rather than the Cuban one flying over the harbor. She performed the Cuban national anthem, a version that included a verse asking Cuba's patron saint, La Caridad del Cobre, to ease the suffering of Cubans. She choked up a little, as she sang it.

At one point, during that weekend recording session, I leaned into the microphone, adopted what I must have thought was a sultry voice, and said in English, "Hi, there." I could perform, too. I was almost a teenager, after all. And sometimes I chafed against the relentlessness of so much Cuba—the way my parents were constantly comparing everything to what they had known before, and especially the way they used old norms from there to determine what I could and couldn't do here and now. My sister and I developed a habitual rejoinder for when our parents tried to impose those views on us. It went something like: "This isn't Cuba!" or "We're not in Cuba anymore!"

But maybe my mother insisted on telling us her stories, on making her recordings of Cuban songs and poems, on invoking Adelino and Tatá and all the others, because there was something she didn't want to lose. It wasn't her memory. She didn't have to cling to that to retain it; it was just hers. But in New Jersey in the 1970s, proud as she saw my sister and me making our way in this country that still felt so foreign to her, I think she sensed that everything had moved too far, too fast. Our present would never be hers, and her past would never be legible to us. Her own daughters did not know her world, or the people who had made her. And without such knowledge, could they ever really know her? Perhaps it was that loss she wanted to foil, that continuity she wanted to ensure with her small acts and gestures and stories.

I can venture with more certainty that in the moment, as she sang for us in front of the tape recorder, she never imagined me, half a century later, searching for traces of her, gathering fragments, imperfectly sketching an outline of her life across two countries, perpetually wishing that I could see her world less in her arms, as she always loved to hold me, than through her eyes.

# NINE

# Mother Hunger

**When Poly was fifteen,** he began signing his letters to my mother with a graffiti tag, adding quotes around his name, turning the tail of the *y* into an arrow and adding the last two digits of the year below that. I used to try copying the style myself when I doodled my name.

Occasionally, he'd include a little wallet-size portrait with a dedication on the back side. The face on the portraits was no longer that of a boy. It was a harder face, baby fat long gone, chin stubbled. He reminded my mother to send razors because he shaved now. He still told her about his baseball games, but, in general, the news he shared was no longer a boy's news. He sold his blue Hungarian bicycle to buy a wristwatch. A few months before he turned fifteen, he declared that he had a girlfriend.

Her name was Marisol; she was one year older than him, and Tía Niña approved, because she was "a good girl who liked

school." I imagine my mother would have been less happy to read Poly's occasional mentions of beer, rum, and cigarettes.

The letters let me glimpse what I never saw in real life: my brother growing up, my grandmother as something other than a ghost. For that reason, Poly's letters, his childhood chronicle of family separation, are like his gift to me.

For all the unexpected scenes painted in Poly's letters, however, there is something very clearly missing from them. It wasn't references to the family members no longer with him and now with us, nor to the businesses that disappeared from his world and then suddenly appeared in mine. It was instead the very thing that had always marked time for me: namely, the steady, predictable progression from school year to school year: third grade to fourth, fourth to fifth, fifth to sixth, and so on.

As a boy, Poly attended one of the most famous schools in Cuba: Ciudad Libertad. It was founded in September 1959, on the campus of what had been Camp Columbia, the largest military installation on the island, the place where my father had sometimes worked, the place where a white dove had landed on Fidel Castro's shoulder as he promised Cubans a new future. The new school on those grounds was to be a symbol of that future. Instead of army uniforms, there would be school uniforms; instead of rifles, pencils; instead of war, culture and learning. Thus did Poly go to school at a showcase for the revolution.

Some of the students in the model school were the sons and daughters of ministers, but they were a very small minority. Together with the children of professionals who attended the school, they accounted for

Scene from Ciudad Libertad, c. 1968.

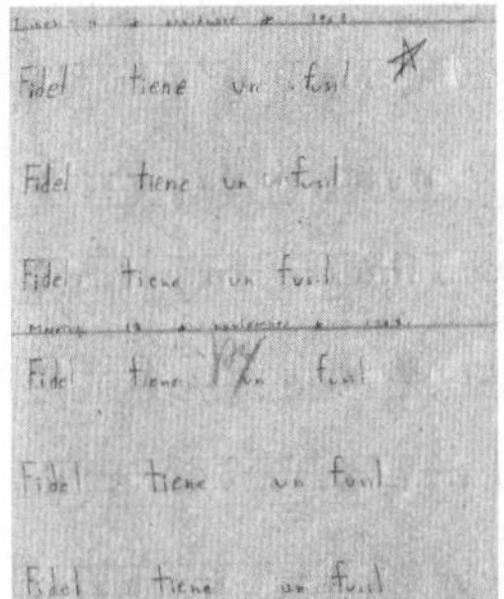

Pages from student notebooks, Ciudad Libertad.
*Left:* Fidel has a rifle. *Right:* I love mother.

about 20 percent of the student body. The vast majority of the students—Poly and my cousins among them—came from very different backgrounds. As a teacher from the school explained, "We have here a poor neighborhood, quite poor. . . . In addition, Marianao is characterized by a social environment that is not the most select but rather one of fairly humble extraction, and those are the students who come to this school." It was a challenge, yet also perfectly in keeping with what the revolution touted. *Cuarteles en escuelas*—barracks into schools—Fidel had proclaimed years before taking power. Everyone would receive a free education, and the children of humble neighborhoods like ours deserved that just as much as anyone else.

But real life is always more complicated than a slogan. And it definitely was in Poly's case. He was nine years old when we left, so he should have been in fourth grade; or, given his birthday in December, perhaps in third. Five months after our departure, he wrote to my mother that he had been left back—an early toll of our leaving—but he didn't mention in what grade. In September 1964, soon to turn eleven, he announced that he had been promoted to fourth grade. The following fall, he told my mother proudly that he was doing quite well in fifth grade. He had six subjects and four teachers. He caused something of a ruckus in school one day, when he distributed some greeting cards that my mother had sent for his classmates, and the girls began arguing about which card was the prettiest.

After that, Poly never mentioned passing from one grade to the next. The years went by, new Septembers rolled around, yet he never seemed to have advanced to sixth grade. It is difficult to piece together exactly what happened. He never explained it, and the letters I have from my aunt to my mother do not provide much by way of explanation either. Recently, I found some contextual clues in a 1969 interview with one of the teachers at the school. She estimated that about 10 percent of the fifth grade at Ciudad Libertad was held back every year. The teacher blamed the parents and families. She said that they preferred to keep their children home to run errands, or they didn't want to deal with the problem of getting them up early or sending them to school in the rain. "We have these kids who spend a year without going to school and two years without going to school." Then, after missing a year, the child would suddenly reappear. And it was hard to know what to do with them, academically and socially. A child in that situation, she said, was "marked." Even if he stayed in school, he would always be noticeably older than his classmates. She regularly over-heard students taunting those kids, saying things like, "How come you're in this class if you're so old?" Is that how they mocked Poly, twelve, then thirteen years old and still in fifth grade?

It was about that time that Poly left Ciudad Libertad to attend what everyone called *la beca*. The term literally means scholarship, but in Cuba in this period, it was used to refer to state boarding schools in the countryside, established in 1966 for students starting in the sixth grade and then extended to students in the fifth grade in 1967. The schools combined the study of traditional academic subjects with agricultural work and political education. Their purpose was to produce new kinds of Cubans, young communist subjects willing, in theory at least, to embrace manual labor for the collective good. The government believed it was easier to do that in a rural boarding school setting, away from parents whose values might still reflect a past unsuited to the present.

Poly seemed to like the new arrangement. The food was good, he wrote to my mother, and school officials gave the students clothes and equipment to play baseball. He took a test on Cuban history and thinks he aced the question about the Pact of Zanjón, an 1878 peace agreement that (mostly) ended Cuba's first war of independence again Spain, without achieving that goal. (The pact would play a prominent role in my first book, published in 1999.) Poly was certain that he'd passed all his exams, and he knew that that would make my mother happy. He was also proud to report that he had been designated "vanguard" of his "platoon," along with twenty-seven other *compañeros*. The boys marched down the street in formation, and everyone who saw them "was blown away." The school year ended, but neither he nor a family member picked up his grades. He never reported whether he'd been promoted to sixth grade or not.

When the next year started, Poly was at a new *beca*. He offered no explanation for the change. He studied academic subjects in the morning followed by work in the afternoon, planting corn and beans, cleaning the school, doing whatever else was needed. Poly liked this *beca* better, he said. Maybe it was the setting: This one was prettier than the other one. Or maybe it was the people: "I want to tell you that I feel very happy with my *compañeros*, we get along well, and we love one another," he wrote to my mother. But there was one major problem. His grades from the previous year were lost. They gave him a test to decide on his grade. He didn't share the results with my mother, which makes me think that he did not pass. That would mean that, at almost fourteen years of age, he was still stuck in fifth grade. Yet, that fall, living at school, he seemed happy.

Then came December. Like May with Mother's Day, December was never a good month for Poly. His birthday, December 6, fell on a Wednesday that year. He secured a pass to go home the weekend before. But when Monday, December 4, rolled around, he did not want to leave. So he stayed a few extra days to spend his actual birthday at home with Tía Niña and our grandmother. The following Monday, he felt the same way still. It was almost Christmas, after all; he might as well just stay through the holidays. The school kicked him out. When my mother found out and wrote him a scolding letter, Poly defended himself. I don't deserve that, he wrote, it wasn't my fault. Instead, he blamed his father, who was supposed to have written him a note justifying the absence. At the end of that school year, which he never finished, Tía Niña wrote to my mother, frustrated, "Let's see if we can manage to get him to start and finish" the grade next year.

A relative tried to secure a spot for him at another *beca*. This one paid students a modest stipend for their labor. But it never seems to have worked out. He had been ready to go, he explained to my mother later, when his father showed up with the head of school (which school I'm not sure) and told him to wait, that he had a spot for him at a better *beca*. That failed to materialize, too, and he seems to have missed a whole other year of school.

Again, Poly blamed his father, to whom he referred by his nickname: "Polo is trying to get me caught up having to do my military service or to be sent to a state farm, but I won't give him that pleasure." He continued, if "I end up having to do my military service, I'll get through it, but when I get out I won't ever look him in the face again, and if he shows up to pester me, I'll hit him, even if he is my father, which for me he is not." He knew that my mother would be upset at those words, so he responded to her disapproval preemptively: "But, Mother, what he has done to us is not something that a father, nor even a human being, would [ever] do; only an animal can think the way he does."

That mental argument seems to have loosened something in Poly. He made his case against his father again in his next letter: "Understand that when you left, I was nine years old and in fourth grade." According to his letters at the time, he was actually in third. "Today I am almost 16 and I still haven't passed fifth grade." He continued:

> He's made you and me suffer, but he will pay for it, if it is true that there is a GOD so great in Heaven, [one] that can bring us together again, little mother of mine *[madrecita mía]*. With all that Polo has done, I know that you love me and I know that you would give your life for me to be by your side, just as I would give mine . . . I love you and I will continue to love you all my life, because there is no love like that of mother and son.

The next school year, things got off to a much better start. Tatá's son, Carlitos, found Poly a spot with him at another place. This one was farther away, in the province of Matanzas in a town called Pedro Betancourt (named after a very handsome general from the Cuban war of independence, who happens to appear on the cover of my first book). At this *beca*, as well, Poly worked and studied, but his coursework was more specialized, focusing on the plants and animals that caused damage to crops. He weeded under the hot sun, chopping away the undesirable plants, eating guavas and oranges as he worked. His *compañeros* were all men, and they got along well. Carlitos was with him, the older cousin who had told my mother years before that he was the only one who really understood Poly.

Discipline was not military, but "each according to his conscience," he explained, and they had the time to watch movies and to play baseball and dominoes.

He was less happy to have to spend his birthday doing voluntary agricultural work, harvesting tangerines from six in the morning to six in the evening. At night he'd hung out with the others, but they hadn't even been able to drink. Poly blamed Fidel Castro and something called the Ten Million Ton Harvest. It was, as the name suggests, a massive drive to produce a ten-million-ton sugar harvest, the largest in the nation's history. According to the Cuban government, the success of the gargantuan harvest would produce the means necessary to carry out industrialization and defeat underdevelopment forever. Castro called 1969 "The Year of the Decisive Effort," a year of eighteen months, he said. Christmas and New Year's would be postponed until the end of the harvest in July 1970. Everything would be geared toward that goal, and, to help, the sale of alcohol was suspended. For that reason, it was impossible for Poly to get a drink for his sixteenth birthday on December 6, 1969.

Around Christmas, Poly had an accident with a machete and needed three stitches on a finger. He wrote to my mother, "It is in moments like that when one knows that one's mother is not at one's side to offer consolation. How sad it is. It is like when a blind man wants to see the dawn and cries because he can't. But I didn't cry, because you taught me not to. Every day my love for you is greater, and every minute of the life I have, I will dedicate to you, *madrecita*."

The following month Poly wrote again about his immense love for our mother and for my sister and me. That was his last letter from that school. Maybe he got tired of working so hard; maybe he was bored; maybe he just missed Tía Niña and our grandmother. Whatever the reason, he picked up one day and left without telling anyone. The next weekend, Carlitos got a pass to go home and found my brother sitting on the porch. That's not for me, Poly told him.

In May, Poly wrote to my mother from home. For the first time since we left in 1963, he had forgotten to send her a Mother's Day greeting. It made him want to cry. But he reassured her that even though there'd been no letter that year, he loved her more than ever. "You know that in my eyes, your image is always reflected . . . deep inside me lives the name of my absent mother."

A few months later, Poly was at a different place; this one combined study with work in the textile industry. To be a student there, however, one had to be under seventeen years of age, and Poly had just turned seventeen. He applied to stay on as a full-time worker. That same year, the government criminalized laziness; men between the ages of seventeen and sixty who were not studying, working, or doing military service could be sentenced to unpaid labor on state farms. The stakes were getting higher. I don't know what happened with Poly's application to continue working at the textile factory. But his days as a student had come to an end.

Poly was seventeen, and he had never finished fifth grade. My mother never told me any of this, not then, not ever. Neither did Poly. As he struggled there, I was already an excellent student here, near perfect attendance, always assuming I would go to college because that was what my mother told me and because that was what I wanted. In my wildest dreams, I could never have imagined that my brother could be seventeen years old and not ever have finished elementary school. Maybe that was why they didn't tell me; it was their shared secret, their shared shame. Poly's was also the kind of story one would never read in a Cuban history book.

As Poly's schooling was paralyzed, his letters became less frequent. More and more, he began his missives with apologies for his silences. He was lazy when it came to writing, he said more than once. More importantly, he admitted to wanting to write only when he had good news to share, when he was doing well in school, and therefore able to make my mother happy from a distance. But those times were becoming rarer and rarer.

There were no letters at all in 1972, the year I turned ten— or none that survived anyway. The following year, Poly turned twenty. In one of his three letters that year, he purposely left out the date. At the top, where he

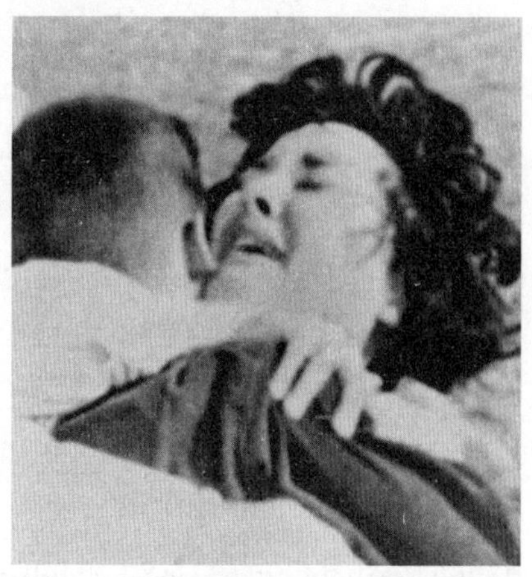

Cuban mother and son reunite after a long separation, Miami, 1966.

would have normally indicated the date, he wrote instead, *Para qué fecha si mi corazón ni mide ni marca el tiempo.* "For what purpose a date, if my heart neither measures nor marks time." He apologized for not having written and reassured my mother that his silence was no indication that his love for her had waned. "In my mind, you are always present . . . you are like a light that guides me on the path of good . . . I love you with all the strength my soul gives me; yes, you, mother of my soul." Did his intensity stun my mother a little, as it did me when I first read the letters? "I am fine," he concluded, "given the circumstances. I say that because I will only be well when I have you at my side."

To say the letters are hard for me to read is an understatement. Sometimes I have to get up and leave them behind for a while. I want a respite from the shame I feel reading them—shame for him, for my mother, for all of us.

In 1974, Poly wrote only one letter, and used the same heading on top: "For what purpose a date, if my heart neither measures nor marks time." In this letter, Poly gave his suffering a name. Trauma. "You have to understand that my life is full of the great trauma that I suffered." What did that trauma mean for him in daily life? He explained: "Everything feels heavy, I have little will, even when I'm determined to follow a path, everything falls apart. And I ask myself, why, without ever reaching a convincing answer. But let's change the subject." Then he added, *son cosas de esta vida.* "They are things of this life." Not of life in a generic sense, but of *this* life, *his* life.

Our grandmother Rita died in 1975. I would never know the grandmother in all my mother's stories, the grandmother she insisted loved me so much. Migration can sever so much. The call came in the middle of the night, at an hour when the ring alone portended something terrible. She had been declining for some time. My mother had requested permission from the Cuban government to visit before she died. There were exceptions made sometimes for reasons like that. But her petition was denied, and she was devastated—devastated by her death, devastated by the fact that she hadn't seen her mother in twelve years, devastated that she hadn't been able to say goodbye, to hold her hand, or stroke her hair, or kiss her forehead, as I would later do with my own mother when she was dying. I imagine that Poly, too, was crushed by our grandmother's death. She had helped raise him after we left, lying in bed with him at night when he was sad and missed our mother. The year she died Poly wrote no letters to my mother.

In 1977, Poly wrote only one letter to my mother, and in it he included one to me. I was turning fifteen. My parents could not afford the fancy *quinceañera* ball that many Cuban American girls had. But we rented a ball gown, long and pink with a hoop skirt, for a set of professional photographs. Poly wrote to me one month before my birthday so that the letter would arrive on time. It was hard, he said, to express in words his profound love for me. He felt sad and happy at the same time. Sad, he said, because he could not share the special day with me, with us. Happy, because I was becoming a woman, more able to help my mother with chores. (Two years earlier, the Cuban government had issued something called the Family Code, establishing that the work of the home corresponded equally to both partners. Housework would no longer be women's work. My brother had not taken the dictum to heart.)

In 1978, Poly wrote only one letter. He reported proudly that he had been at the same job for more than two months. The job was working as an assistant to an accountant in a state construction company. His main responsibility was to keep track of workers' vacation time. He liked it. He earned good money; he wasn't working in agriculture under the grueling sun; he had to dress professionally. "Think about sending me some clothes, because your son has to be well-dressed at work," he wrote to my mother. At the top of the letter, right next to the year, he added a heading. He was copying the Cuban government's practice of naming years: the Year of the Agrarian Reform, the Year of Education, the Year of Solidarity, and so on. The government called 1978 the Year of the 11th World Festival of Youth and Students. Poly, whose schooling had stopped long before he earned a high school degree, gave the year his own title. It was a hopeful one: "The Year of My Absolute Consecration." Did he believe that this was the year in which God would finally look down on him and bless him, or the year in which he would himself become more devoted to work, family, God? I do not know. But he did not last long at his new job.

Living in West New York, I used to poke my head into my parents' room and sometimes find my mother lying in bed in the late afternoons after work. She wasn't exactly crying, but I could tell she was not happy. The room was dark, the heavy curtains obscuring the view of the fire escape out the back window. On the dresser at the foot of my parents' bed, I could see the portrait of my brother, the one where it looked like he was wearing makeup. He was older now in real life, but she liked this picture better; he still looked like a boy in it.

My mother was not a depressive person. She was lively and warm; she smiled easily and made people around her feel welcomed and good. But when I used to find her lying in bed looking miserable, she would look up and tell me softly, *Tengo la cabeza mala.* Literally, I have a bad head or my head is bad, the phrase could refer to a headache or anxiety or depression or just general malaise. She would have been nearing fifty, starting menopause. Her mother had died, and she hadn't been there with her, which broke her heart. The long dark winters did not help, surely. Perhaps my father was straying, as Cuban husbands of his generation were wont to do. I have no idea. But something was very much troubling her.

Now, as I sit with Poly's letters in front of me, correlating their dates with the trajectory of my own life and my mother's, I can see that her short bouts in bed corresponded with the growing intensity of Poly's letters: his melodramatic declarations of love, his threats against his father, his insistence that he would only ever be fine if he was at her side. Maybe she had just finished reading one of his letters that time when she told me, as I sat on the edge of her bed, "I wish I'd never left Poly." Then she asked me to leave her alone for a while.

Still, my mother never stayed long in bed, never sulked, never moped. Her way was always to try to outrun all possible sadness with activity, with a project. In this case, she redoubled her efforts to bring Poly to the United States. On November 1, 1977, she filed a new application for a Relative Immigrant Visa for Poly. It was approved four and a half months later on March 18, 1978. Because there was no US embassy in Havana, the newly approved petition was sent to the US Consul in Toronto for the issuance of the visa. The approval she received also warned that visas were limited, that demand was very high, and that they would be issued in chronological order. Patience, lots of patience would be required.

It was a kind of double bind. Poly was always waiting, always expecting to leave. His visa process was underway. He filled out paperwork, waited to hear about interviews, asked my mother to send him clothes for his journey to be with her. Without any kind of guarantee, he saw his departure as imminent, and he became increasingly obsessed with it. Why go through the trouble of trying to keep a job? Why wake up early and wait for buses that took too long, when he could just sleep, go out, wait, and, then, one day soon, leave and be at his mother's side? That is what Tía Niña suspected. "Many of his friends are starting to have children," she wrote. "Of course, he thinks only about leaving." Everything was perpetually on hold. He felt suspended, deferred, as if his real life—the one that mattered—had not yet started. It would not begin in earnest until he was in the United States with us. "This life"—his life in Cuba, first from school to school, then from job to job—didn't really count. All there was to do was to wait.

# TEN

# Fidel Castro's Surprise

**It was Fidel Castro** who interrupted the monotony of everyone's waiting. In September 1978, the bearded, middle-aged leader (the same age as my mother) stunned Cubans on both sides of the Florida Straits by inviting exiles to visit Havana to speak with him personally. Cuban Americans loved to lambast the man, and the loudest did so on radio, television, and newspaper pages. Negotiating with Castro, they said, was to legitimize his authority. But that was far from the only view. In fact, Cuban Americans flooded Cuban government offices with telegrams volunteering for the talks in Havana.

My mother would have never thought to do that. She wanted me to enroll in college, study diplomacy, become the kind of person who could play a role at a historic summit. She would have felt that she could play no role there. Still, I know she would have thought that should Cubans in the United States actually engage in a dialogue with Fidel Castro, that maybe, just maybe, something immovable might at last budge.

She was right. As a result of the meetings, Castro authorized family reunification visits. For the first time in almost twenty years, Cubans in the United States would be allowed to visit their families on the island. Even as hardliners balked, throngs rushed to take advantage of the opportunity to return home for the first time since their exile began. Political ideology was one thing, family devotion another. Travelers paid heftily to renew their Cuban passports, which the Cuban government required for the visits. They rushed to complete their US residency paperwork so they could reenter the United States without problems. They were going to Cuba, but whatever fantasies they might have once harbored about a permanent return, they knew their stays would last just a week, the limit imposed on the visits by Castro's government. Over one hundred thousand Cubans living in the United States made trips back to the island in the first year, laden with gifts, cash, and love. My mother and her sister Lucrecia were among them.

In Havana, Tía Niña was ecstatic when she heard of her sisters' plan to visit. She had been worried that with Poly in the process of leaving, she might never get to see her sisters again. She explained to my mother that she wasn't telling the extended family about the trip. The family was too large, and everyone would have requests. I know the trip is expensive, she said; you don't have to bring anything, just for Poly, of course. Poly wrote to my mother expressing his own happiness at her imminent arrival in Cuba. "I am very happy to know that I will see you, even if, for now, it is only for a few days. It will soon be 16 years that we have been apart." Sixteen years, nearly a generation in time. He made requests as well: a suit, an overcoat, and shoes (for the trip to the United States, which everyone believed would happen soon). If possible, he added, bring, "two jeans, Lee or Lois [*sic*] brand, a pair of sneakers Adidas or Trax, two T-shirts for the jeans. The pants without pleats and wide at the bottom. The last ones that you sent I didn't like at all." At the top of the letter, after the date, March 6, 1979, he added a heading of his own making: *Año de mi Felicidad*. Year of My Happiness.

When my mother decided to make the trip, she was working as a seamstress; my father still worked as a short-order cook in a Manhattan hotel. Their combined gross income that year was just under $14,000. The trip to Cuba, with all its associated costs, was not something they could afford. But it would have been inconceivable to her to not go. So she did.

Despite Tía Niña's insistence not to, my mother spent every spare minute and dollar buying and preparing gifts to take to people. Most were for Poly, but she felt she had to bring presents for family members, as well: for her two brothers, Ñeñe and Herminio, still living in her hometown of San Cristóbal; for Tía Niña and Tía Tatá, who would be home from Mazorra for her sisters' momentous visit; for a few of her favorite nieces and nephews. She even thought of old neighbors and acquaintances, packing little things for them as well: razors and combs here, bottles of nail polish there, a short stack of small bills for when her stash of inexpensive consumer goods ran out. She took one cowboy hat, and that was for Poly.

My mother at work at the Peppi Spina factory in West New York, New Jersey.

I remember the items laid out on her bed, as she sat, pen in hand, writing the names of each item's recipient on a tag or label, so that there would be no confusion when she got there. It was early spring of my junior year of high school. I was an honors student, receiving brochures for colleges with beautiful leafy campuses, places wholly unlike anything I knew. I was already making lists of where I might apply. My parents were not involved in that process, but they approved of my living at school, so long as it was not too far away: New York or Washington, DC, maybe Boston or Baltimore, some place like that. As my mother prepared her trip, I was already certain that that would happen. Yet I used to like to ponder what-ifs, to think about how things might be otherwise if an earlier event had unfolded in a different way, either by design or by chance. So as I made lists of colleges that year, I remember wondering what would have happened if we hadn't left Cuba. So I asked my mother to please photograph the University of Havana for me, because that is where I would have gone if we had stayed, I told her. I also asked her to bring me back some Cuban posters. Much later, when I began going to Cuba on my own, I met cousins who remembered my mother's trip. When they found out about my requests, they had teased her, or maybe they said it behind her back: She had left Cuba fleeing communism and now she had raised a communist daughter in the United States, in the "belly of the beast." I wasn't a communist, though, just intensely curious about this place where I was born but could not remember.

I remember the first time I used that exact phrase, the first time I voiced the hollow place between my birth and my memory. It was 1977, less than two years before my mother's first return. I was just finishing my first year of high school, and I was sitting with my parents and my sister in the living room. We were hushed, gathered around the television to watch Barbara Walters's interview with Fidel Castro. The program started, and immediately our living room was awash in scenes of Havana. At one time, my parents' eyes might have moistened at the images, but they didn't. I was riveted, almost holding my breath, and then I started to tear up. My parents stared at me unbelieving. They weren't crying, why was I? And I recall with absolute certainty what I said in response: "Because I was born there, but I can't remember it." I still railed against my parents' prohibitions by reminding them loudly that we were not in Cuba. We still argued, and I still rebuffed their nostalgia. But something was changing. I was becoming more interested. What was this Cuba beyond my parents' longing? What was the Cuba that, under other circumstances, might have remained mine?

So as my mother packed for her long-anticipated return, as she fretted about what gifts to take, I wanted her to bring me back a little piece of it. A photograph of the university, a poster, maybe some other little thing from the house. I think my grandmother would have understood. After all, she had buried my first nail clippings under a rosebush by the house; she'd given me little spoonfuls of sweet Cuban coffee, she'd made an altar for me with the toys I'd left behind so I would find them waiting for me when I returned.

I don't know what it was like for my mother and Poly to see each other again for the first time after sixteen years. Did they cry when they first embraced? What does a mother say to a son she knew as a boy of nine and is now a man of twenty-five? What does he say to her? How does he hug her when he can't climb into her lap?

Even though I can't imagine the first encounter between the two of them, I can easily picture my mother in her old house, becoming one with her people. A gaggle of Celedonio's boys pinched her to make sure she was real; a cousin played the guitar for my mother to sing; another took her for a ride on the back of her bicycle, Tía Niña looking on with her hands to her head in alarm. The newly reunited sisters would have stayed up late into the night, delighting in telling old stories, remembering their long-ago *travesuras*, stealing pineapples from a neighbor's farm, decorating another's fence with old bedpans.

The trip wasn't only about nostalgia though. Tía Niña would have described the death of their mother to the two sisters now visiting. I am certain that my mother shared stories about her life in the United States, about my father, and about Aixa and me. There were new things to learn, new people to meet: children born over the last sixteen years, and new spouses found in that same interim. Among the latecomers at the house was Tía Niña's partner, Onelio. A funny man, his face pink and pockmarked, he did not appear in any of my mother's photographs from the trip. He joked that it was because she had been afraid his countenance might break the camera lens.

My mother was always happy—*alegre*—in public. Back home in Cuba, surrounded by loved ones she hadn't seen in sixteen years, she would have been unable to contain her smile, her laughter, her lightness. Yes, I can picture her there, and she was buoyant.

What did Poly make of it all? Did he remember her the same way from when he was little? Did he think she was too happy given how sad he was? And what did he think when my mother talked about my sister and me? She would have sounded proud; she would have mentioned that I was soon going to university, and that I wanted a photograph of the University of Havana. Poly went with her on that outing. He might have been the one who took the photograph of the wide staircase before the main entrance.

I don't remember my mother telling me much—or anything—about her trip when she returned; though, surely, she must have. Back home in

New Jersey, back at her job sewing coat collars, she sometimes felt like the trip hadn't happened at all. In Havana, Tía Niña agreed. "We're all fine here, just like you, feeling like it was a dream that we saw you." The rice cooker and the espresso pot my mother and Lucrecia had left behind were my aunt's daily reminders that the visit had in fact been real. Tatá did nothing but talk out loud to herself about having seen her two sisters, so long away. For his part, Poly wrote, even before Tía Niña did, to say how very happy he was to have seen our mother, imagining, he said, how happy my father, my sister, and I must have been when we welcomed her back. "I would have loved to see everyone, but soon we will all be together. ¡*Verdad, Mami*!" Right, Mommy? He had never called her that in a letter; it made him sound little again.

Sometime that year Poly sent a postcard just to me. On the front was a photograph of a concert on Cuba's most famous beach, Varadero. On the back was a poem of his own making:

*Nada soy, nada reclamo.*
*Nada tengo, nada espero.*
*Sino el limpio*
*desespero de mi amor*
*por lo que amo.*

I am nothing, I demand nothing.
I have nothing, I expect nothing
But the pure
desperation of my love
for what I love.

He closed, "Para Adita, de su hermano 'Poly'/79."

I wonder now if it was motivated by my mother's visit, from hearing my name on her lips, from seeing before his eyes the person absent from his life for so many years, the person I had had all along. In their separation, Poly had become a man. But my mother had changed as well; she became someone he didn't know, someone who was mine in a way she might never again be his.

# ELEVEN

# Exodus

**In November 1979, Poly filled out** his application for a Cuban exit visa. No one was legally permitted to leave the island, even for short trips, without permission from the government, a policy that remained in place until 2013. The Cuban government denied Poly's application: he could not solicit his exit visa until after December 31 of the year he turned twenty-eight, in his case January 1, 1982. Many young people were leaving, and the government was limiting the exit of men of military age. Poly, who had not yet turned twenty-six, would have to wait at least another two years to reapply.

Tía Niña counseled patience to both mother and son. There is no need for your desperation, she wrote to my mother more than once, even as she added, "I understand, though." She understood because, as her own letters show, she often felt just as desperate and exhausted. In January 1979, a few months before my mother's trip to Cuba, she wrote, "Here there are no problems except the ones of always: your son and the fact that I am older, more tired, and that my nerves are fried. The doctor says I'm neurotic." The letter was a continuation of a longer conversation:

> I am not angry about Poly's plan to leave. As I told you on the phone, I always knew it would happen. Besides, I am only interested in his happiness, and here he will never be happy. If I came across a little strangely [on the phone], it is because I worry that it won't happen, that he won't be able to leave. Of course, very happy and contented, I cannot feel. You will understand me; I love him, perhaps too much, because I have ruined him. It is difficult, Adela, to explain this in a letter. I very much wish for him to achieve what he wants, because all that interests him is reuniting with you, and I understand it. . . . *Ya yo no sirvo para nada.* [I am no longer good for anything.]

Five weeks later, she wrote with another call for patience. Calm down, she told my mother. "Think always that things have worked out well for you, that everything you've set your mind to do, you've done. Remember that I am the one who is the nothing of the family." *Soy yo la poca cosa de la familia.*

I met my namesake aunt eventually. I came to know and to love her. She was a matter-of-fact woman. She was not melodramatic, nor was she inclined to feel sorry for herself. Clearly, this was a very difficult time for her. She wanted Poly to go. She loved him, and that was what he most wanted. His leaving, she also certainly knew by then, would make her own life easier. Not long after my mother's visit, Poly had brought a woman into the house to live with him. I don't know anything about her, not even her name. But Tía Niña's partner, Onelio, wanted her out. Poly refused; there were fights. My aunt had no way to make Poly do what she wanted, and she would never make Poly leave. So Onelio left instead. Those months, she later confessed to my mother, *fueron terribles*. Terrible in Spanish is a much stronger word than in English. Maybe if Poly left to join his mother, Onelio would return.

"Your son no longer has any clothes for his trip," Tía Niña wrote to my mother in February 1980, referring to the clothes my mother had taken for him. "He sold everything, even the shoes." She urged my mother to send more clothes for his trip, because she worried that his visa and passport might arrive and he would have nothing to travel in. She promised to hide the new clothes from him, so that he would not sell them again. "I lament telling you these things; that is why I had not written earlier. He cannot know that I have told you." She knew how to tiptoe around him. With Poly in the United States, her life would have less stress, fewer burdens, more peace. She sensed that.

Still, she knew with all her being that she would miss Poly deeply. He was, after all, a son to her. She also worried that Poly's expectations about the United States, even about our family, were so high as to be unrealistic. Inevitably, he would be disappointed. What would happen then? Years later, she told me that she had sometimes cautioned Poly against leaving. She told him that it might be difficult for him in the United States, that he might not get used to it, that he was already too set in his ways to adjust to life in a foreign country, even if that country was where his mother and sisters lived. But Poly would hear none of it. Neither would my mother, had my aunt shared those misgivings with her. So Tía Niña reverted always to the same message: patience and more patience.

Poly's Cuban passport was issued in April 1980, almost exactly a year after my mother's visit. But that was still more than a year and a half before he'd be eligible to apply for the Cuban exit visa. Again, a call for patience. My brother was familiar with it, so was my mother. By that point, so were Cubans in general.

In 1980, my mother and brother suddenly got what they both wanted. All their waiting and anguish notwithstanding, Poly's departure from Cuba, when it came, was unexpected and quick. Poly had not yet received either his US visa or his Cuban exit permit. Neither did he get to travel in a suit sent by my mother.

His journey, so momentous in the life of my family, was but one small episode in a crisis that made front-page news in both countries. It all started on April 1, 1980, when six Cubans stole a city bus, crashed it through the gates of the Peruvian embassy, and requested asylum. Located on embassy row in Havana's posh Miramar district, the embassy had Cuban guards around the perimeter. When the bus crashed the gates, the guards opened fire, and one guard accidentally killed another. The Cuban government demanded that the embassy return the gate crashers to its authority, but the ambassador refused. In response, Fidel Castro announced that the Cuban government would no longer protect foreign embassies that did not cooperate with it. The next morning, embassy staff awoke to the sound of bulldozers demolishing the sentry boxes at the main gate and removing the large boulders blocking the driveway. Then the guards abandoned their posts. The embassy stood completely open and unprotected. The ambassador was sure that Cuban forces were about to storm the embassy and remove the asylum seekers by force. He was mistaken. Instead, Castro's government did nothing.

As Cubans learned that authorities would not prevent people from entering the embassy grounds, hundreds began heading there. Buses whose routes ran near the embassy became fuller and fuller at each stop. Riders did not chat and joke as usual; they rode in silence. Then at the stop closest to the embassy, everyone got off and began walking in the same direction. In the forty-eight hours that the embassy stood unprotected, over ten thousand Cubans entered the grounds, all of them seeking asylum and a way out of the country. There were so many people that some sat on tree branches and the roofs of buildings in the compound. Days went by, but no one could figure out what to do with all those people; no one knew how to get them out of Cuba.

In mid-April, Castro decided that he had found a solution: he would allow Cuban Americans to sail to the island to pick up relatives, provided that they gave passage to some of the people from the embassy. The port selected for the operation was Mariel, about 25 miles west of Havana and roughly 125 miles from Key West.

Within hours of the announcement, many in Miami and in other Cuban American enclaves like West New York began withdrawing savings, borrowing money, planning to hire boats and captains to carry them to Cuba to pick up their people. The first vessel to make the voyage was a forty-one-foot yacht named *Ochún,* the Afro-Cuban deity of love and fresh water, syncretized always with Cuba's patron saint, La Caridad del Cobre. When it arrived in Key West with Cuban refugees on April 21, 1980, the Coast Guard captain on duty barely noted the arrival. After all, occasional boats with people leaving Cuba had been arriving in the small port since the 1960s. It did not take long for officials to realize that something extraordinary was afoot. Within days, there were thousands of boats between Key West and Mariel. One observer remarked that if someone lined up all the boats one behind the other, their relatives would be able to walk from Cuba to Florida.

In Cuba, the response to the government's announcement was perhaps even more dramatic. Castro labeled the asylum seekers as antisocials, using epithets like "scum" and "worms." The government also mobilized its citizenry to humiliate them publicly. When word leaked that someone on the block was leaving, the Committees for the Defense of the Revolution organized protests outside their home. "Acts of repudiation," they were called.

Of course, not every Cuban who wanted to leave had relatives in the United States. Nor did every Cuban American with family seeking to leave have the resources to make the sea journey to retrieve them. Some would-be refugees, even if they had kinfolk willing or able to pick them up, feared that the whole operation might be stopped before their relatives made it to Mariel to get them. Since the government had labeled those who were leaving as antisocials or social misfits, some Cubans began appearing at police stations calling themselves that and requesting permission to leave the country on that basis. Antisocial, however, could be a capacious category. Sometimes, people went to the police and confessed to being gay, which served as one reason for the granting of an exit visa. Sometimes, they just pretended. Other times, people eagerly confessed to prior arrests, or the fact they were not working or in school. Poly had not finished school; he had not served in the military; he was chronically out of a job. At least once, he had served jail time for vagrancy, as I later found out. It would not have been hard for him to convince someone in authority that he was a bad seed.

Meanwhile, in New Jersey, it took my mother a little time to make arrangements and get the money together. But in early May 1980, she boarded a Greyhound bus to Miami. From there, Tía Lucrecia drove her to Key West, where she contracted with a man named Gene Brenner, captain of the *Polaris*, to take her to Mariel. She paid $900 for her round-trip passage to Cuba and Poly's one-way passage to Florida. My mother was always afraid of the ocean; she had recurring nightmares about drowning; she had never learned to swim, not even on those childhood outings to local rivers. But my mother knew how to pray.

The boat launched on May 8, possibly May 9. One of the other passengers was a coworker from the coat factory where my mother worked. Like her, the woman was heading to Cuba to pick up a son left behind. At one point during the voyage, the captain had misgivings due to bad weather and announced that he was turning around. A passenger took a machete out of his duffel and threatened to kill the captain if he didn't continue on to Mariel. My mother reached for the rosary beads in her bag and led the women passengers in prayer.

When she arrived at Mariel, the panorama she surveyed was almost beyond belief. Hundreds of boats jockeyed for position. Unable to secure moorings, new arrivals tied their vessels to others already there. Every captain handed Cuban officials a list of the people his passengers wanted to pick up. It took time for the government to locate them, and the boats sometimes had to wait for days, even weeks. A nightclub was set up aboard a government ship to entertain impatient sailors. Other Cuban vessels patrolled the harbor, while guards on the shore pointed their weapons toward the water. At night, floodlights illuminated everything. Amid this unnerving scene, my mother managed to disembark, find a phone, and call the house (well, the neighbor's house, be-

Mariel Harbor, May 1, 1980.

cause there was no phone in the house). She needed to let Poly know that she had arrived to collect him.

My sources say different things about what happened next. A letter from Tía Niña suggests that she was at work when my mother called and received the message only later. My mother, however, always recounted that she called and talked directly to my aunt, who said, "No, *mi hermana*, your son is already there, since Mother's Day." But Tía Niña couldn't have known that. In fact, when my mother was calling from the phone in Mariel, no one actually knew where Poly was. A neighbor who worked at the port told my aunt that she had seen him there at six in the morning on May 6 but not after.

I don't know how my mother ascertained that Poly had already gotten on a boat bound for Florida. But she did. Then, because the *Polaris* was staying longer to collect the people it had come for, my mother decided to head back to Florida without waiting. She wrote a letter to Tía Niña, posted it from Mariel, and then talked (and paid) her way onto a different boat.

There were four of five other women aboard the small speedboat, all returning alone, because their sons, like Poly, had either already gone or had not been allowed to leave by the government. Our story, after all, is not singular. The captain offered the women pills for seasickness; my mother pretended to take one, but didn't. Awake and feigning sleep, she saw a man shining flashlights into the purses of the sleeping women. At night, asea, the boat ran out of gasoline, and they were stranded. It was my mother's worst nightmare: death by drowning. But another boat came along and shared some gasoline. The fumes made my mother sick. But she thanked God.

She made it back to Key West and boarded a bus to Miami. The bus made a quick stop at a Burger King on the way north. Many of the other passengers didn't speak English, and my mother translated for everyone in her own stilted English, running out of time to buy and eat her own meal. The bus driver, an African American woman, told her to buy something and eat it on the bus. My mother told me this story twice, once in person, as she was recovering from surgery in a Miami Beach hospital, and again a month or so later by telephone. She was a little confused sometimes; the surgery had given her voice a trembling quality that never went away entirely. In person, when she first told me the Burger King story, she wondered aloud if maybe the reason she hadn't gotten to eat at the restaurant was not because of a lack of time, but because they didn't serve Blacks, something that in 1980 would not have been legally possible. When she told me the story on the phone about a month later, she didn't mention that again.

Maybe all my questions had confused her during our hospital conversation. Or maybe it was just the effects of the anesthesia that brought her uncertainty to the surface: a woman in her nineties still unsure of where she fit in this country where she had lived most of her life but where she never really felt like she belonged.

The bus took her to Miami, where she stayed with her sister Lucrecia for the night. The next morning she took another bus back to New Jersey, back to us. She traveled alone, arriving home with no Poly for us to welcome.

# TWELVE

# Camp Liberty

**Poly always told us** that he arrived in the United States on Mother's Day, May 11, 1980. My mother and Tía Niña said the same thing, too: Poly arrived on Mother's Day, like a gift.

But the past, someone once observed, is like a game of telephone. Truth is elusive, and archives don't always provide the answers. Poly's immigration records are full of contradictory information. In one, he entered the United States on May 10, in others May 9; in another it was May 3 (even though we know that he was seen at Mariel on May 6). Not one of the records I have seen indicates that he arrived on Mother's Day. Maybe Poly and my mother both fudged it a little. May 9, May 10, May 11, what was the difference? It might as well have been Mother's Day. In any good story, it *would* have been Mother's Day.

Whatever Poly's exact arrival date, by the time he made it to Florida—perhaps three weeks into the Mariel Boatlift, as the seaborne exodus came to be called—approximately 37,000 Cubans had landed in Key West. About five months later when it ended, the number was close to 125,000. For context, consider that the total population of the city of Miami (not Miami-Dade County) was then under 350,000. Consider also that the Mariel refugees represented about 1.3 percent of Cuba's entire population, the departed gone by sea in just a few months.

Unable to process all the arrivals in Key West, the federal government opened multiple processing centers in Miami. Krome, a defunct missile base on the edge of the Everglades that had been built in 1965 to protect the United States from a Soviet attack launched from Cuba, was repurposed to process the arrivals. (It remains today an immigrant detention center, long among the most notorious.) But even Krome was not enough. Cubans not yet claimed by family members or other sponsors were sent to a makeshift camp in the bleachers and parking lots of the Orange Bowl. Some were placed in a tent city, hastily erected on an old baseball field under the I-95 overpass, between Little Havana and the historically Black neighborhood of Overtown, where it remained for many months.

Still unable to handle all the newcomers in South Florida, the government established processing centers in military bases as far away as Wisconsin and Arkansas. Over 60,000 of the Mariel immigrants were housed at these camps while the government determined what to do with them. Some were there for just days, as they waited to be cleared for entry and for their relatives to sponsor them officially. Many others—without family or of uncertain admissability—waited much longer. It was quite a welcome to America.

Poly ended up at a hastily built camp at Eglin Air Force Base in the Florida Panhandle. Authorities there first learned that Eglin had been chosen to function as a refugee processing center on May 1. The first group of Cubans arrived only two days later, long before the camp was ready. They came with nothing but the clothes on their backs, and some of the refugees had already been wearing those for days, if not weeks. The Cubans were initially housed in Building 19, an empty dormitory slated for a renovation that had not yet begun. When that filled, officials used hangars, a temporary solution until the camp was fully operational.

By May 15, the camp consisted of 413 tents, of which 370 were "sleeping tents," each with room for up to thirty refugees. A designated "captain" among the thirty oversaw the distribution of cigarettes, newspapers, and other items in each tent. There were six latrines, three shower tents, and three permanent shower facilities. At the center of the camp stood the mess hall tents, where workers were soon serving more than thirty thousand meals a day.

To keep the Cuban arrivals busy and entertained, camp authorities and other

Aerial view of sleeping/tent area of Camp Liberty, Eglin Air Force Base, 1980.

organizations organized recreational activities, such as Ping-Pong, baseball, magic shows, and movie screenings. They published a newspaper that included some of the refugees' own writing, as well as useful information about things like obtaining drivers' licenses, learning English, calling family, and more. Priests said Mass in an outdoor theater, and local charities and churches sponsored clothing drives for the destitute arrivals. All of this on a forty-two-acre lot that was now home to almost ten thousand Cubans, 85 percent of them men, and 70 percent of the total between the ages of twenty-one and forty.

Authorities titled the whole endeavor "Operation Red, White, and Blue," and gave the refugee installation the name "Camp Liberty." The gate by which the refugees would exit once officially admitted to the country was christened Freedom Gate, the "golden door for life in the United States," in the words of one Eglin general. That was where Poly suddenly found himself at the age of twenty-six, still young, but a lifetime away from the boy we had left behind.

On arriving at Eglin, Poly was given a small envelope with his name and A (or Alien) number. On the top right corner, in different ink, was the notation "urgent." In the center was his new address in Camp Liberty: Row P, Tent 08, Bed 0230. Inside the envelope was a three-by-five-inch index card, lined only on one side. It looks homemade, improvised, the makeshift effort of local officials and volunteers unprepared for the avalanche of migrants before them, making it up as they went along. The card looks, dare I say it, Cuban, socialist even. On the unlined side, in red marker, someone has written "1S, 1P, 1 jabón," which I think means that Poly was given a bottle of shampoo, a tube of toothpaste, and a bar

of soap. There is a stamped circle in the middle of the card; inside the circle it reads May, then 1980, with a blank space in between. An arrow points to a ten, but it's not clear whether that indicates a date or an hour. On the bottom left corner of the card is another stamp, an incongruous one: a cartoon angel with wings and a halo, reading a sign in English that says "Please Follow Instructions." I found the card only recently, among papers of Poly's that my mother saved in a brown, fake-leather briefcase with a zipper that gets stuck every time I open or close it.

In the Washington, DC, suburb of College Park sits a large gleaming building, its front an arc of floor-to-ceiling windows. Known as Archives 2 of the US National Archives and Records Administration, it holds among the millions of documents in its possession twenty-three boxes of records from the camp at Eglin Air Force Base set up for people like my brother. I scour them looking for Poly and find what researchers often find in archives—inconsistencies. I begin with lists that have titles such as "Cubans in the computer as of now," but there are major gaps. Poly does not appear among the refugees in the camp on May 13, 1980. I find him, though, on the next available list, dated May 17, third name from the bottom, in old-fashioned dot-matrix ink on horizontal, lined computer paper: Hipólito Cabrera Fernández, assigned to Row P, Tent 08, Bed 0230, just as his little card said. Studying the map of the camp, I note that Poly's temporary home is seven tents away from the men's latrine in one direction; in the other, four tents away from the perimeter fence of this unusual camp named Liberty.

If we assume the lists are accurate, Poly arrived at Eglin between the thirteenth and the seventeenth of May. By then the camp had been in operation for about ten days. On the one hand, it was a picture of order and efficiency: perfectly spaced tents; schedules for eating and showering; detailed rosters of all staff; protocols in place for almost any eventuality.

On the other hand, the whole thing bordered on mayhem. On May 16, right around the date of Poly's arrival, there were 9,800 refugees in the camp. It was a typical day. One refugee, "attempting to be humorous," got his hands on a loudspeaker and announced that he was a communist agent. "A small disturbance ensued." The same day, two other refugees separately went to camp police to denounce two different Cubans as Castro informants. They might have just been wanting to get them into trouble, but each time such accusations were made—and they occurred often—camp security and the FBI had to investigate. Later that day, camp police brought in two other Cubans for "alleged homosexual acts." Extensive interviews were conducted, multiple forms filled out, because until 1990, homosexuality was actually grounds for exclusion from the United States. Later, a woman arrived at the police tent to say that her common law husband had threatened her with bodily harm. The man was questioned, and the couple sent back to their tent.

The next day, and the ones after, offered no reprieve. The woman who said her partner had threatened her came back. Yes, the man had assaulted her. Across and two tents down from Poly, a refugee was hit from behind on the head and had to be treated for lacerations. Over on the F row of tents, two men were detained for lighting matches and spraying an aerosol can on them to make torches. Three Cubans wearing sheets over their clothes were seen leaving the mess tent. When confronted, they ran away, bread and crackers falling to the ground from underneath the sheets. Another refugee escaped from tent M-9 and was later found near Mia's Pizza Parlor in town.

Poly applied for asylum on May 17. All the forms were in English, so he, like all the others, would have had help filling them out. On the biographical information sheet collected by the Immigration and Naturalization Service, the only job he listed was the one he had as an assistant accountant in 1978, the one he liked because he didn't have to work out in the sun. He lied about his level of education and said he'd completed ninth grade at Ciudad Libertad, the revolution's model school, the former barracks, the first place where Poly was left back.

A scene from Camp Liberty, Eglin Air Force Base, 1980.

As a petition for asylum, Poly's application was not particularly convincing. The person translating for him mostly checked no to questions about whether he was suffering persecution in Cuba. For question 17, which asked "If you return to your country, for what specific reasons do you believe you will be persecuted?" Poly checked the box that said "Political Opinion." "What do you think would happen if you return?" the application asked. The person filling out the form, translated his answer: "I would be jailed b/c I'm not in agreement w/ the government there." That was his answer, even though when he was asked if he or his family had suffered because of his political opinion, his response was no. Elsewhere in the application he admitted that he had been arrested and served three months in jail for violation of the Cuban government's vagrancy laws. He was imprisoned "because [he] wasn't doing anything." The medical report that accompanied his petition showed that his blood pressure was perfect; his pulse, 92, perhaps a little high. The nurse or doctor jotted down that he smoked half a pack of cigarettes a day. He had smoked in Cuba. At the camp, staff issued two packs a day for every tent of thirty people, so he smoked there, too. Now, with his asylum petition complete, all Poly had to do was wait. But he'd been doing that already most of his life, and his patience was running thin.


Everyone's was. Many area residents were furious about the camp in their community. Yet the refugees kept arriving. More of them jumped the fence every day in vain attempts to escape. All were caught. In fact, most returned to the camp of their own volition. Where were they to go in the Florida Panhandle, when they had no money, no English, and nothing other than the clothes on their backs? But their capture did not soothe the anger of the camp's neighbors. On May 18, two locals tried to crash into the main gate with their vehicle. Another day, thirty robed Klansman held a rally of about two hundred people outside the camp. They burned a cross, and from a hired plane flew a KKK banner over the scene.

Of course, it was the refugees who were the most frustrated of all. Many had been wanting to leave Cuba for years or, as in Poly's case, almost two decades. In Cuba, some had endured public shaming ceremonies at the hands of their neighbors; they had crowded onto boats and ships loaded beyond capacity. They had been sleeping with strangers for weeks, waiting and waiting for their release. The detainees felt like prisoners—discouraged, exasperated, unsure when or if they would be allowed to leave.

On the eve of Poly's application asylum, the camp was housing 9,997 Cuban arrivals. Yet at that point, only 159 refugees had been released. Camp authorities understood the risks the situation entailed. Major General Robert M. Bond informed his superiors on May 16 that "the slow rate of refugee out-processing will have an adverse effect on refugee morale and, subsequently, the internal security of Camp Libertad."

On Saturday, May 24, the flimsy peace broke down. The day didn't start out any differently than any other day four weeks into the experiment that was Camp Liberty. One soldier was apprehended for alleged possession of marijuana, another worker for possession of alcohol. Two Cubans were separately detained for suspicion of being Castro agents. Another Cuban was threatened by the other residents of his tent, who accused him of stealing clothes and cigarettes and vowed to kill him if he didn't return them by 11 a.m. One Cuban man tried to slit his wrist after a fight with his boyfriend. But sometime that morning, amid the ordinary extraordinary, a group of residents living in three rows of tents in what authorities called Sector A of the camp—precisely the people who had been there longest—got together and organized a hunger strike. "We do not want to eat," they insisted. "We want to leave."

When the security police detained the alleged organizer of the movement, over one hundred refugees "tried to rush the gate to save their friend." He was released, but with the situation tenser than at any point before, camp authorities announced that they would hold a meeting to address the refugees' concerns. At 6:30 p.m., two officers began their oration in the camp's outdoor theater before an audience of "several thousand refugees." Some began chanting and jeering at the speakers. Less than twenty minutes into the event, "approximately 100–200" people carrying signs painted on sheets joined the spectators, and the situation grew even more restive. The two officers onstage, concluding "that the refugees would not be satisfied with anything except the promise of an immediate departure from the camp," retreated.

Then a crowd surged toward the gate that separated the refugee tents from the command buildings and the police and military tents. "Up to two thousand refugees" pushed against security police trying to hold a line against them. That face-off lasted about a half hour, with refugees shoving police and pelting them with rocks. "At one time, a parking sign that was on the roadway was used to ram into the police line, but it held." Some protesters used the metal rods from the cots in their tents to face off against camp police and military. Meanwhile, other refugees siding with authorities joined in and began throwing rocks at the refugees who were attacking the police. Though reinforcements were called immediately and all the gates locked, many refugees took advantage of the melee to jump the fences. Order was restored by 8:55 p.m. but camp authorities did not immediately know how many people had escaped.

In response to the disturbance, US Marshals took responsibility for security, and camp officials sped up the pace of out-processing. Less than a week later on May 30, Poly was officially authorized to enter the United States. June 1980 was two days away. I was about to graduate from high school, about to turn eighteen.

When I went to look for Poly in the National Archives, I was not sure what I expected to find, besides confirmation that he had been at the camp. When I saw the level of detail contained in police blotters and other records, I wondered if I would find Poly's name there, perhaps even among the records created in the wake of the May 24 disturbance. The records, however, give no indication that Poly participated. Perhaps he was at the outdoor theater when the two officers held the public meeting, one among "several thousand" frustrated that he was still there rather than free and with his family. I don't know if he attacked the police line, but he is not mentioned among those detained for doing so. Perhaps he tried—or even succeeded in—jumping the fence, as so many did, even though in almost all cases, they were quickly recovered and returned, their names not always recorded. In fact, no matter how hard I looked, I found no evidence at all of Poly doing anything untoward. (Though, of course, that in and of itself is not proof that he didn't.)

I close my eyes and picture him: a young man sleeping in bed 230 of Tent 8 in row P of Camp Liberty, his world suddenly turned upside down, thinking of our mother, our aunt, wanting—trying—to be

Refugee, possibly Poly, looking at national map with volunteers.

good, knowing that he was on the cusp of getting what he'd been waiting for almost all his life.

I found a photograph in the archives that might be Poly. It shows a young man standing next to a table talking with two middle-aged women volunteers. They are looking together at a map of the United States. The young man leans over the table, his face visible only in profile. I think it is him. Maybe he has just asked the volunteers to point out New Jersey on a map. He wants to see how far our mother is, how much farther he will have to travel to be with her.

In his letters from Cuba in 1979, Poly had written, "Year of My Happiness." Maybe now, in 1980, paroled into the United States, he wondered if he'd just been off by a year. Poly was aching for that happiness to begin. He called my mother on the phone. "Pick me up," he begged. She probably wanted nothing more. So, seventeen years after having left Cuba, she finally went to get her son and bring him home. My father went with her.

"You remember the rest," she said to me when she was ninety-two.

# PART III

# Strange Changes

# THIRTEEN

# Hello, Goodbye

**I don't think my parents** ever figured out American geography. When they went together to pick up Poly at Eglin Air Force Base, they took a plane to Miami then a bus north some 630 miles to the Florida Panhandle. Or that, at least, was how my mother remembered (or misremembered) the trip a year or two before she died. When they made the journey, she was almost fifty-four, a mature middle-aged woman at the end of menopause, recently recovered from frozen shoulder. Poly was a man, almost twenty-seven, waiting to be released from a US military camp to go live with his mother, her husband, and their two teenaged daughters, his sisters.

Aixa and I were excited—and nervous—to finally meet our brother, the person we'd been waiting for our whole lives. He had shaved off his mustache before he left Camp Liberty. My mother called it his first gift to her in the United States. She, meanwhile, gave him lots of gifts, buying him clothes, shoes, cologne, whatever he might need or want. After all, he had arrived from Cuba with absolutely nothing. She bought him novels by Corín Tellado, the prolific Spanish romance novelist, whose work inspired many *telenovelas*. In Cuba, Poly and Tía Niña had shared the little paperbacks between them. My sister and I bought him presents, too, but I can't remember what.

Given how long we'd known about Poly, how long my mother had led us to anticipate the moment of his arrival, it is surprising that neither Aixa nor I remember much about our initial glimpse of him. Neither of us remembers him walking through the door for the first time, nor the embraces we surely gave him. We have no idea what we said to him that first day, or what he might have said to us. Aixa remembers that our relatives came to see and welcome him, everyone squeezing into our modest living room. She also recalls awkward attempts at conversations when company was not around. My own memories are of the kitchen table. My mother prepared big meals, all the things she was always so good at cooking: beans and rice every night, with it something like *ropa vieja*, chicken fricassee, fried pork, salt cod stew on Fridays, on Sundays her *boliche*, the pot roast she used to slice so thin back when her family had a restaurant in their Havana home behind the military hospital. We did not have a dining room, just a table against the wall in a small eat-in kitchen. We pulled it out to make room for Poly, and still we were cramped.

I asked him things about Cuba over dinner, but I can't recall what he responded. I probably asked him about school, about what he had liked to study. I might even have asked him about Cuba's famous Literacy Campaign, in which young people taught peasants to read and write. Poly would have been too young to participate, but the idealistic teacher in me would have liked it if he had. I realize now how much he must have hated my questions. One night with all five us around the dinner table, I shared the news that Mayra, one of my two best friends in high school, had a young uncle arrive on the boatlift and move in with them. I met him that day and liked him. He was an architect, or maybe an architecture student. Soon after, my mother pulled me aside and told me to please stop asking Poly questions about his life in Cuba. It was making him feel bad about himself, about the fact that he had not gotten an education. I thought at the time she was referring to the fact that he had not gone to college. I know now, because I have read his letters, that it was because he had never finished fifth grade.

I started keeping a journal that summer. But I wrote of Poly only twice that whole season. The first mention is dated more than two months after his arrival and is mostly a long run-on sentence that doesn't even use his name. "I'm very irritable today. . . . This house [we often referred to our apartment as a house] always smells like cigarettes & beer now. Thanks to you know who. He really gets on my nerves sometimes, like when I come home and find him using this notebook, or [when he] leaves my albums lying around or in the wrong covers or acts like my calculator is his and I need permission to use it or when I'm listening to something on TV and he starts asking a lot of questions so I miss it, or when he sings Beatles songs." I added something in parentheses right after that. But I crossed it out, heavily and in different ink, so that all I can read is an "etc." at the end.

Poly was not the brother I had imagined. He was not the born architect I had conjured because of the shape of the A's in his writing, not the kind of older brother with friends who inspired crushes. In my daydreams, Poly had been something other than the brother who now stood before me: smoking, drinking beer, talking in a voice that always sounded angry. We were probably not what he expected, either.

What did my parents make of it all? My parents never drank, or not until much later when my father, in his nineties, began having a few sips of red wine with dinner. Neither of them ever smoked. They raised their voices sometimes, but not too much. They always made us aware that we had neighbors, that they could hear us, that we didn't want to bother or annoy them. It is not hard to imagine that the things that bothered my sister and me likely bothered them as well. My father had gone with my mother to pick him up and bring him home. He would not have let her make that journey by herself. He had known Poly as a little boy, but did he like him as the man now before him? My sister remembers my father being very quiet around this time.

Figuring out how my mother felt is impossible. The relief of finally having her son at her side was deep. A high school friend reminded me recently how happy and excited my mother was. Just look at her smile in the picture of the two of them sitting on our couch right after his arrival.

But surely, she understood that her son was also something of a stranger to her and, even more so, to us. Did she look at Poly and feel doubts? Given his troubles in Cuba, did she wonder if he would adapt? Was she already thinking then what I know she believed for much of her life: that he was the way he was because of her? Did she gaze from Poly to my fa-

ther, looking sterner and more silent than usual, and recall Tía Niña's letter, the one where she complained about how Poly had driven away her partner, Onelio?

Soon after Poly's arrival, the family dinners

in the cramped kitchen stopped. My sister and I went back to eating dinner as we had before, in front of the television, watching reruns of *M*A*S*H* and I can't remember what else. Sometimes we could hear my mother at the dining table, trying to lighten the mood, to be jaunty and funny. I don't think my father and Poly said much. Poly was often loud, but he could be silent, too.

On Sunday, August 24, 1980, I wrote in my journal again. This was my only other mention of Poly that summer. I was leaving for college the next day, leaving home for the first time. "I don't know what to write, because I don't know what I'm feeling," I confessed. Then I added a PS: "I really love Mami, Papi & Aixa, and I very much love [my best friends] Georgia & Mayra. And I guess I love Augustine, Cocuzza, Segali, Wilson [my favorite teachers]. I'm not sure about Poly."

In the morning, as my parents loaded the car downstairs, I lingered behind, alone in my room, sitting on my bed. The radio was still on, and I could hear the song "Sailing," by Christopher Cross, then number one on the *Billboard* Hot 100 chart and today regarded as a classic of "yacht rock." The subject of the song was so far from anything I knew that I misheard the line "The canvas can do miracles." In my head it was, "The campus can do miracles; just you wait and see." I took it as a sign, looked around, blew a kiss to my room, and left. Five of us loaded into the car for the roughly two-hour journey to Vassar College: my parents, my sister and I, and Jorge, a cousin on my father's side who lived in our building.

Poly didn't come. As I gave him a hug goodbye, did my excited departure confuse him? He had just come from a world where state boarding schools were mandatory, where students usually went home on weekends, where even those who attended university often lived at home. I wonder now if he resented my leaving, thinking that the long-awaited arrival of my long-lost brother should have been reason enough for me to stay.

# FOURTEEN

# Tía Niña

**When Poly left Cuba** in May 1980, he didn't say goodbye to Tía Niña. She returned home from work that day and found him gone. Eventually, a neighbor came by to tell her that she'd briefly caught sight of Poly near Mariel, at the camp set up near the port for people waiting to leave. Now Tía Niña had no idea where he was: if he'd managed to leave, if he'd arrived, if he'd been arrested somewhere, if he'd drowned at sea. She couldn't sleep; she wasn't eating, she was shedding pounds. Finally, on June 3, my aunt Lucrecia in Miami called Havana to let her know that Poly had arrived safely and that my mother was on her way to pick him up. Thank God, Tatá said aloud to herself over and over, driving Tía Niña mad.

Poly felt a little guilty about having gone without taking leave of Tía

Niña. It was what my mother had done to him. Don't worry, my aunt reassured him. "It is better that way. Goodbyes are sad."

I don't know if she meant it, or if she was just trying to assuage his guilt. By then, she was used to doing things for Poly, to telling him white lies, to brushing off his slights. Over seventeen years, she had raised him, seen him grow into a man, struggled with his difficulties. She had done that as she cared for my grandmother, as she cared for Tatá, visiting and taking her food at Mazorra or attending to her in myriad ways when she was home. She raised her nephew Carlitos, as well, because Tatá could not. Without biological children of her own, Tía Niña became a mother to two boys. The only one of my mother's eleven siblings who went beyond the sixth grade in school, Tía Niña had a good job. Before the revolution she worked at the Sears Department Store in Marianao, walking distance from the house. Later she worked as a cashier in the stores that the revolutionary government opened for foreign diplomats and staff. She joined the Committees for the Defense of the Revolution and the Federation of Cuban Women, both formed soon after Fidel Castro's rise to power. She was an upstanding citizen, not remotely militant but still cooperative.

Her first true love was a revolutionary, bearded like Castro and nicknamed Pepe. She eventually left him because he wouldn't change, she told my mother, though I don't know what it was he was doing: drinking, maybe, gambling, cheating. She met Onelio, her second partner, some years later. And when Onelio got tired of living with Poly's problems, Tía Niña gave up her lover for her inherited son. She had put up with a lot from Poly over those seventeen years and given up a lot, too.

Poly's departure, then, left a deep mark in her life. She had always known he would go immediately if given the chance. Now it had happened, and she wanted to be happy for him. As she wrote in her first letter to him after he left, "I am happy when I think that you are already with your mother, like you, and we, so much wanted."

A reluctant correspondent, Tía Niña probably wrote more letters to Poly after his departure then she had ever written in her life. She peppered him with questions: How are you feeling? Are you eating well? Does your head hurt? "You must be thrilled spending these months with your sisters who are on vacation," she wrote in August, referring to the fact that his arrival had coincided with the start of our summer. Are they teaching you English? She heard from my mother that he had a job, and she was thrilled. Tell me what you do at work? Do you like it? Tell me everything, she seemed to say. "Poly," she wrote in September, "I want you to be happy. You have cause to be, you are with your mother and your sisters." Tell me, are you happy?

Tía Niña looked for signs one way or another. But it was hard, because he wasn't answering. She nagged him all the time: I'm writing to you again, without having received so much as a scrap of paper from you. "*Chico*, seriously, are you never going to write me?" she asked in August, three months after his departure. She begged him to write. Your mother gives me news of you, she said, "but it is not the same as hearing it from you, because that way I am conversing a little with you." Was his silence a sign of something bad, she asked herself, or just his customary laziness? My mother had spent years having anxiety dreams about Poly. Now it was Tía Niña's turn. She dreamt that he was well, that he was sad, that he was back for a visit. She scrutinized her nighttime visions, deciphering what they might be telling her about his state of mind, about his life with us.

In late August, Tía Niña received a first batch of pictures from my mother. She showed the photos to all her neighbors and to everyone who came to the house. She even took them to her job to show her coworkers. Everyone—herself included—loved the way Poly looked without a mustache. She stared at his eyes and his mouth, and she was pleased. She wrote to Poly right away, explaining that she had been asking him for pictures because she had wanted to see his face, to study his expression. "I was satisfied. You are happy, and I am very glad. I knew you would be."

Two weeks later, Tía Niña received her first letter from Poly. He was not happy. Because I only have her letters to him, I do not have the exact date of his letter, nor do I know exactly what he said to her. She responded on September 10; that would have meant that he probably wrote his first to her right around the time I moved away to college. "In your letter," she wrote to him, "I noted that you are not too happy." What had he written to prompt that response? She counseled him, "But, my son, the beginning is always like that, it is hard to adapt to a new life." "Don't despair," she added; it will work out. "Your good luck will keep accompanying you."

Why did she use the word *keep*, I wonder. And did he notice that she called him her son? I'm sure he did. He must have loved to read Tía Niña's reassurances, to hear her voice in his head calling him son. Maybe he loved her letters so much that he reread them again and again. I think of him as a little boy in Cuba, sitting with my mother's letters on the porch, writing that receiving them made him so happy that sometimes it made him sad. Suddenly living in New Jersey, receiving letters from Tía Niña, listening to his sisters jabbering in an unintelligible language, watching as his mother went back to work, maybe he felt a little like that again.

What was it like for Tía Niña after Poly left? Poly had driven off her partner, Onelio, so she was alone in the house, even though many nieces and nephews came by regularly. She adopted a stray cat, and that helped entertain her a little. Carlitos, Tatá's son, separated from his wife and moved back in with her for a time shortly after Poly's departure. She also brought Tatá home from Mazorra for a while to take better care of her. But Tatá was driving her crazy, constantly talking to herself and praying aloud about Poly. Tatá offered running commentary on everything she saw on television. She was obsessed with the cosmonaut Arnaldo Tamayo, part of the Soviet space mission Soyuz 38 and the first Latin American and the first person of African descent to make it to space. Maybe Tatá hummed the special song about the cosmos that the government had commissioned for the occasion of a Cuban in outer space.

Yet even with all those distractions, Tía Niña missed Poly terribly. She memorized the few letters he wrote her, stared and stared at the pictures my mother sent. In the one she liked "best of all," she wrote, "you have a smile; it looks like you dedicated it to me, right?" The photographs she had of him were fading, she said rhetorically, because she looked at them so much.

Still, there must have been a part of her that, however much she loved and yearned for Poly, was a little relieved not to be responsible for him anymore. She did not have to worry up close about his drinking and gambling, about the fact that he wasn't working, about his constant courting of trouble. Even Onelio, whom Poly had helped drive away, came back to her. "I feel good and at ease," she wrote to Poly in May 1981. Do you want to know why? she asked. Three of Poly's friends had just been arrested. One was released quickly, but the other two remained imprisoned. Tía Niña couldn't stop thinking about what would have happened to Poly had he still been in Cuba when it happened. He would have ended up in jail, she was certain of it. "See why I feel so calm now?" she explained.

Surely his absence, even if painful, could sometimes feel like a source of quiet and peace. When I finally met Tía Niña ten years later, that was one of my impressions of her. She was a woman who lived in peace.

# FIFTEEN

# Exit

**Many things—history, fate, circumstance,** our parents—conspired to set Poly and me on radically divergent paths. Yet it is also true that our lives seemed to share a chronology. The turning points came at the same time, inextricably linked. In 1963, both our lives changed when our mother left him and not me. In 1980, both our lives changed again. He achieved his long-sought reunification with our mother and landed in a world completely alien to him. I pulled off my long-sought departure from the constrictions of my parents' Cuban nest and suddenly entered a world radically new to me.

I arrived at Vassar a few days before my two roommates. In our two-room triple I chose neither the best nor the worst bed and location. My mother and I unpacked together; she made the bed, and we all went for a little walk around campus. It was my parents' first time seeing it. Then without meeting my roommates or any other students, they drove back to New Jersey.

In those first weeks, as people sat around getting to know each other, lots of people asked me where I was from. New Jersey was not the answer they were seeking. Where was I "from from"? they wanted to know. Some asked *what* I was. In one gathering, someone said their mother was from the Fiji Islands, and another person in the group chimed in, "My family owns one of those." My new companions had spent time in Europe on exchange programs, alone backpacking and traveling with Eurail passes, or touring with their families. Their parents were diplomats, violinists, lawyers, fashion designers, artists, surgeons, professors. It was a world full of people I thought of as Americans, people who to my young eyes never questioned their place in the world that surrounded them. (I know now that the truth was more complicated than that.) Caught between two worlds, I did my best to keep them apart. At Vassar, Poly was my shameful secret. In a place like that, even my parents were something of a secret.

While still in high school, my two best friends and I used to write letters to each other as if we were already in college, a strange exercise in anticipation and speculation. Georgia was headed to Barnard, Mayra to Bennington, me to Vassar. In those letters, we imagined ourselves as student activists, sometimes as writers. When I got to Vassar, though, I couldn't even open my mouth a lot of the time. In my freshman English class, our first assignment was to write a two-page essay on the role of fairy tales in our childhoods; the professor suggested we write about some favorite books our parents had read to us. But my parents never read to me. Until I started buying one or two a month at the Scholastic Book Fairs and storing them in a dresser drawer, we had no books at home. So I wrote about the only thing I could: television, about watching *Cinderella* on TV at the age of four or five and crying when it ended. My father had pretended to call the television station and then consoled me with a white lie. *Cinderella*, he said, would be on again the next night. My professor loved the essay. The following week, without asking for my permission or letting me know ahead of time, she shared copies of it with the whole class. Someone said my use of the phrase "left much to be desired" was trite. Someone else said that my life followed the arc of a fairy tale, from my so-humble origins all the way to Vassar. I did not speak for the rest of term.

That first semester, I tried joining a left-leaning political club. It was a relatively small group. When people found out I was Cuban, they asked me how much property my family lost to the revolution. In that moment, I recalled one of my favorite high school teachers, Mr. Augustine, who had once encouraged Georgia, Mayra, and me to cut school and go see *Hearts and Minds* in a Greenwich Village movie theater in the middle of the day. He always said that the most important rule in politics was "to know who your people are." I decided that the club wasn't for me.

In my dorm room one night, trying to fall asleep in the dark, I could hear what sounded like water moving through pipes. But somehow the sound of the water turned into the laughter of a man and a woman. They were laughing at me. I sat up in bed, trying to call out to my roommate Elisa,

In my dorm room freshman year.

but no sound would come out of my mouth. Another day, I was in the library heading to my work-study job in the Reserve Room. I opened the door to the basement floor, where the room was located, and saw a young woman sitting at a desk against a wall. I could only see her back; her long black hair was down, wavy and frizzy like mine. Her height and weight mirrored my own. And I remember thinking something like, "Oh, good, there I am; we can finally talk." I started walking toward her, but halfway there realized that she wasn't me. (I recently found myself thinking about that girl, a figment of my imagination, wishing I could talk to her about this book.)

Vassar was beautiful, though. I had never seen a place so beautiful in my life. I went for walks a lot. Autumn was glorious. On family weekend in October, my parents visited; Poly came with them. But I only know that because he reminded me about it much later. I had completely blocked it out. They came for only part of the day, didn't attend any of the college-sponsored events, and left before dinner. We probably all preferred it that way.

In the age before VCRs and streaming, the college screened films every Wednesday, Friday, Saturday, and Sunday night. I went at least twice a week, sometimes more, and saw films such as *Being There, If . . . , The Harder They Come*, and *It's a Wonderful Life*, the last one shown shortly before most of us left campus for winter break.

A few days after my return home, I noticed that PBS was airing it for the holidays. I wanted to watch it with my family. Poly wasn't home. But my mother and sister didn't want to see it. I don't know why it meant so much to me, or why I cried when they said no. Maybe in that moment, I hadn't wanted to keep my two worlds separate. I wanted to share something of my new world with them. My father always hated to see me cry, and sometimes when he saw me cry, it made him cry. And that's what he did with me that night in my room. Then we went back out to the living room, and the four of us watched the movie together. A day or two later, on our first Christmas Eve with Poly, we all ate roast pork, *congrí*, and yuca and exchanged presents by the tree.

When I returned to Vassar in January, I began thinking seriously about visiting Cuba for the first time. I got in touch with a group of Cuban Americans called the Brigada Antonio Maceo, named after the famed Afro-Cuban independence hero, about whom I would later write. The "brigade" was composed of people, mostly a generation older than me, who had left Cuba as children and teens and had returned for the first time in 1977. Thereafter, they organized yearly trips for Cuban Americans and held regular meetings in preparation. I attended a few, taking the train from Poughkeepsie, the subway down to the gatherings in the East Village, and then a bus home to New Jersey to sleep before returning to school in the morning. More than the meetings, I was interested in the trip. But participating required a screening. The woman who conducted my interview—a psychologist, I think—told me to be honest, that I could share anything with her, any concerns, doubts, criticisms. I was young, impressionable, curious, yet constitutionally skeptical of dogma. I wasn't sure where to begin, so I asked about the treatment of gays in Cuba, the subject of a reading I had recently done in a Spanish class. I knew they were scorned, prohibited from joining the Communist Party, sent to reeducation camps, and so on. To my surprise, the woman interviewing me justified the government's conduct; she told me that homosexuality was both a disease and an unwanted legacy of capitalist decadence, or something like that. She can't possibly believe that, I thought to myself. So why was she saying that other than to parrot government propaganda?

I stopped going to the meetings soon after and did not go to Cuba that summer.

Is it strange that I can date my interest in returning to Cuba to scarcely six months after Poly's arrival in the United States? Perhaps. But I sense that it may have also had something to do with my being at Vassar. Growing up surrounded by people who were mostly like my parents and me, my sense of being different was more abstract. I was never alone in that difference. At Vassar, I felt my otherness in so much of what I saw around me everyday; I heard it in occasionally stilted introductions to someone's family. (Doesn't she look a little like María, said one girl to her parents, before turning to me to explain that María was their maid.) Leaving my New Jersey version of Cuban America and entering the privileged world of an elite American college, I had to confront my difference all the time. In one way, that pushed me to think about its source, about Cuba and the root of my uneasy presence at a place like Vassar. Yet even as I struggled with my sense of apartness there, I think I could already tell that the place was also widening the distance between me and my parents.

# SIXTEEN

# Vengeance

**Before I ever went to Cuba,** I went to Miami. It was our third family vacation there over the course of about a decade. We always stayed in South Beach, though this was well before it became gentrified and trendy. At most of the hotels on that stretch of Collins Avenue where we stayed, the guests were almost all people like us, Cubans from up north, taking a few weeks off in summer, low season in Miami and the only season most of us could travel.

In July 1981, my parents rented two hotel rooms at the Bancroft Hotel on Fifteenth Street and Collins. My sister and I stayed in the same room as my parents, which had two double beds. My brother stayed in his own room, but I never saw it. Relatives came to visit, and Poly sat at the pool drinking beer with old friends from Havana, like him also Mariel Boatlift arrivals.

My sister and I spent our days swimming and tanning, our evenings playing Ping-Pong and pinball in the game room. I was there one night when my sister came in crying. Poly had been looking for her because he needed the key to our room, and he thought she had it. When he found her walking on the beach with a boy, he slapped her.

I was furious. With the righteous energy of a girl-woman just turned nineteen, I stormed off to find him. He was in our room, my parents' room, but they were not there. As soon as I came in, before I could utter any of the words I was already planning to say, he came toward me, shouting, *¡Y tú!* (And you!) Then all I remember is him hitting me: I fall to the ground; he stands over me, his beer belly already protruding, the mustache he'd regrown drooping over his top lip, set in anger. He starts kicking me.

A cousin, who happened to be in the room, shouted for him to stop. "Call the police!" I shouted back. She picked up the phone, and then, finally, he desisted. I have no idea how long the episode lasted. I was crying; he was shouting, roaring that he had the right to hit me, because of his *hombría*, because he was a man. Then he threatened me: If I told my parents—or was it just my father? I can't remember— *va a haber muertos.* "There will be dead people." Then he added that he had done it before: He had killed before.

I believed him when he said it. Now I wonder if he made it up. I imagine him puffed up in anger, maybe feeling a little alarmed by what he had just done to me, worried about what the consequences would be, trying to scare me, because maybe he had just scared himself.

I told my mother right away. The only thing I remember of the conversation is that she told me to never, ever tell my father. She was scared, too. Maybe more than I was, more than Poly was. She could imagine consequences way too easily. My father would confront Poly and kick him out of our home. That would be like abandoning her son all over again. Or my father would confront Poly; then there would be words, blows. Maybe there would be dead people, as Poly had forewarned. Or perhaps she imagined that what Poly had just done would go on some kind of invisible ledger my father kept, a ledger of reasons to leave, as Onelio had left Tía Niña because of Poly. My father could have any woman he wanted, she always thought. Why would he put up with Poly's mess? I never told my father.

Back home, a week after the incident, I wrote about it in my journal. "My brother tried to beat me up," I began. "We have not looked at each other for a week (exactly)." Immediately after, I bring up my mother. Even now, it's almost impossible for me to think about my relationship with him without thinking of her. "He's bent on making Mami suffer," I wrote. "She's not to be forgiven for her 'abandonment.' This is his revenge—he's making up for lost time. . . . I see him standing over me, hitting me, and I HATE him."

Reading the entry now, I think immediately of something my mother told me that Poly said to her soon after his arrival in this country. I thought about it a lot after that summer. He told her that, just as she had ruined his life by leaving him in Cuba, he was now here to ruin hers. His very presence would be his vengeance.

But vengeance, like memory, is a strange animal; it can bark with more than one mouth. In this case, the person it would most come to hurt was the same person bent on inflicting it.

# SEVENTEEN

# Guns, Knives, and Books

**In 1981, shortly after we returned** from the family vacation in Miami, my mother found an apartment for Poly in our building, a small one-bedroom two floors down from us. Maybe my mother thought a little distance would be good. She furnished the apartment, buying a sofa and a bed when he first moved in. A few months later, she bought him a refrigerator, a table and four chairs for the kitchen, two lamps, a coffee table, and two side tables for the living room. All of it was new, from Colony Furniture on Bergenline Avenue, costing a total of $1,120.35, which at the time was more than two months of her salary. My mother took pictures of the apartment and sent copies to Tía

Niña in Cuba. In one, my sister sits on Poly's bed, neatly made by my mother.

My mother prayed that the accountability of a home would teach him to keep a job, to learn the habits of life that he had not been able to master in Cuba. By then, he was on his second job in the country, working at a local factory called Richie Embroidery Corp. In the 1950s, West New York (and neighboring Union City) were home to about 90 percent of all machine embroidery in the United States, with more than four hundred factories scattered across the two towns. The industry was smaller by the time Poly arrived, but it was still a mainstay of the local economy. Wages were relatively high; English was not required, and some of the factories were walking distance from our apartment. Poly's title was "watcher"—they were the workers who, in the days before the job was mechanized, literally watched the machines to monitor for thread breaks. In his first year at the job, he earned $8,650. Poly paid or helped with rent on his new apartment. He had a bank account, and he bought himself clothes. He was trying to look good.

Maybe her plan would work: Her mothering and her love, even if they came two decades late, would fix him. She saw proof of it not just in his job or his newfound care with this grooming. It was evident also in the fact that he was helping to take care of other people. He sent a new pair of eyeglasses to Tía Niña in Havana. He paid for my sister's first pair of contact lenses and bought her an Atari console as a Christmas present. When the time came, he even contributed toward the cost of her high school graduation photos. My mother felt so proud.

Like the Cuban mother she was, like the Cuban son he was, they both fell into predictable roles. She still shopped and cooked for him, did his laundry, cleaned his apartment. One time when my mother was cleaning for him while he was at work, my sister keeping her company, she found a gun in his dresser. My sister and I don't think she ever told my father, but she told me. At Vassar, I was distressed and frightened enough to share the news with my new (and first) boyfriend. That is the only time I recall ever revealing anything like that to anyone there. My sister remembers the gun vividly, tucked in the back of the first drawer of his bedroom dresser. She remembers the weight of it. My mother begged him to get rid of it, and he did. But later she found a large knife hidden in a drawer, too.

During those first years with Poly, my mother developed a great fear of knives or, rather, of him with knives. It was a fear that lasted for decades. One time, while I was away at college, she hid all the large kitchen knives. She gathered them up, wrapped them in a brown paper grocery bag, and hid them in my father's bedroom closet. My sister, who would have been fifteen or sixteen at the time, found them by accident one day, quickly put them back, and shut the closet door.

I myself remember another episode involving my mother's fear of knives. There was an argument. All of us—except my father, who was at work—were standing in the hallway, between our bedroom door and my mother's closet. (She gave my father the larger closet in their bedroom and used the smaller one in the hallway for herself.) I don't know what we were arguing about, but my brother stormed off toward the kitchen. He was going to get a knife. That was what my mother thought. I can't remember if I thought that, too, or if that became my memory after she gave me hers. She collapsed suddenly, and all three of us—my sister, Poly, and I—rushed to help her, the altercation forgotten. My mother told me later that she had only pretended to faint. She had wanted to make sure that Poly wouldn't go to the kitchen for a knife. The moment stayed with me forever: my mother pretending to faint to keep her son from stabbing one of us. For most of my adult life, I have imagined terrible scenes unfolding in our family. Those imaginings took root then, in Poly's first years here, after the incident in the Miami Beach hotel and as my mother began telling me (some) things from a distance.

My sister remembers an argument in that very same spot, in the hallway, in front of my mother's closet. In Aixa's memory, however, I was not present, and it was only the three of them arguing. She can't remember what the argument was about or how it ended. But she feels certain that my mother did not collapse, neither in earnest nor intentionally. Instead, my mother stood in front of her closet, wearing a housedress, holding a pretty box in her hand. As my sister tells me all this, I try to get her to focus on the box. We are talking on Zoom. On the screen, she moves her hands to indicate its dimensions. "Like a memory box," she tells me, orangish, brownish. I very clearly remember a brown box my mother kept in that closet. It was originally a case for a Fabergé perfume set, once a gift and then simply a pretty box in which to save old letters. She always told me that the letters she kept in it were the ones she and my father had exchanged after he left Cuba and she stayed behind pregnant with me. Could this be the box Aixa remembers? And what kind of argument might a letter box have provoked? As an adult, after I became a historian, I once asked my mother about the letters. She said she'd thrown them out. I think it was around the time Poly arrived that she did that. Maybe she hadn't wanted him reading my parents' love letters or their conversations about reuniting in the United States, when Poly knew very well what that had meant for him.

My sister and I have been talking about Poly lately. We have commiserated about him before, of course. But it is only now, as I turn to her for help with this book, that we revisit our first years with him, that we say out loud what we were each thinking and feeling at the beginning of our family's reunification.

Two years younger, Aixa was left to deal with Poly after I went away to college. She couldn't escape his beer drinking, his smoking, his perpetual aura of anger. She remembers how nervous she used to get as she approached our apartment on her way home from school. He had taken to drinking during the day at a corner bar on the ground floor of our apartment building. She feared he would see her through the window and come out to talk to her drunk. She told me of another memory recently, a vivid one. Our parents were so scared of Poly that one night they barricaded themselves in their bedroom, pushing furniture in front of their door to impede his entry. "How do you know that?" I ask. If she was home and they were that scared, they would not have left her alone in her bedroom at the other end of the apartment. Was she in the bedroom with them? Or was this something my mother told her later and that she can now see in her mind's eye as if she had been there, panicked alongside them? I press her. Our mother told her, she concludes a little later. Even if Aixa and I sometimes struggle to differentiate between first- and secondhand knowledge, one truth was very clear: Something was wrong, and we were scared. My sister pauses and then adds, sadly, "It was miserable."

Shortly before going home for Christmas my junior year, in 1982, I watched *Sophie's Choice*, the new Meryl Streep movie that told the story of a mother coerced into making an unthinkable decision. At Auschwitz, she was forced to choose which of her two children would be sent to the gas chamber; if she refused to choose, both her children would be murdered. So she chose. Living in Brooklyn, yet another immigrant, this was her secret and cross to bear. My mother's situation was different, of course. There was no gas chamber, neither of her children would be killed. But, still, the film, and the idea of a mother having to make an impossible choice between her two children, affected me deeply.

A few months later, I had to draft a short story for a creative writing class. I returned to the incident at the docks in Havana, when my mother had the chance to leave Cuba on the spur of the moment with both Poly and me and had chosen not to. I turned in the nine-page, double-spaced story on March 28, 1983, exactly one month shy of the twentieth anniversary of my mother's and my departure from Cuba. I keenly remember writing it, recalling specific scenes I invented for it. But as I read the story now, I am still surprised.

I begin with my grandmother watching her daughter—my mother—put a newly arrived letter from my father in New York in her purse and then head out with her two children for an appointment at an immigration office. I include a scene with Poly's father, who watches the three of us from a second-story window as we head off on that same errand. Benny Moré's "Yiri Yiri Bom" wafts out an open window. Construction on a new hospital site makes my mother detour toward the docks of Old Havana. There, the scene is pandemonium. Crowds are gathered near two large ships. At a hastily set up table, two women take the names of people boarding. My mother sees a neighbor and learns that the vessels, which have just arrived from the United States with medicine, are willing to take Cubans aboard for the return trip. There is pushing, and a soldier tries to corral her into the line. Poly—who in the story I call Marcos—tugs at her skirt, as I start crying. She's thinking of my father, of being with him in a matter of days. She's thinking of Poly's father, of never having to humiliate herself before him again, never having to beg and cajole him. She thinks of her mother, my grandmother, whose age I put at eighty in the story, but who was really seventy-five then. "It would be so easy to leave. . . . She moved toward the table with the lists. She couldn't," I wrote. In that moment, my mother made a choice. She made it, as we all make choices, without knowing everything that would come after. And by then, as a young woman writing an assignment at a place my mother could barely imagine, I was starting to grasp that decision's consequences; I was already struggling to understand.

When the semester ended, I lingered at school, avoiding the return home. Though I was only a junior, I stayed for commencement. Meryl Streep, having just won an Academy Award for her performance in *Sophie's Choice*, was the commencement speaker. She told the graduates that real life was more like high school than like college. And I remember wondering if that was good or bad. In high school, Poly was still in Cuba. In high school, I had known who I was.

When my own commencement came around a year later, in 1984, my parents and Aixa attended. Poly, I think, was in Miami. To pick up a cap and gown, I had to fill out a survey. I think we had filled out a version of it when we first arrived at Vassar; this was a follow-up one on the eve of our departure. Among the questions was one about future plans followed by a very long checklist of possible careers. One option, maybe on the middle of the page, read "College Professor." I remember an instant moment of recognition and excitement. I thought, "Yes! That is what I want to be." I had not finished formulating the sentence in my mind, when I said to myself with equal certainty, "But, no, people like me don't do that." I marked undecided instead.

While I was at Vassar for four years, Poly tried living in Miami a few times but always returned. Tía Niña worried about his rootlessness and chastised him, "I hear that you're in Miami again. You don't feel good anywhere. . . . you have to settle down someplace for your own good." But maybe Poly was just trying to recommit to the project of living in the United States by staying away from his family and the heaviness they made him feel. Tía Niña just didn't understand, didn't know what it was like to be him among us.

Besides, many of his old Cuban companions—men he'd been hanging out with since childhood and who left during the Mariel Boatlift—had settled in Miami. He probably felt more at home there with them than he did with us. Through the mothers and girlfriends of some of those friends, Tía Niña sometimes heard indirect news of Poly; she knew he was hanging out with the brothers Jorgito and Miguelito, as well as someone nicknamed El Purry, old neighbors and friends from Marianao. Tía Niña thought this last acquaintance was worrisome, and she was forceful with her advice: "Don't have any more relations with Purry. You know I don't like him, I've never liked him, he's a nasty piece of work." Stay away from him, she commanded; "he casts a bad shadow."

I don't know if it was one of those friends who was with Poly on a twenty-four-foot Sea Ray named *Sun Drifter* off the coast of Bimini in the Bahamas in December 1984. Poly and his companion were heading back to Miami when they encountered another boat, in distress and with ten Cubans aboard. The *Sun Drifter* rescued them and radioed the Coast Guard to let them know. The Coast Guard dispatched the *Cape Fox*, a Type B Cape-class cutter, which was frequently used to rescue stranded seafarers, as well as to confiscate shipments of illegal drugs and detain the traffickers. The crew on the cutter searched Poly's vessel, but their report makes no mention of drugs. They in-

Poly (*right*) and a friend.

terviewed the stranded migrants, all of whom answered "freedom" when asked why they wanted to come to the United States. Or that was how the person recording the interview summarized their reasons. The migrants would have then embarked on the process of formally requesting asylum, and as Cubans there was no reason to suppose that their petitions would have been denied.

But Poly's own fate was not as clear. He was technically "an immigrant without a visa." He did not have his I-94 card, the documentation given to people who are not US citizens or legal permanent residents on admittance to the country. In fact, he had no "suitable travel document" at all. He was detained as potentially "excludable" and sent to Krome, the defunct missile base on the edge of the Everglades turned immigrant detention center. Interviewed there, he swore that this trip to the Bahamas was the first time he had left the country since he'd been admitted in 1980. He confessed to traveling without appropriate authorization. Asked if he wanted to add anything to his statement, he said, "I don't want to lose my parole," referring to the permission to remain in the country while his immigration case was decided. "I want to get my residency."

There is remorse in his voice. He could still be the same young man who wrote to my mother from Cuba, wondering why things always went wrong for him, anguished that even when he tried to be good, to steer a clear and righteous path, he was unable to stay there. Everything always falls apart, he had written back then. Poly spent almost three weeks detained at Krome. He was released on January 8, 1985, given a new I-94 card to replace the one he had lost, and summoned to appear before an immigration judge for exclusion proceedings on April 1, 1985.

He never showed up. Instead, he returned to New Jersey and our mother. Whether he told her everything that happened, I am not sure. But I know that she was hell-bent on helping him. She hired an immigration attorney to handle his case and apply for US residency. I have the receipts, literally: $2,500 paid to the lawyer. The case was held up because my mother's name on Poly's birth certificate did not match her name in the United States. When she sent the certificate of her marriage to my father as proof of her name change, it was a family affair. My father handwrote, "I'm sending a copy photostatic of my certificate of marriage. Thank you," and then my mother signed in her own hand. Underneath, I recognize my own small handwriting: "Also please note my new mailing address," I wrote as if I was Poly. The address I added was our own.

By then, I was back at home, too, having graduated and taken a job as a paralegal at a New York City law firm. I took the bus and subway every day, looking around at the other commuters and wondering, "Is this it? Is this the rest of life, an expanse of seemingly unending time no longer broken up by school years?" I wasn't sure I liked it at all. But I was reading like crazy. I binge read Thomas Hardy and Honoré de Balzac, long novels in which the failings of parents were often visited on the children. When those got too heavy, I retreated to Jane Austen. I read *War and Peace* and reread *One Hundred Years of Solitude*—I can't remember if in English or Spanish. One night when my sister, Aixa, was home from college for a visit, I finished Anne Moody's *Coming of Age in Mississippi* at 3:30 a.m. in the kitchen, so as not to wake her. During a trip to London in 1985, my first time traveling out of the United States, I purchased a book titled *Novel with Cocaine*, a Russian work of uncertain authorship translated into English for the first time in 1984. I read it back in New Jersey, thinking about Poly's long pinkie nail right away.

When I was alone in my childhood bedroom at night, I always closed the door but couldn't lock it, because it had no lock. I would hear Poly come into the apartment late at night, hear him climb into the cot my mother prepared for him in our living room every night. I heard the sounds he made, his soft moans. Was he in pain? Was he masturbating? Was he crying? Did he know I was awake and listening?

I had no idea about his recent arrest, or about the possibility of his exclusion and deportation. Neither did I know that he had recently suffered some heavy losses. Sometime in 1984, Poly lost his father in Cuba. Tía Niña waited a few months to tell him, wanting to confirm that the rumor she had heard was true. But after Poly's aunt, his father's sister, stopped by her job at the store to tell her, Tía Niña wrote to Poly with the news. His father died of a heart attack. He'd lain down for a nap during the day, and "passed from sleep to death." "The bad die well," she mused. There was no love lost between Poly and his father, but I know that the loss registered for him. Many years later, Poly once lashed out at me for not having expressed my condolences to him on the death of his father.

Not long after his father died, Poly lost his good friend Miguelito. Miguelito and his brother Jorgito had left Cuba during the Mariel Boatlift. Tía Niña talked and visited regularly with both Miguelito's mother and his partner, Anita, and all three women would fill each other in on news of their beloved young men now in the United States. When Poly moved to Miami in 1984, it was Miguelito and Jorgito who welcomed him. He hung out with them, drank with them, sometimes worked with them, and got into trouble with them. In 1984, Miguelito was brutally murdered, his body chopped to pieces and stuffed into the trunk of a car. Then in 1985, Poly's friend Purry died. Whether it was murder or a natural death, I do not know. Tía Niña expressed sadness at the news, even though she had never liked him and had warned Poly that he was a bad influence. It was a useless warning. Poly loved bad influences; he had long since become one himself.

Whatever else Poly may have been—sad, angry, dangerous—I now sense that he was also scared: of the law, of the future, maybe of himself. That's what he sounded like lying in the cot in the living room. But listening from my bed in the room next door, I myself was too afraid to realize it.

# EIGHTEEN

# History Moves

**I did not like living at home.** I hated living with Poly. I hated taking buses from the Port Authority in the wee hours of the morning after seeing friends in the city. I hated commuting to my job at a law firm, though I was happy to use one of my first paychecks to buy a tall pine bookcase for my bedroom. I had taken the job supposing I might become a lawyer but quickly decided I didn't want that. I quit after a year and went to London hoping to stay for a bit, but when my father had a medical emergency, I returned and moved back home. For a while I worked as a research and personal assistant for a writer and philanthropist. Sometimes, she gave me her tickets and invitations to gallery openings, screenings, performances. Once, when I was out with friends at a movie, Diane Keaton said hello to me because she recognized me from having seen me regularly at PEN readings by Norman Mailer, Joyce Carol Oates, Kurt Vonnegut. I always sat in the seat in front of her, *Playbill* in hand, scanning for names like mine even though there were none to be had, something I knew even before looking.

School beckoned, I thought. But I couldn't justify going back to school to read more British literature. I came up with an alternative that in some ways was closer to home and in others completely new. Because I was from Latin America but knew next to nothing about it, I decided to learn about it. My wealthy employer wrote one of my letters of recommendation. She shared a line from her letter with me, something about how I was turning what might have been a mere footnote—my first ten months of life in Cuba—into inspiration for study. My plan was to do a master's degree in Latin American History and then perhaps go to journalism school. I would become a journalist who covered Latin America, I told my parents with resolve. The University of Texas at Austin, which admitted me with full funding and a stipend, was to be the start of that journey.

In June 1986, a few months before I headed to Austin, my parents moved to Miami. My father had been talking about moving there for a while. Miami was, after all, the mecca, even more so for aging Cubans with joints starting to ache in the cold. My father had just turned sixty-five, my mother would soon turn sixty. My sister, recently graduated, went with them. Poly, I have no idea why, stayed behind in West New York.

I am nothing if not adaptable. In Texas, I made friends who gave me mixtapes featuring Hank Williams and George Jones. I bought a turquoise bolo tie, though I put it away after wearing it just once. It was a strange place to go to get closer to Cuba, but I did take whole courses on Brazilian slavery and the Mexican Revolution that first term, a far cry from all the Victorian literature I had read in college and later on my own. My second term I took a course on the Caribbean and an independent study of my own design on the history of Cuba.

It was then that I developed the habit of calling my parents every day. I remember once after studying a map, calling to tease them. I found my father's home, Jarahueca, on the map. But the place my mother called her childhood home, Chirigota, was nowhere to be found. She must really be a *guajira*, I teased. They were born in 1921 and 1926, so when I read about things that had occurred within their living memory, I often called to ask them about it. Did they remember? Did they witness it? Did they participate? When I read about the Constitutional Convention of 1940, of the way "the country" zealously followed its progress, I discovered that my parents (and their parents) hadn't. When I read about the multitudes who attended the first massive rallies of a victorious Fidel Castro, I learned that they hadn't. When I studied the agrarian reform that had nationalized so much land and asked my parents about their experience of it, their answers were again a version of no. No, my father said, our farm was too small to confiscate; no, we had no land, said my mother. When I read Castro's speeches, many broadcast on television, and asked my parents what they had thought as they watched, they reminded me that they didn't have televisions. They never joined; they never participated. They had no "history" to tell. I was inevitably disappointed, like the teenager I had once been, searching for Spanish surnames on lists and never finding them or the recognition I imagined they might bring.

I didn't realize then that the problem wasn't in my parents' answers, much less in their lives. History is often written in the collective, the names of countries (or classes) made to stand in for so many human beings. And what I was discovering, without yet being able to put it into words, was the gulf between the history of Cuba I was learning and the history of the two Cuban people who were my parents. There were probably many fewer people who showed up for political rallies and such than there were people like my parents: utterly ordinary people, always on the margins, absent less as a matter of ideology than from an unconscious sense that history did not belong to them. My parents' story, like that of so many others, could not "be absorbed into the central one: it [was] both its disruption and its essential counterpoint." And it was precisely in that misencounter between the history I was reading and the history of my own family that I found the seeds of how I myself would come to write about the past and its people. But in all those unusual phone calls about history and experience there was something else, too. Embarking on a journey that would catapult me to worlds way beyond my parents', I longed to keep them with me.

Our own immediate family history was changing at the same time. My mother's sister Lucrecia, the only one of her many siblings to join us in the United States, died unexpectedly. She was the first person I knew who died. She had gone into the hospital for a routine procedure and encountered one complication after another. My mother was devastated. She also told me that Lucrecia's death made her remourn all the people she had lost in Cuba after leaving, the people whose care and death she had not been present for, the people she hadn't said goodbye to. She kept thinking of her mother, she said.

Our family was growing, too. During my first Thanksgiving in Austin, I met my future husband, Gregg. He was there visiting his sister, a new friend, who like me had recently relocated from New York City. His eyes looked so deep and beautiful with the red plaid shirt he was wearing when he appeared on my doorstep. We were both reading books about the causes of revolutions, and we bonded as we washed Thanksgiving dishes. At the time, he was caring for his father, who was dying of AIDS and whose longtime partner had died earlier that year. Gregg had absolutely nothing to do with Cuba. But he understood the matter of family, and I fell in love.

The summer after I started the MA, I stayed with Gregg in New York City and took him to meet Poly in New Jersey. We met him at a bar near the embroidery factory where I think he was working off the books. He was playing pool when we showed up. We talked over a beer and calamari salad in the late afternoon. The visit wasn't long; Gregg remembers thinking he was brusque, not particularly friendly. He remembers, too, how nervous I was on the bus ride there. It surprises me that I took him at all, and I have no memory of what prompted me to reach out to Poly then. Maybe my mother had told him I'd be there, and she begged me to see him. Maybe from the distance of Austin, Texas, I wanted to give my relationship with him another chance, though I doubt that. However ill-tempered and sullen Poly appeared, I think I knew him well enough to know that he liked that I took my boyfriend to meet him, liked that we had calamari salad, which my mother never served, but which, it turns out, we both liked.

Soon after that, there were more moves. My parents stayed in Miami. My sister moved to Washington, DC, to join and marry her boyfriend Adrian, an African American man from Newport News, Virginia, whom she had met in college. They had a daughter in 1987 and blessed her with the name Nailah. With no childcare and not much money, they went to Miami, where my parents could help. Soon after, Poly moved to Miami, as well. Now all of them were there: my mother and father, Aixa and her young family, Poly.

I never joined them. Instead, I finished my degree in 1988, returned to New York, and moved in with Gregg. The following year, we were married at the chapel at Columbia University, where his father had taught before he died and where he himself had gone. I invited Poly to the wedding because I had to. My mother told me not to worry, that he would never attend. And she was right. A few months after our wedding, Gregg and I rented a moving truck and headed for Ann Arbor, Michigan, where I would get a PhD in History, specializing—it should come as no surprise—in the history of Cuba.

# PART IV

# Discoveries

# NINETEEN

# Long-Lost Brother

**My father always wanted** to be somewhere else. When he was in Cuba, he wanted to be in the United States. When he was in New Jersey, he wanted to be in Miami. After they moved to Miami, he pined for New York. Later, he began fantasizing about a permanent return to Cuba. Neither happened. He lived in Miami for the rest of his life, and there he became a new man.

Che Guevara loved the idea of the New Man, a figure who was both a motor of revolution and its most sublime product, a man who had defeated all the vices and limitations of the past, in the world around him and in the depths of his own being. My father hated Che Guevara. My father became a new man without the capital letters, and he did that not by overcoming the past but by revisiting it.

Indirectly, it involved a woman. Her name was Elia. She was the woman whose brothers had once vowed to kill my father, the woman whose pregnancy in 1945 had set in motion my father's decision to leave his home in the Cuban countryside, a decision that ended up being permanent. After my father absconded, Elia carried the infant to term hidden from public view, secreted away in the manner that women of respectable families gave birth to illegitimate, metaphorically fatherless children.

When the baby was born, Elia named him Juan José.

By the time my parents moved to Miami in 1986, Elia had already died. But Juan José was in Cuba, living in a small rural town not far from my father's people. Perhaps it was my father's perpetual longing for something else that led him to seek contact with a son he didn't know. Perhaps it was something of a feeling of mortality as he approached seventy. Sometimes, though, I wonder if it had something to do with Poly. Maybe in the years since Poly's arrival my father had come to wonder more intensely about the fate of his own son. Perhaps seeing Poly made him think that he needed to parent the son he had abandoned. Maybe, just maybe, he thought he needed to give my sister and me a different brother.

Aixa thinks she first learned about Juan José's existence while still living in New Jersey with my parents, which meant the conversation occurred no later than the summer of 1986. I wasn't there, she tells me. I, meanwhile, remember a conversation with my father in Miami in the summer of 1987. He was asking for my advice, for permission perhaps. He was thinking of getting in touch with Juan José. What did I think? To me, the idea was full of legitimacy and promise. His son. My brother. In Cuba. I loved the idea. Of course, he should contact him, I told him. Maybe I wanted the chance at another brother, too.

My brother Juan José was born on February 16, 1946, in his maternal grand-parents' home in rural central Cuba. When he was still an infant, his mother went to work in Havana as a live-in domestic servant. Initially, Juan José stayed behind with his grandparents, and Elia visited and sent money home for the family. Eventually, she took him with her to the capital. Maybe at that point, she still imagined making a family with my father. Many years later, she would tell her daughter-in-law, Juan José's wife, that she had gone to Havana because my father was there. I'm not sure how old Juan José was when she met and married another man who gave Juan José his own last name. Together Elia and her new husband had another son, Juan José's half brother.

Juan José always knew that he was not the son of the man who was raising him. But no one ever had a conversation with him about it. He knew it only from hushed rumor and unfeeling gossip. In Havana, my father saw Juan José as a young boy a handful of times. He would get in touch with Elia, she would bring Juan José to a corner or some other designated place, and they would talk for a little bit. Her husband found out, however, and soon forbade the meetings. He had contacts in the police and said he could make things hard for my father. So contact ended there.

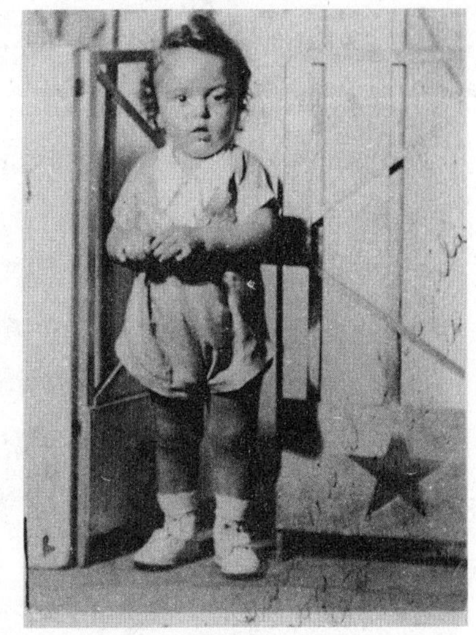

Juan José, my brother.

On March 4, 1960, shortly after Juan José's fourteenth birthday, my father ignored the warnings. That day, the *Coubre*, a French ship loaded with munitions from Belgium and docked at the busy port of Havana, exploded without warning at 3:10 p.m. The upper structure of the ship was almost completely destroyed; fires immediately broke out in the surrounding docks and buildings. Forty-five minutes later, with everyone rushing to put out the flames and tend to the wounded, a second explosion rocked the area. All told, seventy-five people were killed and over two hundred wounded. Juan José and his mother lived near the explosion. My father went to make sure they were all right, which they were.

My mother accompanied him that day. So, by then, she knew that my father, like her, had a son with someone from an earlier life. They were my two half brothers, one son for each of my parents: Poly, my mother's, and Juan José, my father's.

Less than a year after the explosion of the *Coubre*, Castro's government launched its famed Literacy Campaign, a vast mobilization that was to eradicate illiteracy across the country. Nineteen sixty-one became "The Year of Education." Of Cuba's roughly 7.3 million inhabitants at the time, approximately 1.25 million took part directly in the campaign, either as teachers or students. Close to three hundred thousand people volunteered to teach peasants to read and write, many traveling to the island's remotest corners. So many young people volunteered for the campaign that the government organized them in special youth brigades.

Juan José, living in Havana, rushed to join the effort. Volunteer teachers, however, needed their parents' permission, and his mother hesitated to let him go. She finally acquiesced but put a condition on her consent: that he serve back in her home province, in the Escambray Mountains, which were close to some members of her family. He agreed. But when he appeared for service, he told no one of that preference. In fact, when they asked for volunteers to go to Oriente, Cuba's mountainous eastern region, he immediately stepped forward. They assigned him to Sagua de Tánamo, to a tiny recondite corner of it accessible only by canoe and pack mule. A report prepared by Cuban Presbyterians who established a camp for children there in early 1959 gives a sense of the region's poverty: Every single child within the mission's jurisdiction suffered from parasites.

Juan José loved teaching people there to read. He stayed for almost six months between June and December 1961, living with a large extended family in a one-room house, forgoing milk with his coffee at breakfast because there was no milk for the family. After he left, the family saved the little jar he used for coffee as a memento on a shelf. A few times, long after the experience, he ran into someone whom he had taught to read. He was proud, gratified, humble about it, like my mother was when she ran into people whom she had baptized a lifetime before in the countryside of western Cuba. For decades after, Juan José saved his badge and pin from the campaign. Today, they sit displayed on a bookshelf behind my desk at home, the metal pin faded and discolored, the coating on the badge peeling and wrinkled, the words barely legible.

Living in Havana in 1967, Juan José happened to go to a New Year's dance in a small town in the middle of the island. He spent all night dancing and talking with a young woman named Hilda, whom everyone called Hildita. He was twenty-one years old and doing his obligatory military service, but every

Juan José and Hildita in the yard between their house and her parents' house.

weekend after they met he took the train to visit her. The military recruits could board only after everyone else got on, so he often made the trip standing the whole way. Ten months after their first meeting, they married.

Though they started their married life in Havana, they soon moved to the small rural town of General Carrillo, where they had met at the dance and where Hildita's family lived. Juan José built a house in the backyard of her parents' old colonial home, and they made their lives there. Both became schoolteachers, she teaching English, he Spanish language arts and literature. They had two children, a boy, Alain, born in 1970, and Aymara, a girl, born in 1971. A family of four, like we had been before Poly's arrival.

The town of Carrillo was just about five or six miles west of Jarahueca, where my father's family farm was located. Juan José was aware of the Ferrers. He knew my father's siblings were his biological aunts and uncles, even though no one acknowledged it. My father's youngest sister, Orelia, used to go to Carrillo regularly. When Juan José and Hildita had their first child in 1970, Orelia approached the new mother one day in town. She said that she'd like to come by their house and meet their son. Hildita said yes, of course. But she did not tell Juan José. She knew he would not like the idea; he had no interest in establishing relations with the family of a man who had never been a father to him. When Orelia went for the visit, Juan José was out. Hildita made coffee, and the two women bonded over the new baby. Juan José came home, saw what was going on, barely greeted Orelia, and left. Orelia, though, kept coming around, and eventually Juan José softened—some. Hildita knew that would happen, he was constitutionally unable to sustain the rudeness for long. The story reminds me of my father. He would have done the same thing in the beginning and come around gradually, if not completely.

I have no idea if my father knew about that contact or not. But in 1988—living in Miami, retired, with a lot of time to think—he decided to reach out himself. He didn't do so directly at first. He wrote to his cousin, Emelanio Ferrer, who lived around the corner from Juan José. I don't have my father's letter, just his cousin's response. He had been shocked to receive the letter, because there had been no contact between them for many decades. "I didn't think you even remembered my name," he wrote to my father. After receiving the letter, Emelanio talked to Juan José to gauge his openness to hearing from my father.

Juan José didn't want to decide alone and asked his family for their opinion. Were they interested in a relationship with his biological father and his family? All three of them supported the idea. After all, his wife had already been championing some kind of relationship with my father's sister Orelia.

Emeliano reported back, "It all depends on you; he holds no grudge against you." Emeliano also shared Juan José's address and some basic information on his family: Juan José and Hildita were both teachers, their children, Alain (eighteen) and Aymara (seventeen), were both in school. "They live well." He added: "Your son is named Juan José," which my father already knew.

The first letter from Juan José to my father arrived on July 15, 1988.

Juan José was forty-two, my father sixty-seven. I don't have a copy of the letter my father wrote, just Juan José's response. The salutation was simple: Ramón. No *querido* (dear), no *estimado* (esteemed), certainly nothing like *father*. Just Ramón. He begins, "Today I, too, will be brief," so we know that my father's letter was not long. "Two things force me to be brief," he wrote. "First, good sense. Another: man cannot live his whole life with a bitter feeling burning in his soul. And since I feel this way, I fear that in a mad rush of recklessness, foolish words will pour out. Moderation imposes itself, and I now subordinate myself to it." He told our father a little about his family, said he liked receiving the pictures of Aixa and me, and, as my father had asked, he was sending some of his own family, though he had no recent ones.

He told my father that he loved reading, that he'd done "some" over the years: "Reading is a source of inextinguishable pleasure and knowledge." But even with everything he'd read, he said, it was a particular poem of José Martí's that came most often to his mind. He didn't quote it in the letter, but it is Martí's best-known poem, and it goes like this:

> *Cultivo una rosa blanca,*
> *En julio como en enero,*
> *Para el amigo sincero*
> *Que me da su mano franca.*
> *Y para el cruel que me arranca*
> *El corazón con que vivo,*
> *Cardo ni oruga cultivo:*
> *Cultivo la rosa blanca.*

> I tend a white rose
> In July as in January
> For the sincere friend

Who offers his hand frankly
And for the cruel one who tears
The heart with which I live
Neither thistle nor thorn do I grow
For him, too, I tend a white rose.

Juan José said he liked its musicality—it sounds more musical in Spanish—
and the humanity of its sentiment. He thought it spoke to him in that moment, as he communicated with his father for the first time in his life. "So,
in our case, I leave the path open and we will see if Martí's words, written
with so much love, have merit." With that Juan José put the ball back in
my father's court. In 1945, my father chose to abandon the woman he had
made pregnant, to not recognize the son he had fathered. Was the hand he
was now extending to that son offered sincerely, frankly? Or would Juan
José's heart be broken by pursuing the relation?

The correspondence seems to have started slowly. I have found no other
letters between them in 1988. Instead, I found a copy of a letter that I wrote
to my newfound long-lost brother. I found it among my father's papers, so I
must have sent him a copy. The letter is typed, and in it, I asked forgiveness
for any errors in my Spanish. I informed him that when I first learned of his
existence, I was overcome with curiosity and peppered my father with questions: "Who is my brother? Where is he? What does he do? Does he know
you? Who is his mother? What happened?" I suppose that by sharing my
response to my father, I was also asking Juan José the same questions. I told
him I was happy that my father had overcome his fear of rejection and finally
reached out to him. I told him that my father had been unbelievably happy
to receive his letter, that he had learned it by heart (like Poly had learned my
mother's, and Tía Niña learned Poly's). Our father was a "good and sweet
man. And it weighs on me that you do not know him," I wrote.

I introduced myself to my brother. I gave him a brief synopsis of my life, including my attendance at Vassar, which I described as having been founded in 1861, as a pioneer in women's education. I might have told him that José Martí wrote a beautiful essay describing a graduation ceremony at the college in 1884, but I did not know that yet. I continued my academic curriculum by recounting the subject of my master's thesis on education in Cuba during the US military occupation of 1899–1902. I also told him about Gregg and about Aixa and Adrian's then eight-month-old daughter, Nailah. I did not mention Poly. I wonder if I thought of including him and then decided to leave him out; or if the thought never even entered my mind at all.

Letters between Cuba and the United States move slowly. Juan José's response to me is dated November 6, 1988, almost three months after I penned mine to him. But it may have been more than the slow mails that caused the delay. "I received your letter some days ago, and since then, I have thought every day of responding." He continues the letter in a fashion that I would come to recognize as very much his. He loved to speak and write in questions. "Why hadn't I replied?" he asks. "Did only one reason impede me? Can you imagine a deer serene in the forest? Isn't he wary of everything around him?" Then he switches from interrogative to indicative mood: "I do not want to be like the deer; that is not my nature, but life has forced me to be that way. I want and need to believe that this phenomenon that is opening up before me is not a mirage." Juan José tried to answer my questions about what had happened. I was really asking for the story behind his very existence. But he didn't have much to share. He had always sensed that it hurt his mother too much to talk about it all, and so he hadn't asked.

I can't remember now how I felt reading his letter then. What did I think of his seeming caution in the face of my father's sudden reappearance?

What did I make of the questions he asked? What more could I say to him about this reencounter between two grown men? Reading his letter now, I am surprised, less by his caution than by other questions he formulates later in the letter. He addresses them to me in the third person:

> Was it Ada who effectively always showed an interest in know-ing about her brother? Was it not Ada who was the vehicle that prompted Ramón—forgive me for calling him that, but I feel that in that regard I was born a few months ago, and in that time, it is not possible for me to call him father—to find the path that had been lost for so many years?

What had my father told him? Why did he think I was the primary mover of the reconciliation between them, between a parent in the United States and the son who had stayed in Cuba?

Juan José did not write to my father the rest of the year. On Febru-ary 17, 1989, the day after his forty-third birthday, he wrote in response to a letter my father had dated November 29 of the year before. Juan José confessed doubts. "Why haven't I replied before?" he asked, always asking. "It is something difficult to explain, something that happened to me also when I received Ada's letter. A thousand ideas have come to mind over all these days . . . but of all of them, the one that worries me most, the one that hounds me most and always occurs to me as a question without an answer is: Where are we going with this relation-ship?" I don't know what my father replied. Juan José's next letter to him is dated more than six months after that one. He acknowledged my father's most recent letter, a brief one. "I understand," he wrote, "because as you say, you haven't heard from me in a while."

It is strange to read just one side of the conversation. I hear the trepidation, the doubt in Juan José's writing. I imagine my father a little reticent. It is like they are each asking for something the other is not yet ready to give. Juan José wants to reassure my father. "When Emelanio first discussed the subject with me, I thought long and hard before answering that I was willing to establish contact with you. From that moment on, my decision has been firm." He confesses that he thinks he has always had a desire and a need for that contact, even though he had never admitted it to himself before. "There is no reason, then, according to my criteria, for you to have any doubt as to whether or not I want more direct contact. . . . The doors of my modest home, the heart of my family and my own are open to you, my sisters and your wife." What, if anything, we do now to establish direct contact depends on you, he told my father. I think Juan José was essentially saying that he wanted to talk with my father.

It should not have been that hard. But neither was it easy. To call from Cuba, one had to call the operator and request a collect call. Sometimes the call went through, sometimes the operator informed you that all lines were busy. And that was from Havana, calling from a private phone. Located in a small rural town in central Cuba, and without a phone in his house, making and receiving calls was even more difficult for Juan José. In that same letter to my father, he offered an alternative. My father could call the one public phone in town, someone would go get him, and then they could talk. "I hope there will soon be a personal conversation between us; sincerely, I wish it with all my heart, so I pray it will happen."

If my father tried calling, he was unable to reach my brother. But I'm not sure that he did call. He always hated talking on the phone. And the technical hurdles would have made him waver even more. Maybe because Juan José had been expecting a call and didn't receive one, he started to worry that communications had come to a halt between them. When he received another letter from my father on October 28, 1989, he was relieved. Again, I don't know what my father said, but whatever it was, Juan José took the letter's contents as a sign that the relationship was taking a more "concrete character." Still, he asks, "Please, where are we going? If you have been sincere, and I believe you have been, it will be easy for you to understand my uncertainty, especially as I feel that my hands and feet are tied, and I can only wait calmly—which is not easy—for your decisions."

Why did he say that he felt like his hands and feet were tied? He couldn't visit the United States to meet my father. That would have required an invitation from a close relative. Since my father was not legally his father, that would not have sufficed. And my father had not issued one, in any case. Juan José said it was nearly impossible to make a phone call out from Carrillo. He couldn't do more than what he was doing—writing letters. My father, however, could do more, at least in theory. He could call; he could even visit Cuba. But he wasn't doing either. That left Juan José waiting for and wanting more. I think my father wanted more, as well. He wanted something he could recognize as unequivocal forgiveness. And Juan José's letters seemed short of that, too.

This particular letter, however, ended with something new. "I am very happy to hear that Ada intends to come to Cuba. Surely, we will see each other, God willing."

# TWENTY

# First Return

**In the summer of 1990,** more than a quarter century after I left Cuba, I returned. This was the trip I'd been waiting for, in one way or another, my whole life. In the beginning, when I was little, my parents had always made that return seem both inevitable and permanent. As I grew out of childhood, I rejected that idea. I might not consider myself fully American, I thought, but there was no way I was moving back to Cuba. In 1990, the decision to return was my own. I was twenty-eight, just recently married in a wedding that neither of my brothers attended. I had just finished my first year in a PhD program in history at the University of Michigan. I was becoming a historian of Cuba, and, obviously, one cannot be a historian of Cuba and not go to Cuba.

Neither government made it easy for me. From Havana, I needed a new Cuban passport, a requirement for anyone born in Cuba who had left and wanted to visit. In addition, I also had to secure an entry permit specifically for Cuban-born persons residing abroad and visiting Cuba for professional reasons, a PE-6 it was called at the time. Given the US embargo and travel restrictions, I needed permission from that government as well. I decided that the easiest way to go was with a group. I contacted the Center for Cuban Studies in New York and signed up for two back-to-back tours, each two weeks long. The first was a general Cuban history tour, while the second was devoted to Afro-Cuban culture. The Center negotiated all the permissions, the fact of my Cuban birth making my visa significantly more complicated than that of the other members of the group. Somehow it worked, and all the powers that be agreed to let me go.

Just because I'd been waiting for that trip forever does not mean that the reality of it did not scare me. As I prepared to return for the first time to my birthplace, to a country off-limits to almost everyone in the United States, to the place my family had always taught me to both love and hate, I know that I would have bitten my nails, suffered from stomachaches, had trouble sleeping. About a month before the trip, I dreamt that Cuba was a life-size cutout map. It stood vertically, rather than horizontally as it lies in the Caribbean Sea. I approached it and wrapped by arms around it in an awkward embrace, my feet parallel with Guane on the island's western tip, Baracoa looking down on me from its eastern tip, a few inches above my head. Cuba, flat and abstract like a cardboard cutout, was about to become real.

At 8 p.m. on Friday, June 29, I checked into Haiti Trans Air flight 8506 from Miami to Havana. I think of the first line in Joan Didion's *Miami*: "Havana vanities come to dust in Miami," and I wish for a line like that to describe the scene at my departure gate. A woman wore multiple straw hats, one atop another, the top one covered in hair barrettes and studded with earrings and any number of baubles she could give to loved ones for their own use or for them to resell. Some men wore two or three jackets, their linings lumpy from all the little gifts sewn into them. Cuban authorities allowed one to travel with only forty-four pounds of luggage, so there was incentive to load up one's body, literally. I can't remember if the family trying to stuff take-out food––Cuban sandwiches, steak with chimichurri sauce, ham *croquetas*—into their carry-on bags was from that trip or a later one. Everyone posed for pictures and talked to their gate mates. Some passengers tried to size up our tour group waiting to board with them. The tour group members would have looked back, perhaps chuckled derisively under their breath at the sight of the hats and the suits and the overstuffed valises, not realizing that this, too, was Cuba.

I know now that it is impossible to understand Cuba without understanding Miami Airport and its once-secret departure gates for Cuba. But I didn't know that yet in 1990. So, I sat there nervous but observant, gawkily occupying my habitual place: in the middle, part and not part of both groups at the same time.

On the plane, I sat next to an older couple, Cuban, who had just spent six weeks with their daughter in Miami. They warned me that I would find the coffee in Cuba to be not nearly as good as the coffee in Miami. (They were right.) They told me they had visited an old friend who lived in subsidized housing for the elderly and that they had been impressed. I had the window seat and craned my neck as we descended to glimpse the island for the first time. But it was a nighttime flight, and I wouldn't have seen much. I remember climbing down the stairs from the plane to the tarmac, looking at the young men and women in their uniforms, seeing the low building before me, a nondescript rectangular block, faded modern.

Large block letters, I think unlit, read José Martí International Airport. An airport named José Martí. It gratified me.

The room one first enters is very plain; it is the place where lines of passengers go through the immigration control booths. It is not a first world airport. There are unframed posters on the walls—Che Guevara, tourist must-sees, bikini-clad women enticing viewers to visit Cuba, even though everyone who laid eyes on the posters was already there. To this day, I get nervous as I choose a line to wait in. I fret about what to say when asked about the purpose of my trip. There is never only one. There is always research; there is always family. But I fear that saying more than one thing might raise questions, hold up the process. Sometimes I've encountered delays, suspicious questions, seeing my passport whisked away for the unhurried inspection of a supervisor behind closed doors. On my first trip, there were barely any questions at all.

On the other side of the immigration booths are the baggage claim belts and all the customs officials standing before tables and scales, ready—eager even—to weigh and inspect all those overstuffed bags. When it was my turn, the inspector asked me what I was bringing into the country. I smiled (as my mother would have done) and said I had clothes, books, papers, and toiletries. Did I touch my earlobe to feel for the gold posts my grandmother had once given me, the ones another official in the same airport had unexpectedly let me keep? The official waved me through without opening my bag.

The first Cuban Cuban I met by name was the tour guide who welcomed us at the airport. Her name was Alina. I remember immediately saying to myself, "I'd forgotten that name," thinking back to several Alinas in my high school. "I like it. If I have a daughter, maybe we should name her that." And we did. Alina, the tour guide, was pretty and slight in build. The Cubans around me spoke of her in the diminutive as a *mulatica*.

Sometimes when our group arrived places, the people expecting us and looking for someone who fit that description, assumed I was her.

It was midnight by the time we got to the Capri hotel that first night. Everyone was tired; people sat around the lobby chatting and getting drinks. Some just went up to bed. I could do neither. I had arrived in Cuba, the place that had defined so much of my life, and I was back because I wanted to be. I longed to grapple with something, even if I wasn't sure what. I didn't want to go to bed or hang out with Americans in the lobby. I wanted to go out, walk around, see it with my own eyes. No one was in the mood. I headed out by myself, but a few of the others joined me at the last minute. We ended up at the Malecón.

Cuba may be complicated, but the Malecón at midnight is magical. It certainly was on my first night in Havana. The beautiful seawall and promenade that ring part of the city hummed with conversation and music. Ocean spray curled its fingers over the edge of the wall, a salty mist blanketing the sidewalks. But the damp did not deter people from spending their evening sitting on the wall. Some looked out over the Atlantic, which from that point reaches northward about ninety miles to Key West. Others sat facing in toward the city, noting the Soviet Ladas from the '70s and the much older Chevies and Buicks drive by, watching families stroll, lovers kiss, and a few tourists saunter over from the aging hotels nearby, hotels I have come to know over many years and many trips: the Habana Libre (formerly the Hilton), the Riviera (built by US mobster Meyer Lansky), and the Capri (where I had just arrived). I drank it all in. Walking along the Malecón, young Cubans sought us out. They could tell we were not locals, and they wanted to talk to us. We met a group of Black university students who had just finished their semester, and we talked and talked. "When they found out I was Cuban, they hugged me, asked me questions, called me cousin," I wrote to Gregg. It felt like a homecoming. Back at the hotel, a roommate asleep on the bed next to mine, I was still too excited to settle down. I slept for only an hour that night.

A very odd thing happened the next morning. I was waiting by the elevators near the breakfast room when a repairman approached me. It was Pupi, one of my cousins, son of my mother's brother who had had seventeen children, long-ago playmate of Poly's. He had recognized me from Tía Niña's photographs. Incredulous, I asked him if he'd known I was coming, and he said no. Even now, it seems implausible, like the stars, or the ancestors, had indeed arranged a homecoming for me.

It was on my second or third evening in Havana that I took a taxi back to the house where we had lived before we left. Calle 116 #3522, between Thirty-Fifth and Thirty-Seventh Avenues, right behind the military hospital in Marianao. On the way, I made the taxi driver stop so that I could take a picture of Maternidad Obrera, with the towering Madonna and child over the front entrance. The statue's creator, I would later learn, was the Black sculptor Teodoro Ramos Blanco who portrayed in monuments many of the same people I would soon start to render in writing. A few minutes later, the taxi turned down our old street, and I began trying to make out the numbers on the doors. Tía Niña and Onelio came out as soon as they heard the car to embrace and welcome me. I walked into the living room and noted the framed poster of Fidel Castro in profile, aiming through the scope of his rifle. Pictures of the family hung on other walls. In the middle bedroom, three portraits hung side by side: one each of my maternal grandparents and one of my mother as a young woman. Onelio kept referring to the house as mine. It sounded strange on his lips. I wasn't there to reclaim property, and anyway we were just renters when we lived there.

As much as the house, it was Tía Niña that I was coming back to. I was named after her; people always told me I resembled her. When I was younger and angry at my mother, I had often fantasized that she was my real mother. I think the fantasy was also about making Poly and me even. If I belonged to my aunt, then Poly was with my real mother, and I was with his. The abandonment was canceled out, the debt repaid, the cause for guilt annulled.

Meeting each other for the first time as adults, Tía Niña and I had a lot of ground to cover. We began with presents, sitting together on her bed to open all the things my mother had sent with me. On every trip I made to Cuba after that, we repeated this ritual. Everything was always perfect. My mother sent the kind of shoes Tía Niña wanted in the perfect size, even though my aunt hadn't asked for them. Bras always arrived just as her old ones were wearing out. My mother hid things in unusual packages: *tasajo* (dry-cured beef) sealed tight in Christmas cookie tins; spices like cumin and oregano and bay leaves in medicine bottles; popcorn kernels or needle and thread in Metamucil jars. Sometimes it felt like an old game between the two sisters. With every surprise, my aunt squealed like she was thirteen, like it was my mother and not me on the bed next to her. "My sister knows me so well!" she would say over and over.

We spent a lot of time sitting on the bed together poring over old photographs and documents. I remember the feel of the mattress sinking in the middle, springs stubborn under our frames, a rotating fan near the headboard, occasionally causing the papers to flutter across the bed and to the ground. I studied the old photographs my mother had sent over the years of my sister and me as children, pictures dedicated on the back to my grandmother and to Poly. Both were gone, so they were Tía Niña's now whether she wanted them or not. She also had piles of letters, mostly from my mother, including all the ones she had sent to Poly over the years.

I didn't read them, but I mentioned them in an essay I started (but never finished) writing in Spanish after that first trip. I always thought I'd go back and get them, take them home, read them.

Sometimes Tía Niña and I would lie together on her bed and just talk: about family members, about work, about politics, about relationships. When it came to Poly, I wasn't completely honest with her. I don't think I confessed my fear of him or that sometimes it felt like I hated him. But we did talk about his troubles, his temper, his anger. That was when she told me that she had warned Poly that it might be hard for him to adapt if he left Cuba. She said that Poly, after he was with us, once told her that I was cold and difficult, that Aixa was easier to get along with.

Tía Niña was my personal gateway into the Cuba of my mother's large family and our old neighborhood. She took me around the corner to meet my godmother, Inés. Another neighbor we visited was about to move permanently to the United States to join her family in Miami. In her living room was a portrait of Jesus Christ, in the dining room one of Fidel Castro. Tía Niña summoned Poly's friend Machi, who had served in Angola, who was peeved that Poly had never written to him after he left. I took a picture with him and his son to show Poly. I met his mother, Fefa, who owned the phone my mother always used to call Tía Niña who had none. I gave her a little money as a present.

I had too many relatives to meet them all. Tía Niña worried that if people in the family found out that Adela's daughter was there, that Adita was there, I would be overrun with visitors at the hotel and with petitions for help and for gifts. So she curated my contacts as best she could. I met La Nena's two daughters, Paco and Rache. (Years later, Paco's daughter in Miami helped care for my parents in their final years and days.) Pupi, who I had met at the hotel by chance, also came around to see me with a few of his brothers, among them Papito, who took me to his house and gave me his porcupine quill from Angola as a present. I met other cousins on that trip, maybe a dozen of them, a tiny fraction of the hundreds still living in Cuba.

Tía Niña also arranged for me to meet my mother's brothers and sisters, those still living. One day, we went to San Cristóbal and Chirigota, site of the farm where my mother and her siblings had grown up. I saw the church where my mother had spent so much time. We stood on the land where their house had been, and Tía Niña made me take a picture of the mango tree that sat in what used to be their yard. I met her two brothers, who still lived there: Herminio and Ñeñe. We ate breadfruit (which they prepared only when other things were scarce) and tamales made from corn they had milled. At one point sitting outside talking with them, Ñeñe—very skinny, tall, with thick, black-framed eyeglasses—reached over, grabbed my bare foot, and shouted to his siblings, *¡Mira, el pie de Adela!* "Look, Adela's foot!" I never saw him again after that trip, because he died soon after. Herminio I saw a few more times over the years; he even visited Miami once, and Gregg and I took him sightseeing.

Another day, Tía Niña took me to see Tía Tatá in Mazorra, the psychiatric hospital. I had heard about her all my life. I found her perhaps worse than I imagined. Her mouth didn't quite seem to close right; her eyes wandered; she mumbled. But she understood that I was my mother's daughter. "She recognized me" and was happy to see me, I wrote to Gregg. The hospital itself shocked me. "Women in dirty white robes, walking around with tin cans begging visitors for coffee. Flies everywhere." Better than it was before, my aunt told me. I didn't think that said much.

Everyone I saw—close and distant relatives, friends, neighbors, and busybodies—asked after my mother and Poly. About Poly, I always answered vaguely. People always assumed that we were close. I replied in ways that did not give away how not close we were.

For all the people I met, however, it was Tía Niña that I always came back to. When I could get away from the tour group, I went to the house to visit her. Sometimes I stayed overnight in the same room where I had once slept in a crib. She'd bring me coffee in bed in the morning, and we'd lounge around chatting. She welcomed me back, protected me, loved me. I had finally met my other Ada. In Cuba, she was my anchor, the home to which I always returned.

# TWENTY-ONE

# The Milky Way
# with My Brother

**Cuba, of course, is more** than my mother's family. It is also my father's. The first person I met on my father's side was his son Juan José, my brother who was not Poly. Juan José came to Havana with his son, Alain, and his daughter, Aymara, to see me at the Hotel Presidente, where my tour group was staying then. I told him he looked like my father; Aymara looked a little like me. We sat on the large terrace of the hotel, talking for hours.

I don't think I realized until then that though my father and Juan José had been writing to each other for almost two years, they had never spoken on the phone. Cubans were not allowed in hotel rooms; in fact, back then, they were usually not allowed in tourist hotels at all. More than once, I had a doorman stop me at a hotel entrance to ask if he could help me. The assumption was that I lived on the island, so had no business in a hotel where all the guests had to be foreigners. But that night with Juan José and his kids, I knew I had to get him up to my room to call my father. I can't recall whether I snuck him upstairs, or whether I asked a receptionist to make an exception. However it happened, we made the call. I remember feeling like the ease with which I called did not correspond with how hard it had been for them to make that move. For the two of them, before that, there had only been obstacles, or perhaps things that their apprehension had turned into obstacles. Especially for my father.

The following weekend, I hired a private taxi and made the trip to my father's countryside, to meet his people and visit the farm where he grew up. I went first to Juan José's, and that was where I spent most of the weekend. His family made up a bed for the driver, who ate with us all weekend and then drove me back to Havana late on Sunday night, so that I could be at the archives for research on Monday morning. His name was Hugo; there's a good chance that he doesn't live in Cuba anymore.

Juan José and his family lived in the house he had built himself in the backyard of his wife's parents' house. It was cement and cinder block with wooden louvered windows. He had also built some of the furniture inside it, the cabinet where they kept their TV and some framed photos, bookshelves sagging under the weight of books. Most of the relatives I knew did not have bookcases. We ate late that first night and did a long *sobremesa*. The mood was light, buoyant even. There was so much to talk about, so many questions to ask. I walked around the little town with them. I rode a bike. At night, a sky made of black velvet revealed things I'd never before noticed. Juan José pointed out the Milky Way. That was the first time I learned the name for it in Spanish: *Vía Láctea*. It felt magical to be with them. I loved Juan José almost from the moment I met him, and I think he felt the same way about me. He had a high forehead like my father, and a mustache, trimmer than Poly's, elegant like José Martí's. We talked about politics, about family, about history and literature. He was humble and eloquent. He was warm and noble. I suppose that he was everything one could want in a long-lost brother.

The next day, or maybe the one after, the driver took me to meet my father's siblings, my uncles Gregorio and Joseíto, and my aunt Orelia. Juan José and his family came with me. Though Juan José had met Orelia before, the trip he made with me that summer was the first time he was being welcomed as a member of the family, as *el hijo de Ramón*, arriving alongside Ramón's daughter, me.

We went first to Gregorio's house in the town of Jarahueca. I had heard about him my whole life as a stern man, an exigent, exacting man. *Resabioso* was how I had grown up hearing him described. When I was difficult, picky, irritated, my parents used to call me by his name. Now I was meeting him in the flesh. He was thin, his chin pointy, his cheekbones high and chiseled, his eyes blue and a little sad. I didn't know then that he had opposed my parents' union.

A big group of us made the journey to the family farm, Jayún. The road was too rough for the taxi, so we went in a horse-drawn carriage. No one lived on the farm anymore; my uncles made the trip daily to work. Gregorio often stayed as late as 10 p.m. and then returned home to Jarahueca on his horse to eat a late supper and sleep. They all showed me around the mostly empty house. My grandparents' bedroom still had a bed, high with a metal frame; I think my father told me that it was the bed on which he had been born. Outside, they asked me to photograph an old cedar tree that they said my father would remember. We all sat around a long wooden table talking under the canopy of an enormous old tree, Juan José by my side the whole time.

I left for Havana later that day, after a huge meal at Gregorio's. As the time of my departure approached, several people stole away to write short letters to my father, letters I would carry to him by hand. That became a ritual on every subsequent trip, too. I have the letter that Juan José wrote to my father that day:

Ramón Ferrer: Having overloaded myself with emotions and now with hardly any time, I write you these lines. I feel happy to have had Ada among us. Today we spent time with Gregorio, José Manuel, and Orelia. I felt good with them, so did my family. It is now time for Ada's departure, and I cannot fathom what to say. Just two words: I had imagined her affectionate and down-to-earth, and I have discovered her better than that. It is hard to put into words the days we spent together. Several times my eyes watered, but out of happiness. I won't go on, the moments fly, my only wish is for us to see each other again soon.

We said our goodbyes, and I got in the taxi to return to Havana. I lay down in the back seat to sleep a little. I was tired, my voice a little hoarse from talking and laughing. It got dark quickly, and I could see the moon through the window. I remembered my mother sometimes saying never to sleep

Juan José writing a letter to my father, 1992.

where the moon could see you. So I switched my head to the other side of the seat and slept the whole way back to Havana.

# TWENTY-TWO

# My Cuba

**On that trip to Cuba** I discovered another unexpected love, not a person, but a place: the Cuban National Archives. That may sound strange, but over the years it became my anchor in Havana, almost as much as Tía Niña. An old arsenal turned national archives, the majestic limestone building sits in a far corner of Old Havana, near the house where José Martí was born. Early in the twentieth century, the neighborhood was a zone of prostitution. In the late twentieth, when I first started going there regularly, the neighborhood was poor and its infrastructure crumbling. When I turned the corner at San Isidro and Compostela, I always had to sidestep a large murky puddle next to the garbage dumpster. But ascending the steps of the archive building felt so good, so right. The lobby, a double-story atrium that seemed much taller than that managed to feel airy even in July. The reading room was modest, about ten or twelve tables in a room surrounded by old card catalogs on every wall, interrupted by tall windows, usually open for the lack of air-conditioning.

The first time I visited, a historian named Fe Iglesias was my guide, showing me around, introducing me to people. She instructed me never to sit at one particular table. It was the table of the venerable José Luciano Franco, a man of color, a self-taught historian, author of many books that I would read over the years and to whom I dedicated my second book. He had died less than a year before my first trip, and, out of respect, researchers were not sitting at his table.

I remember the experience of reading documents there for the first time. Among them was the trial record from an alleged conspiracy of enslaved people in El Cobre, home to Cuba's patron saint, in 1864. The state had to get translators, because not all the witnesses spoke Spanish. Many of the documents I tried to read were themselves like a foreign language to me at first, handwritten in formal, nineteenth-century Spanish. I remember being moved the first time I saw an *X* as the signature of someone unable to read or write. But that brief description doesn't convey the quality of the person's mark. It's not an *X*, I thought, but a cross. The lines were wobbly, the small dips in what for someone else might have been a straight line betraying the fact that the person was unused to holding a writing instrument. A lot of the documents were small, maybe eight by six inches, oriented vertically. The original creators of the documents had treated the page as if it had two invisible columns. The document was folded in half, the author wrote only on the right side of the fold, and the letter's recipient would respond in the blank space on the left. In the archive for over a century, the letters were stored unfolded, as a flat sheet of paper. In the beginning, I tried to read the letters the way I always read, left to right across the whole page, not realizing that it had two columns of writing. I worked hard not to cry in the reading room. I remember asking myself in frustration, "What made me think I could do this?" Staring at the page for what felt like an eternity, I finally figured it out. Now, it's a story I tell my students.

It was in that archive where I first learned how complicated and unknowable the truth can be, even with the sources right in front of you. I found a list of pro-independence rebels, all of them Black. But sometime later I came across a letter from a Spanish official instructing his subalterns to leave white names off the lists of rebels in order to make it seem like the movement was all Black and thus make it less appealing to whites. In another case, I read a witness account of hundreds of rebels attacking a plantation. Elsewhere, however, a rebel testified that they were only a small group; they just kept circling the gate, beating their machetes against it as they passed to make their numbers seem much larger. I knew already that things weren't always as they seemed. But in the archives, I learned that sometimes that continued to be the case even in the face of voluminous evidence, even with hundred-year-old documents in your hands. That only made me love them more.

Cuba's National Library, where I also went during that trip, is in a different neighborhood than the archive. Its address is on the Plaza de la Revolución. Like Havana's airport, the library bears the name of José Martí. My guide there was Tomás Fernández Robaina, a writer, historian, and bibliographer. I met Tomasito (everyone called him by the diminutive) when I went to the library for the first time. He was the one who took me around, showed me how things worked, and introduced me to everyone I needed to know there. I shared with him a request from my PhD adviser, Rebecca Scott, who wanted his help finding a map of a place called Santa Isabel de las Lajas. When I told him that, he started singing Benny Moré's song by the same name: *Santa Isabel de las Lajas, querida. Santa Isabel.*

*Lajas, mi rincón querido, pueblo donde yo nací* . . . Another of my mother's favorites, she sang it all the time; it is on the recording she made when I was a girl. Softly, I began to sing along with Tomasito. It moved him, and he cried a little. (He cried easily, and he'd do that with me on other occasions over the years.)

I remember another Cuban colleague, during a later trip once telling me that I was like a strange encyclopedia, not because I knew so much—I didn't—but because it was like I had the memory of people who had lived in Cuba decades earlier. I did, in a way. I spoke with references that were my parents', things I didn't share with Cuban Cubans my own age, but with older people who remembered a time before. I cannot see myself through other people's eyes. But I think I was something of a mystery to them. Left at ten months, spoke relatively good Cuban Spanish, sometimes with idioms that had gone out of fashion decades earlier, sometimes with quirky errors that came from translating literally from English to Spanish in my head, a young woman who showed up out of nowhere and parked herself in a chair at the National Archives to study a history that was hers and not hers all at once.

On July 27, 1990, after a month there, I left Havana for Miami. At the airport, I called Tía Niña to say goodbye and tell her I was on my way. I wanted to call Juan José, too, but there was no phone where I could reach him quickly. I bought Poly a case of his favorite Cuban cigarettes, unfiltered. When he tried them on my return, he didn't like them as much as the Marlboros he was now accustomed to. But every time I went to Cuba, I bought him a pack.

Over the course of the trip, I had taken rolls and rolls of film. I developed them in Miami so that my parents and I could look at them together.

My father did not stop staring at the ones of the son he had seen only a handful of times as a boy, of his grandchildren, of his brothers and sisters, of the farmhouse. My mother delighted in seeing the church in Chirigota with her siblings and me posing in front. She immediately recognized the mango tree that stood in the yard of her once-upon-a-time house. She loved seeing the photo of me with Tatá in Mazorra, even if it made her a little sad. But, unlike my father, her own long-lost son was not there anymore, he had been with her now for ten years. Some relatives came over to see my photographs, too—my mother gracious as always, my father eager for the company to get going, as was his way. I don't think I showed Poly the pictures. I made duplicates of all of them and gave them to my parents. My mother probably showed some to him.

Less than a year later in 1991, I returned to Cuba again, this time with my mother. It was her first time back since 1979. I remember wondering if Poly might be jealous of the fact that my mother and I were returning together, just as we had left. Given his struggles in Cuba, was he jealous of my being there at all? Was he starting to realize, as I was, that even in Cuba I would have opportunities that he had never had? Whatever the answer to that question, I knew by then that I would return, that I would keep showing up, summoning into being a Cuba that was my family, but also something more, something mine.

In Havana, my mother and I stayed in Tía Niña's house. The two of them often stayed up late talking every night. Her brother Herminio came from the countryside, and Tía Tatá was home from Mazorra for our visit. One day at a large family gathering, my cousin María Elena brought out her guitar, and my mother sang. She was in her element, where she had once belonged, becoming one with her people, and I got to see it with my own eyes.

We took a car to my father's part of the island. She met my brother Juan José, saw my father's siblings, including Gregorio who had long ago scorned her as my father's choice. At one point, she donned a Cuban cowboy hat and posed for a picture with a yoke of oxen. Like all trips to the Cuban countryside, it was a rushed affair. Time in Cuba was never enough for all the people and places there were to see. On the ride back to Havana, our taxi ran out of gasoline. My mother was sure it was some kind of scam to rob us, or kidnap us, or worse, but it wasn't.

My plan for the trip had been to spend a week with my mother and then stay on doing my own research. But Cuban bureaucracy can be an insurmountable hurdle. I had entered the country with a visa for Cuban-born people visiting family. After I was there, I couldn't change it to one for a Cuban-born person visiting for professional reasons. So I went back to Miami with my mother.

At the airport, as we waited to board our return flight, I went to buy some cigarettes for Poly. My mother had lost her voice from all the talking and laughing with her family. Walking back toward her, I could see how exhausted she was. When I took the seat beside her, she rested her head on my shoulder and looked at the cigarettes. She spoke softly. Had she known what her departure would do to Poly, she said, she would never have left. I imagined that alternative, asking myself then, as I would do many times to come: Was my good fortune built on Poly's suffering?

# TWENTY-THREE

# Motherhood

**A few years ago,** I read a book by Sarah Knott called *Mother Is a Verb* about the history of motherhood. By the time I read it, I had two daughters, grown or practically so. Alina was born in 1995, a few years after my first trip to Cuba and the same year I finished my PhD at Michigan and began a tenure-track job at New York University. Lucía was born in 2001, just as I was coming up for tenure at NYU. She was with me in her stroller when I saw the first plane hit the World Trade Center on September 11.

Motherhood, the book suggests, is, among other things, perpetual interruption. Midthought, midsleep, midgesture, midtask inevitably come the child's summons. The morning after I read that, I was sitting down to write something new, and twenty-year-old Lucía called out from the kitchen as she finished breakfast, "Mommy, come hang out with me before I leave." Settled down at my desk, later in the morning, Alina, twenty-six and living in Miami, texted, "Mommy, I'm sad. Can you talk?" "Of course," I said. And I remember smiling and thinking: Yes, motherhood *is* perpetual interruption.

Before having Alina and Lucía, I had never thought of myself as particularly maternal. So, how much I loved becoming a mother, how comfortable I felt in the intensity of the feeling, surprised me. I remember sitting by Alina's crib a few days after her birth, staring at her, imagining her perhaps giving birth someday, thinking about my mother giving birth to me, and my grandmother to her, imagining the pain and the wonder of it, going backward and forward in time to mothers and daughters I could not even dream of.

Becoming a mother changed my relationship to my mother. I called her more, even as I got busier with the girls and with the increasing demands of my job and my scholarship. I called to ask her questions, to tell her the latest little thing one of the girls had done. I thought more about my mother *as* a mother, as a woman who had to learn to mother. I imagined her in my place and me in hers. Becoming a mother also changed my relationship to her story of leaving Poly. If I had always lived with it and its consequences, it haunted me more after I had children. Poly's shadow was there in a different way now. I often found myself measuring the progress of my daughters' childhoods in relation to his. Alina is turning nine, I thought, Poly's age when we left him. Lucía's ten; by that age Poly had spent almost a year without his mother. I would look at my girls and wonder what could ever make me leave them. And could I have gone, as my mother had, in secret, without saying goodbye? I couldn't picture it at all.

It is strange, I think as I write this, that I never thought to put myself in my father's place, abandoning a woman he made pregnant, refusing a child that was his.

# PART V

# Archives

# TWENTY-FOUR

# Reading an Alien
# File with My Mother

**2023. Sixty years have passed** since we left Cuba, and my mother is three years gone. I see myself through her eyes. I sit at a desk poring over a 442-page Alien File, for which I had to submit a Freedom of Information Act request. The first page of the file is a random document from 2009, neither the beginning nor the end of Poly's story. The pages that follow are not organized chronologically, nor in any kind of order I can decipher. So I must impose one. I print the file and have it spiral-bound. Inside, I number the pages in pencil, on the front only. If I cite something from the back of a page, I think as I thumb through the thick binder, I can use v. for verso, something historians do all the time. As I read and reread the file, the pages become dog-eared, heavy with highlighting. I pose questions to myself in the margins. I make a note of names that appear in the documents (perhaps oversights by the people redacting the documents to comply with my request), and I look for them on Google, Facebook, LinkedIn. On the first page of the bound volume is a title page I created myself in 16-point Times New Roman font:

**Poly
A-File
FOIA**

It looks like a tombstone.

Elsewhere on my desk, I have more of Poly's papers, documents that my mother kept in the fake-leather briefcase where she saved all his papers. I've sorted them by year and then within year, by theme: encounters with police or the criminal justice system, with government benefits agencies, with immigration officials, and (somewhat to my surprise) with mental health professionals. Little pieces of paper sometimes fall out of the folders—unfilled prescriptions, old traffic citations, an obsolete bank book for an account long ago emptied and closed. Sometimes there are envelopes or scraps of papers on which my mother jotted down the name of a lawyer, or a social worker, or a doctor who might be able to help somehow.

Family separation produced the letters I used to reconstruct something of Poly's life as a boy without our mother in Cuba. To reconstruct his life as a man living in the same city as her, this is what I have: an archive produced by the linked infrastructures of policing and incarceration, immigrant detention and public health.

A Complaint/Arrest Affidavit in Poly's A-file reveals that late on Monday afternoon, July 1, 1991, not long after my mother and I returned from Cuba together, Poly and a companion showed up at an automotive body shop. They started arguing with the man inside. Things got heated. My brother pulled out a Thompson semiautomatic with an altered serial number, fired twice, and missed. The man returned fire and shot my brother in the hip. When the police arrived, they found my brother bleeding on the ground. The emergency room at Jackson Memorial Hospital in downtown Miami is listed as the site of his arrest on the affidavit.

My mother always answered the phone saying "Hello?" It was one of the few English words she used with unambiguous confidence. Her tone was always positive, friendly. When she was expecting my call or my sister's, she was even more upbeat, answering with a funny accent, turning the *H* into a *Y*, so that it sounded like the word *yellow* but with the /l/ sound a little more intentional and the *o* at the end a short vowel. On hanging up with Poly that night, she would have called my sister, who lived less than a ten-minute drive away. My mother always called her right away when Poly got into trouble. Living in Miami, Aixa had the boon of my parents' nearness and the strain of our brother's. She took my mother to the hospital to see Poly, but because he was under arrest no one would let her into his room. Aixa, who worked at a prominent law firm, got her boss to go in to see him on their behalf. This way my mother would be reassured that he was okay, and Poly would know that she had not forgotten him, that she was always there, his mother trying to take care of him.

The case went to trial in January 1992. Poly wore new clothes that my mother had bought him for the occasion. My parents and Aixa attended. All I know about the case is the verdict: The jury acquitted him of the attempted murder and manslaughter charges and found him guilty of being in possession of a firearm while in the act of committing a crime. The judge dismissed the jury and then changed the third verdict to not guilty. If the finding on the first two charges had been not guilty, there was no crime being committed when he had the firearm, I suppose. Poly was released.

In the five months that Poly spent in jail, my parents moved out of the two-bedroom apartment they had shared with him and into a smaller one with no room for him. They chose Miami Beach. My mother, who never learned to drive, liked that she could walk places. Back then, there were still stores where she could buy fabric and sewing notions to make dresses for Aixa's daughter, Nailah. There was a *botánica*—part apothecary, part religious goods store. She appreciated being able to go there without having to bug anyone for a ride, so that she could buy things for Poly, something to help guide his way, to protect him, to protect all of us.

But it was less the amenities of Miami Beach that attracted my parents than the fact of being able to put distance between them and Poly. He was often explosive, always unpredictable. One time, my parents, Aixa, Adrian, and Nailah all checked into a hotel room to hide from him, because he had threatened to hurt my parents. The five of them squeezed into one room; Aixa thinks she turned on the television to distract Nailah. Nothing happened, and they left before the night was out. Perhaps not sharing a home with Poly made the fear feel a little less suffocating, though it was there nonetheless.

My mother helped Poly find a studio apartment in Little Havana. She gave him money every month to pay the rent, because whatever else he was doing, he was not working. He had not filed taxes since 1990. A document, produced sometime between January 1992 and August 1994, and incorporated into his A-file, indicates that he had not received any income in three years. Every weekend Aixa took my mother to see him. She arrived with groceries and things she'd cooked for him; she picked up his laundry and gave him money. She was going broke helping him. But she didn't mind. He seemed calm, almost tame, she wrote to me in April 1992.

It didn't last. On August 8, 1993, two years after the attempted murder charge, a Miami-Dade police officer observed Poly in his Oldsmobile Cutlass in an alleyway in an "area known for drugs and heavy prostitution." The car was his; my mother had helped him buy it. (Buying things for him to make up for the past was a long-standing habit.) Aware that the police officer was watching him, Poly drove off "in a sudden manner." When the officer stopped him, he noticed "a strong odor of an alcoholic beverage coming from this breath." That was in addition to the "poor balance, blood shot eyes, and slurry speech." He was arrested and charged with driving under the influence, driving with a suspended license, and possession of an open container of an alcoholic beverage.

The charges were dismissed. But less than two weeks later, the same thing happened again. At 5:28 p.m. on August 20, a different police officer saw Poly in his car, drinking from a bottle of Beck's beer. When the officer asked for his license, Poly responded "Don't have one." The judge in the case ordered him to do fifty hours of community service. He never did.

Sometimes, Poly was the victim. In October 1993, someone beat him up with a pipe, for what reason I do not know. An ambulance rushed him to the hospital, and he had to be restrained soon after arriving. The next day surgeons performed a craniotomy. According to a hospital bill my mother saved, the charge for over eight hours in the operating room topped $71,000. He was in the hospital for almost two weeks, and every day my mother went to see him. But when he was released, she did not let him go home with her. She knew if she let him stay, he would never leave. She got him a hotel room for a few nights while she looked for an apartment for him. To punish our mother for not having taken him in, Poly briefly disappeared, and she had no idea where he was. She made Aixa drive her to downtown Miami to look for him under some of the highway overpasses. Aixa remembers parking and getting out of the car several times, calling out his name to no avail. Poly reminded my mother of her refusal almost forever. He would never forgive her, he said.

Maybe it was my mother's unwillingness to take him in that led Poly to the Miami-Dade County Office of Emergency Assistance. The staff there helped him apply for food stamps and also referred him to the Miami Mental Health Center for an evaluation. After that, he saw mental health professionals on and off. I found records of some of those appointments in the brown fake-leather briefcase. The first diagnosis, dated February 17, 1994, was "major depression with psychosis," prognosis: "guarded." The psychiatrist prescribed 5 milligrams daily of Haldol, an antipsychotic, and Zoloft, an antidepressant. He also determined that Poly was not fit to work. A few months later, the doctor doubled his dose of the antipsychotic. Recently, I found the original prescriptions. He hadn't filled them.

On September 18, 1995 (a month and a day after the birth of my first daughter), Poly was diagnosed with "major depression recurrent with psychosis, R/O schizoaffective disorder." Maybe he was in the midst of a crisis when he showed up to the clinic that time, because they gave him a much higher dose of Haldol than before: 50 mg daily for four weeks and then 10 mg thereafter. They also prescribed Cogentin (to help control some of the side effects of the antipsychotic) and Restoril for sleeping. Exactly one week later, the same doctor wrote, "At present, the client is receiving psychiatric treatment—and is unable to maintain a long attention span; also, the client has poor memory, the client, is an active psychiatric ill."

The strange phrasing and punctuation is in the original, which is addressed simply "To Whom It May Concern."

While all this was going on, Poly was applying for public assistance, specifically Supplemental Security Income from the Social Security Administration, which pays a monthly stipend to people with "qualifying disabilities." He was approved for Medicaid benefits starting in fall 1994. When my mother hired a lawyer in 1996 to try to regularize his immigration status, the lawyer described him as "disabled" on the requisite biographic information form. On a later form filled out by Poly himself, he wrote in his broken English, "I got Desability for Mental illness and Diabetic, high blood pressure."

I do not doubt that diagnosis, nor the general contention that Poly was mentally ill. But I suspect that however much he needed help, he also sought a diagnosis and began treatment because he knew that by being classified as "disabled," he would also receive government benefits. As one of his social workers noted years later, Poly had "poor insight into his mental illness."

At some point in the 1990s, I developed a suspicion that maybe I was Poly's trigger. Almost every time he got into trouble with the law or became especially difficult and combative with my mother, it seemed to be shortly after one of my visits to Miami. The attempted murder charge in 1991 came shortly after I visited Cuba with our mother and then spent time in Miami on our return. The other arrests I have been able to find—either in his A-File or in Miami-Dade County criminal records—all occurred in January (so shortly after my Christmas visit), in the summer (I always visited for a week or more in summer), and in one case in mid-September (so possibly soon after a late summer visit).

Again, I think of my mother. I picture her standing behind me, looking over my shoulder, trying to decipher the documents before me, watching as I try to reconstruct Poly's arrests, his appointments with shrinks, his moods, observing as I ruminate about their possible relation to me. She would be curious especially about what I'm finding in the FOIA file. But at the same time, she wouldn't want to look too closely, to remember what she already knows.

I talk to her in my head, pointing out that the evidence of her own tenacity is all over Poly's file. Even though her name has been redacted so as not to reveal her identity, I know she's there when I read things like "Defendant's mother appeared as well," on a handwritten "Record of Action," dated September 7, 1995. (She had just returned from spending two weeks with us right after Alina's birth on August 17.) I recognize my sister's handwriting on a note from my mother to the Miami Office of the Immigration and Naturalization Service in 1998 inquiring about "the application for resident status of my son, Hipolito de Jesus Cabrera," accents missing. When she doesn't hear back, my mother follows up again, and then once more. She would do so as many times as necessary. Most of the letters she sent over and over on Poly's behalf were composed by Aixa in English, sometimes faxed from her office. My sister would have done that only at my mother's unstoppable insistence, grumbling the whole while. *Refunfuñando*, as my mother would say, using one of my favorite words in the Spanish language. *Refunfuñar*: to emit confused voices between the teeth, the word deriving from the onomatopoeia of the sound produced while grumbling. If I had lived in Miami, I would have *refunfuñado*, too.

My mother nags daughters and lawyers and husbands and government officials. She appears before judges, makes sure that they and the juries see her, makes clear to everyone willing to pay attention that Poly is her beloved son and that she stands with him.

Still, she seems disappointed, unsettled. "You are always looking for dead people," she once said to me when I called her from Charleston, South Carolina, where I'd gone following clues about a man who had helped lead an antislavery conspiracy in Havana in 1812. Now the traces I look for are those of my own closest family. Why? she wonders. Have I not carried this with me long enough? Am I not tired yet? But maybe what she really wants to ask is why I hadn't thought to spend this much time trying to understand Poly earlier, when it might have made a difference. And I can think of no answer that would satisfy her.

# TWENTY-FIVE

# Letters to Fidel

**When I was home,** wherever that was, I called my mother often. When I didn't, she phoned me, left me messages, calling me fresh—*sinvergüenza*—for failing in my habit. When I was away in Cuba doing research, or in Spain, where archives and libraries held more Cuban treasures, she wrote me letters. She missed talking with me, she said. My father wrote, too, though not as often. When I was in Cuba, he urged me to eat, to sleep, to rest, to be careful, to call relatives, to write to my mother who was missing me. From Madrid, I sent them both a postcard saying that I wanted to bring them to Spain with me. Except for one visit to Disney World, and the time my mother spent in Mexico with me, they had never been tourists anywhere. I wanted to give them that; I wanted them to see the beautiful things I was seeing and to be with them when they compared it to Cuba, as I knew they would. The expression of that sentiment in my postcard led my father to write me a sweet letter about how moved he felt to know that, in my adventures, I remembered and included them. What more could he ask for, he said, and then he wrote me a poem. Becoming a historian, writing about Cuba, was how I left my parents. It was also how I took them with me.

Except I didn't really. Day to day, they lived alone, making their lives in Miami Beach, a couple, together for many decades, aging and poor. At a distance from me, they changed. I remember picking them up at the airport in New York once in the mid-1990s. I saw an elderly man retrieving a suitcase at the baggage claim and thought, "That is what Papi will look like when he's old." When the man turned around, he was my father.

Back in Miami, my father went out all the time. He was responsible for every errand that needed to be run. He wrote checks and paid bills, walking the envelopes over to the post office a block and a half away. In the morning, he often went to Publix to pick up groceries or to Walgreens to pick up a prescription. Each was about a fifteen-minute walk from home. He did this into his nineties, through Miami's worst summer heat, or in the rain, crossing busy avenues and not always waiting for the walk sign, even after he started using a cane. Every afternoon, he would go out again to the bodega a block from the apartment to get whatever else my mother might need: milk, sweetener, plantains. Sometimes he'd be walking out the door with the list of items dutifully memorized, and she'd call him back to ask for something else she had just remembered. Sometimes she'd remember only after he'd returned home. He'd complain, and I can hear her saying something like, *Viejo, tú sabes como tengo la ca-beza.* "Old man"—they always called each other old man or old woman, and it sounded lovely when they said it—"you know my mind is always distracted." Then he'd go out again and maybe pick up a lotto ticket or two. Sometimes he took the bus (actually, two buses) to place a few bets at jai alai.

When my father was home, though, he was almost always perfectly still. He watched TV: cable news, baseball during the season, sometimes an action movie or a police procedural. He napped every afternoon at the same time my mother did. After lunch, they'd doze off listening to reruns of an old Cuban radio show from the 1940s and 1950s that later became a staple of Miami daytime radio: *La Tremenda Corte* with comedian Tres Patines.

But what my father liked to do most while sitting still was to write. In the 1990s, retired, already in his seventies, he began to write regularly. It became his habit, his vocation even.

He wrote in ink on loose-leaf paper, sitting on the couch, resting the page before him on one of my mother's mail-order catalogs. My sister gave him a clipboard, and the pace of his writing picked up. My mother later bought him a typewriter, and for a while he wrote on that, using carbon paper sometimes to keep copies. He was a good typist, because that had been his job in the Cuban army. Later I tried giving him a computer, but he said he was too old to learn. We gave him blank, bound journals on special occasions. On the first page of one that Nailah gave him on a Father's Day, he wondered what he would do with such a beautiful notebook. "I don't yet know, because sometimes it is difficult for me to arrange my words so that others understand them correctly. In any case, I will try to write something in the hopes that, even if it turns out badly, you will be able to understand the reasons." But he left the pages that followed mostly blank. Maybe he just didn't like the permanence of a bound book. Instead, he kept writing on his loose-leaf paper, using both sides, his pen strokes so firm that I can run my finger along the page as if reading Braille. If he was low on paper, he found an old spiral notebook that had been Nailah's at school and wrote in that. He wrote all the time.

There were no bookshelves or filing cabinets in my parents' apartment. So all those pages my father kept writing and rewriting made a mess. He had a rusty magazine rack behind his recliner, and he kept papers in there. They fanned out from overstuffed ring binders—the three holes on the lined sheets of paper torn, the original pagination lost, all of it overgrowing the top edge of his battered magazine rack. When they no longer fit, he stacked notebooks and other papers on the floor behind the rack. He stuffed some papers in a plastic grocery bag, which he hung from a nail on the back wall of his closet. High on a shelf in the same closet was his own hard-shell briefcase, so full of papers that it was impossible to close.

Among his papers there are poems he composed and then reworked in draft after draft. There are lists of numbers to play in the Florida Mega Millions lottery, which he never won. One time, he wrote his own prayer over three drafts, asking God "to fill [his] heart with faith and love so that [he] could feel happy and share [his] life sweetly with those who surrounded [him] daily."

A fraction of my father's papers, as I sorted them into four (incomplete) piles (*clockwise from top left*): letters from Juan José, tax records back to 1963, letters to public officials, proclamations and essays.

He penned political proclamations addressed "To the People of Cuba" and "To the Cuban Exile Community," the titles written in large, thick block letters on the top of the page. He even drafted a "Free Trade Treaty for the Republic of Cuba." He wrote and rewrote long essays with titles such as "How I See It," "The Island Fidel Stole," "Treason," "The Hypocrisy of the United States." He wrote about US-Cuban relations, about September 11, about Elián González, the six-year-old boy found drifting at sea after the boat he'd been traveling on capsized. Elián was the only survivor, his mother among the drowned. The boy was taken to relatives in Miami, but his father and the Cuban government wanted him back on the island. My father—like my mother, like almost every Cuban in Miami—wanted fervently for him to stay.

My father also wrote dozens of letters to public figures over three decades. He appealed to the presidents of Mexico and Argentina, urging them to help find "a peaceful and just solution to the Cuban problem." He wrote to US presidents and politicians, as well as to local and national media personalities. He lambasted Diane Sawyer after her interview with Fidel Castro in March 1993. The letter was in English, so my sister would have grudgingly prepared the translation. Or maybe I did and don't remember.

Given his penchant for writing to public figures, it is no surprise at all that my father soon began penning letters to Fidel Castro. The first of those letters, typed, is dated April 19, 1993. My father was soon to turn seventy-two, Fidel Castro, sixty-seven. He addressed the bearded leader as "Señor Presidente" and wondered what a letter penned by a "humble Cuban" who had left the island more than thirty years earlier might signify for its famous and powerful recipient. "I think nothing," he immediately answered himself. He wasn't sure Fidel would even read it. He wrote it anyway and dared ask in its last paragraph:

How is it possible that a man like you, of your intelligence, who once counted on the support of the people of Cuba and had the courage to say before half a million of his compatriots, "Here we are communists," can still be determined, after more than three decades of continual failures in almost every aspect of life in Cuba, to continue pursuing mistaken and unjust policies for his people. Mr. Castro, enough already with so much deception for the Cuban people. With the same valor with which you aligned your country to the communist bloc, leave it free now of a system that holds no future for our beautiful island, and once more take up the cause of freedom and progress.

He signed it "Respectfully, Ramón Ferrer." In ink, he added in the margin, "Not sent."

My father continued writing to Fidel every few years. In 1999, he informed him: "It is time to leave the destiny of Cuba to young Cubans." In 2005, appealing to the leader's sense of supreme self-importance, he wrote, "It is never too late to bequeath to history that gesture of greatness that will make you the bravest politician of all time." "It is time, Dr. Castro," read the words my father used to begin his letter. But the time kept coming and passing with no change—for Cuba, for Fidel, for himself. In 2006, when illness forced the Cuban leader to provisionally (and later permanently) step down from power, my father wrote to him again. "Time does not stand still," he philosophized.

Sometimes, my father sat on his chair, thought about life, his family, Cuba, the pain on his side or in his knee, and he picked up a pen and just wrote. Or maybe he'd already been composing the words in his head for a while before he committed them to a half sheet of loose paper or the back of an envelope. One day, he was doing what he always did—weekends and weekdays almost indistinguishable—when he wrote this:

Today is Sunday, the 17th of September of 2006, it is 12:30 p.m. I am in the living room of my house [apartment] in front of the television. In just a few minutes I will hear my wife's voice from the kitchen saying, "*Viejo*, lunch is ready; come to the table." As I do every day, I heed her call, trying not to fail in my obligations to a routine imposed on me without my consent by some universal law faced by all men. The years have trapped me, and very little have I been able to accomplish in order to leave testimony of my good faith. I have carried on my back, without ever being able to become free of it, the name of the beautiful and unrivalled land called Cuba, which I one day mistakenly abandoned forgetting my sacred duty as its good son to defend it always until my death. I left Cuba behind, and with it my life.

It is one of history's major concerns: how people—even ordinary, unpowerful people like my father—can come to feel such a fierce emotional attachment to a nation. I think it took him a little by surprise as he aged. And writing, another surprise late in life, became the perfect vehicle for its expression.

Whatever my father had written to Fidel about the passage of time, for him writing did make time stand still. It was a wrinkle in his humdrum routine of low-income, elderly life in Miami. In 2008, soon to turn eighty-seven, he penned a letter to a radio personality in Miami who had read a poem on air during his show. My father thought it "one of the most beautiful poems" he'd ever heard. It was titled "Cumpleaños"—"Birthday"—but he had missed the name of its author. Please, could someone from the station send him that information? "As you can appreciate, I, too, am at the stage of life when one dies many times too much," he closed, referring to a line in the poem. No one replied. If my father had asked me to find it, I could have identified the author in a minute or two, though maybe I would have told him I was too busy. Here is the poem, written by Spanish poet Ángel González, who had died about a month before the Miami broadcaster read it on the air.

> *Yo lo noto: cómo me voy volviendo*
> *menos cierto, confuso,*
> *disolviéndome en aire*
> *cotidiano, burdo*
> *jirón de mí, deshilachado*
> *y roto por los puños.*
>
> *Yo comprendo: he vivido*
> *un año más, y eso es muy duro.*
> *¡Mover el corazón todos los días*
> *casi cien veces por minuto!*
>
> *Para vivir un año es necesario*
> *morirse muchas veces mucho.*

. . .

> I notice it: how I'm becoming
> less certain, confused,
> dissolving in day-to-day
> air, coarse
> remnant of myself, frayed
> and torn at the cuffs.
>
> I understand: I've lived
> another year, and that is very tough.

To move one's heart every day
almost a hundred times a minute!

To live one year one has to
die many times too much.

As he aged, and to my own eternal surprise, my father became a writer. He loved to write. So much so that he once penned the sentence, "To write in silence is a marvelous thing."

# TWENTY-SIX

# Love Letters

**Every day around 4 p.m.,** a little bit after his afternoon coffee, my father went down to the mailbox to see what had arrived. There was always something: bills, credit card offers, my mother's mail-order catalogs. There was often mail for Poly that came to my mother: Medicaid updates, traffic citations, notices to appear in court, unpaid medical bills, correspondence about his immigration status. Just as often, there were letters for my father, sent from Cuba by his son Juan José. Starting with their phone call from my hotel room during my first visit to the island, they had developed an increasingly meaningful bond. And by the time my father was an old man, that relationship, and the correspondence that came with it, was something he lived for.

Juan José's bookcase.

Juan José wrote beautifully. His cursive was perfect; his sentences enticing. He was a Spanish language and literature teacher, after all. He loved reading: José Martí, especially, but also Jean Jacques Rousseau and a host of Spanish writers: Benito Pérez Galdós, Pedro Calderón de la Barca, Silvestre de Balboa, really almost anything he could get his hands on. He was proud of his personal country library, weathered paperbacks sitting on shelves that he had made himself.

And like my father, Juan José loved to write. He was a terrible sleeper and often got up at odd hours to read and write. His granddaughter, Amalia, remembers how she'd often wake up in the middle of the night and find him sitting fully clothed on the toilet sometimes reading, sometimes writing, the sheet of paper before him resting on a book. He told her it was the only place in the house where he could turn on the light without disturbing anyone.

Among his letters to my father were many written in the early morning hours, during those episodes of insomnia. "It is 4:50 a.m., delicious time for the muses to descend," he wrote one January morning. "It is exactly 5 a.m. . . . I have been awake the last three hours, lying next to my wife, and my ideas follow one after the other at film-strip speed." And often when that happened, he would get up and write a letter to my father. "Without a doubt, this hour (4:10 a.m.) of the morning is for me an invitation to write to you, I sleep the first hours of the night and then, I wake and knock ideas around in my head. And what better than to share them with you?"

What were the ideas that kept him up? It could be anything. One time, the source of his sleeplessness was the mail. Juan José kept thorough track of how long letters between him and my father took to arrive. If he happened to be visiting Havana, he would mail a letter from there, to ascertain how much less or more time it took than the letters he mailed from his small hometown. He wondered at strange markings that sometimes appeared on the ones that arrived from my father. That sleepless morning at 4:10 a.m., he was obsessing about the itinerary of my father's most recent letter. So he turned it into a story fit to share with him. The letter, Juan José explained, had spent five days sitting in a box at the post office, less than a hundred meters from his home, without being delivered. The person who should have delivered it was the same postman who had delivered the newspaper every day. Yet the man never thought to bring the letter when he brought the newspaper. "What do you think of that?" If I complain, he continued, "I run the risk that all my letters might end up in the trash bin." He found out about the letter from a neighbor who had seen it sitting there for days. "But don't tell anyone I told you," cautioned the neighbor, fearing for the fate of his own mail. "And why do I tell you all this?" Juan José asked my father. "Nothing. I'm trying to make you understand a little bit how complicated life is here. There is an absolute lethargy. We face it every day, and if sometimes you find a positive solution, the days go by, and we return to the same thing; everything is a vicious circle. . . . But, well, what cannot be solved is best forgotten."

The middle of the night also prodded concerns about retirement, about how to make ends meet with even less income. Maybe he would go work in Havana for a while to make more money for the family. (He did, but it didn't work out.) Sometimes he worried about his students and shared stories with my father about his teaching. He invented exercises to teach them about literature, language, and life. He had them explore the meanings of last names; he had them look around, choose objects, and then work out as many adjectives as possible to describe them. Nothing too obvious, he warned them.

Sometimes, it was thoughts about his children and grandchildren that kept Juan José awake. When his daughter, Aymara, married, Juan José constructed a tiny house for her in their yard. His own house was in the backyard of his wife's parents' house, a large colonial one. Now Aymara's house became the third house, each one smaller than the one before, like someone had taken a set of nesting houses and put them in a line.

As I read his descriptions of his daily routines, his attachment to his family, and his inner thoughts, an image of him takes shape in my mind (as it would have, I think, in my father's). *Un hombre de bien.* An honest, upright man, a teacher who holds his head high. He tries not to wrong people; he raises his children well. He is endlessly curious, ceaselessly thoughtful. He is the kind of man that people respect, the kind of man who, when the time came, would have the biggest funeral in the town's living memory.

But this man whom everyone in the town looked up to was also a son who had never known his father. And that, too, came across in the letters. "My childhood," he wrote to my father almost twenty years after they exchanged their first letters, "was like the childhood of every other boy who has grown up and become a man without ever having uttered the word *papá*." Maybe for that reason, the relationship he established with my father so late in life always seemed to him like something of a dream. For a long time, he was not sure it would last. He worried that someday, my father might just stop writing, that the new connection would simply evaporate.

So, Juan José's missives conveyed a kind of longing, too. In 1996, he wrote to my father on the eighteenth anniversary of his mother's death and confessed honestly, vulnerably, that he wished he had the magic power to fly and appear at my father's side for a little bit. He couldn't, of course, so he wrote, and he waited for his letters. My father's letters, "when they are long sate me, but when they are short, they leave me with a hunger to know everything." Reading my father's letters and writing his own in response became a central, necessary feature of Juan José's life. In 2008, at the age of sixty-two, he confessed that writing to my father was like "a balm that allows me to keep going." "Don't read weakness into those words, men are men and nothing more."

Juan José treasured the letters from my father. He saved all of them in their original envelopes. Inside each envelope, he placed a carbon copy or the draft of his own responses to them. Then he numbered the envelopes by year. In 2007, for example, he numbered them: 2007①, 2007②, 2007③, and so on through the twenty-fourth letter for that year. More than the letters themselves, I think Juan José cherished what they represented. They were, in a sense, the fulfillment of a lifelong dream: to know his real father. "Ever since I was a child, I grew up with the *secret* illusion of having my real father by my side." I have always needed this, he had told my father in one of his first letters. Now he prized it beyond belief. He expressed the love he came to feel in simple declarative statements: "I hold in my heart the satisfaction of feeling you as my father." It was evident in the way he sometimes signed his letters: "Here goes my heart, I assure you, J.J." or "Hey, really, I love you." Sometimes the love showed less in a declaration or a signoff than in a gesture: "Dawn. The crowing of the roosters near and far . . . and I wonder: How many times did you in your youth have to wake up to that insignificant and now majestic song? I don't know how many times; but I am sure that it happened, and I remind you of it now because I also know that remembering it makes you happy."

He was right; it did make him happy. He made my father happy.

My father loved reading his son's letters, getting to know him, realizing (as Juan José did) the similarities they shared in their ways of thinking and being. Receiving and reading Juan José's letters became the highlight of my father's day-to-day life as he aged. Sometimes, he sensed that a letter from Juan José was waiting for him in the mailbox downstairs, then when it wasn't, he worried that something was wrong. The letters gave him purpose. Reading them made him feel seen.

So, too, did writing them. Educated only to the sixth grade, my father tried to write as best he could to a son who was a language and literature teacher. Sometimes he looked up words in the dictionary; he looked up passages by Martí; he summarized and commented on the latest news—Y2K and the dread that preceded the first day of a new millennium, the cost of a thirty-second commercial during the Super Bowl, the chances of a Black man becoming president of the United States. He composed multiple drafts of the same letter. He tried to write neatly, though his handwriting could not compare to Juan José's. His letters were as beautiful as his son's, even though they tended to have too many commas and not enough periods. Juan José sometimes read them aloud to his family. Once his son, Alain, having read or heard one of the letters, asked his girlfriend to read one. Finished, she proclaimed her agreement: Juan José's father was a beautiful writer. Juan José himself sometimes called the letters "exquisite" and "eloquent." My father had risen to the challenge. He loved it, in fact. More importantly, he also came to love the grown man he was now getting to know as his only son.

Reading the letters back and forth—my father's to Juan José, Juan José's to our father—a memory moves me. I was a young mother with my first child; I was waiting for a walk signal on the corner of my daughter's daycare center. I was the best kind of nervous, eager to see her again after six or seven hours apart, anxious to know how her day had been, hungry for the look she would give me when I walked in and she rushed to me with her arms aloft to be picked up and held. I stood waiting for the walk sign that afternoon and thought, "This isn't just love; this is being in love." In some of the letters between Juan José and my father—middle-aged and elderly, respectively—that is what it feels like I am witnessing, eavesdropping on. My father and my brother were falling in love.

My father was so enamored of his son that he wanted to give him his rightful last name of Ferrer. Other people had denied Juan José his last name: his mother, her husband, my own father above all. But now as an adult with a consequential relationship with his real father, Juan José could—and, in my father's opinion, should—change his last name to Ferrer. My father insisted not only that that was the right thing to do, but that there would be a material benefit to his doing so.

In a twisted Cuban tale, tens of thousands of Cubans, mostly from the central part of the island where my father's family was from and where Juan José lived, came to believe that they were heirs to a three-hundred-million-dollar fortune hidden away in a British bank. The original treasure dated back centuries, when a Spanish nobleman somehow acquired a fortune from the pirates who plied the waters of the island's north-central coast. Some of the money had been hidden in a nunnery, the story went, but most of it ended up in a London bank. Suddenly, everyone was a gene-alogist. People showed up at municipal archives and churches and civil registry offices in search of records that might be mobilized to prove their blood ties to the mysterious nobleman. People hired lawyers to search out the fortune and negotiate with the bank. Rumors swirled that the Cuban government had already recovered part of the money and would start to pay it out to heirs in the year 2000, in the form of a car, a house, and a credit card with which they could withdraw $350 a month for the rest of their lives. It doesn't sound like much, but in Cuba, fewer than 1 percent of people owned cars; housing shortages were rife; and the median salary in 1993 was 223 pesos a month, at the time roughly equivalent to $11. The fall of the Soviet Union in 1991 had plunged the country into one of the worst economic disasters of its history: the Special Period. For people on the island, it was not an abstract proposition: Food and other necessities available through the ration system dwindled to almost nothing; the buses they took to work stopped running; average daily consumption of calories dropped by about a third. Given all that, it is a little easier to understand the craze occasioned by rumors about a secret Cuban fortune in a London bank.

My father's family became caught up in the frenzy. In Cuba, his sister Orelia was one of those reaching out to local institutions for records. In Miami and New Jersey, my father and his two siblings hired a lawyer to help. Among my father's papers are the traces of that obsession: correspondence with lawyers, family trees, copies of birth certificates for people I'd never heard of dating back to the seventeenth century. My father had always put faith in things like the lottery and dog races. Maybe this seemed like a surer bet, the prize more substantial, too. He talked about it with Juan José. If he changed his name, if there was some official process of recognition between the two of them, Juan José and his family stood to inherit part of the mysterious fortune, as well. Their troubles would be solved; for them the Special Period might end up being special in a good way.

But Juan José had his feet firmly planted on the ground. He was skeptical about the inheritance and was eventually proved right. There was no fortune. But even had he stood to gain, he told my father, that was not how he made decisions. He simply wasn't ready to change his name. Changing his name would also entail, among other things, changing those of his children and grandchildren. It seemed to him that the most important thing wasn't sharing my father's name, but sharing in his life. So every time my father brought it up—and it was always my father who did so—Juan José said no, or not yet. He wasn't ready to change his name in 1999, when rumors of the inheritance were rampant, and he wasn't ready to do it when my father raised the issue again in 2003, then in 2005, and once more in 2007. To debate in letters about the question "seems banal and unimportant," wrote Juan José, underlining the words. Of course, my father did not agree. He read and reread the letters. In the case of one of Juan José's refusals in 1999, my father took the letter to Kinko's, made a photocopy, and highlighted in pink the parts pertaining to the issue of the last name. On the envelope, he wrote in capital letters, *OJO: APELLIDO*—IMPORTANT: SURNAME—perhaps to not lose the letter among the hundreds of other ones.

It was the only time in their long correspondence where each seemed a little mad at the other. My father accused Juan José of not giving it serious enough thought. Juan José countered, a little incredulous, testy even. "Since childhood, I have always *remembered* that thing called a *surname*. . . . I repeat, ever since I was a child, I *have thought about it and remembered it*." In one of their back-and-forths, my father wrote—himself sounding a little angry and defensive—"I am not asking that my surname be accepted. I consider it so worthy and interesting that to humiliate it before those who are entitled to it and do not want it would be too sad and painful." Eventually, my father realized that it would not happen anytime soon, and he relented. They agreed to forget about it. Maybe it will make sense down the line, my father wrote, but for now let us leave it. My father had asked, and Juan José had said no. But they kept writing, getting to know each other more profoundly.

Though the letters were the bedrock of the relationship, my father and my brother did get to meet when Juan José made a monthlong visit to the United States. He was forty-nine, my father soon to turn seventy-four. I wasn't there when they first laid eyes on each other in Miami International Airport. Neither do I remember anything either of them said to me about their initial reunion. Did they stay up late talking? Not sure. Did my father take him along on his daily errands and walks? My guess is yes. My sister reminds me that our mother was very happy for them, but stressed out about Poly. What would he make of the fact that Juan José was staying with them, when my mother did not extend the same privilege to him.

But my father and Juan José would not have noticed. I have a photograph of the two of them outside the building where my parents lived at the time. My father looks giddy; Juan José smiles, but a little shyly, perhaps.

My parents, my niece Nailah, and Juan José came to visit me in New York City. I was pregnant with my first daughter, Alina, just barely showing. They visited a class that I was teaching during my first semester at NYU, a general survey of Latin American and Caribbean history. That week was dedicated to examining US military interventions in the early twentieth century. I happened to have one of the nicest lecture halls in the university, one that comfortably seated the eighty students in the class. Juan José could not understand a word I said, but he was impressed, he said: the room, the students asking questions, me at the front of the lecture hall. I can still see them sitting there, in the plush red velvet chairs on the right end of a long row about a third of the way back.

My father wanted Juan José to stay in the United States, as many Cubans did when they came to visit. But Juan José could not leave his wife or his children, he said over and over again.

He made the trip again five years later in 2000. This time he came with his wife, Hildita. They visited New York, just the two of them. I was pregnant with my second daughter, Lucía. It was summer, so there were no classes for them to sit in on. I remember we all walked to Chinatown, Alina riding her scooter the whole way. Again, my father wanted them to stay, but they wouldn't. Hildita would not leave her elderly parents or her children, and Juan José would not stay without Hildita. Nor did he want to leave his children and by then his grandchildren. So they went back to Cuba and told their stories. No one who visits the United States and leaves without seeing New York City has really seen the United States, their granddaughter remembers them saying. (As a New Yorker, I know the opposite is perhaps more true: to come to this country and visit only New York is not really to see this country.)

My father was disappointed at their decision. Many people who migrated from Cuba had to leave people behind. Often it worked out, and family reunification followed. My father knew that. That's what had happened with him, my mother, and me. Of course, he also knew from experience that a completely different outcome might be just as likely. Look at my mother and Poly. But still, as with the issue of his last name, my father and Juan José begged to differ one from the other.

That changed in November 2007, when the US Customs and Immigration Service announced a new policy. Called the Cuban Family Reunification Parole Program, it allowed US citizens and lawful permanent residents to apply for "parole" for family members in Cuba. If granted, those family members could move to the United States without waiting for their immigrant visas to become available. My father could not apply, because legally Juan José was not his son. His name did not appear on the birth certificate, and they had undertaken no legal process to recognize or affirm the relationship. But Juan José had a half brother in the United States; they were in close touch, and he could legally sponsor Juan José and his family.

This time, unlike during his visits to the United States in 1995 and 2000, Juan José was very interested. Why? Things in Cuba were not really improving. Some symptoms of the Special Period had abated, but the major underlying problems persisted, with no solution in sight. For him, the issue was at once economic and political. Around the time he decided the whole family would leave, Juan José and I had a long conversation in Havana. We ended up discussing the meaning of freedom. He explained that there were the usual things: freedom of thought, speech, and so on. But he insisted that the matter was also astonishingly concrete, banal even. Freedom, he said, was also the right to a real living, as simple as buying yourself a pair of shoes or a pair of pants without it having to cost a month's salary, without having to wait for gifts from abroad. But as he pondered whether to stay or go, I think the most decisive factor was his sense of obligation to his children. He was seeing them stymied in what they could accomplish, and he could imagine a different future for them, for his grandchildren. And that was key, because under this new policy, the whole family would be eligible to leave. All nine of them. Juan José and his wife; their daughter, Aymara, with her husband and daughter; their son, Alain, with his wife and two sons. They applied for Cuban passports; they filled out paperwork, and they waited. And waited.

I note in my father's letters over this period something that I can't quite explain; they seem somehow a little less intimate. He barely mentions my mother. He spends significantly more time writing about the 2008 presidential elections than anything else. When he talks about the possibility of family reunification, he mostly expresses frustration at how slowly it's all going. Still, there are moments of love and longing that appear, as always. He sends Juan José medicine and advises him: "be careful with fats; when eating eggs, eat only the whites." And like Juan José, he appeals to God: "I hope that God allows us to have you all here before I am gone, in truth, I don't know where the Lord will send me." (When I read that I could not help but wonder what sins my father was remembering.)

Juan José's letters over the same period feel anxious. He can't sleep at night, though that's not entirely new for him. It's 4:55 a.m. and he lies awake, he says, "a tumult of ideas in my mind." He asks God for guidance: "every time I think about what we're doing, I say, 'God, may your will be done, for whatever is best for my family.' I think a lot about my children and grandchildren." Everything he did, he did for them, he says. Referring to the entire family, he writes, "There is within us a mix of hope, optimism, skepticism, and worry that does not let us rest. . . . We will see what happens. . . . In these moments I can only deposit my faith in God." By then it was September 2009. Almost two years in, the application process was still ongoing, and their waiting continued.

On November 14, 2009, Juan José wrote an early Christmas letter not just to my father, but to all of us: Ramón, Adela, Aixa, Ada, Nailah, Alina and Lucía. "¡Feliz Navidad! ¡Feliz Año Nuevo!" he begins excitedly. And then he lets himself imagine all of us together in my parents' apartment. Aixa and Hildita sit on the balcony talking, each smoking a cigarette. My mother and Aymara are cooking, and my mother is teaching her some of her secrets. Alain and I are having an animated conversation about Barack Obama. Nailah takes charge of all the younger children, who look curiously at the adults, whose joy at being together is plainly visible. Then Juan José asks: "Will my dreams become a reality? Let us pray to God that they will."

The post office stamp on the letter's envelope reads November 18, 2009. But someone wrote over it in pen and changed the 18 to a 19. Maybe it was the first letter of the day on the nineteenth, and the postal worker stamped it before realizing that he had forgotten to change the date from the afternoon before. So he corrected it in ink. Everything was the same, all was routine, interrupted occasionally by moments like that, a worker improvising a correction to an error, my brother vividly imagining a different kind of routine in an alternative future.

A few days later, Wednesday, November 25, Juan José was home in the afternoon, working in the little woodshop that he had built in the yard; his granddaughter Amalia, then ten, was doing her homework at a small table on the back patio. Hildita went out to get the family's daily ration of bread. She returned to take a shower and start on dinner, calling out to Juan José to tell him something, she doesn't remember what. He doesn't answer. She finds him on the floor, and he is not breathing. He had died moments before of a massive heart attack.

# TWENTY-SEVEN

# Letters to a Judge, Letters to a Mother

**January evenings in Miami** are often perfect. Thursday night January 24, 2002, certainly was: 74 degrees and clear. At 6:50 p.m., the sun had already set, and the sky was probably the deep ultramarine blue that has been my favorite color since I was a child. My parents would have been home in the Miami Beach apartment that Gregg and I had purchased for them almost five years earlier. They were likely finishing their habitual five-item dinner of rice, beans, plantains, salad, and some kind of savory meat. Aixa was probably already home from work, getting ready for dinner with Adrian and Nailah.

In New York, Thursday would have been the end of my teaching week. It was shaping up to be a busy semester. I had just been awarded tenure at NYU and was working on a new book. Lucía was almost one; Alina recently turned six. I was preparing to take seventeen NYU students to Havana in the summer and was busy figuring out all the complicated logistics. Gregg and I were also making plans to move the family to Spain for a year, because we both had sabbaticals coming up. He taught on Thursday nights. So, chances are that on January 24, I ordered Chinese or Indian for an easy meal, before getting the girls to bed and, if I was still awake enough, settling into the couch for some television to mark the end of a week's worth of teaching and meetings.

Poly was probably the only member of the family who was out that evening. He was just about a half block from his apartment on West Flagler at a bar called Las Tres Monitas, a picture of three little monkeys on the sign outside. It was a typical Little Havana bar: not particularly well lit, boasting pool tables, video game machines, a jukebox, and plenty to drink. Everyone there—staff and customers—spoke Spanish. The owner, let us call him Danny, was Cuban, a former political prisoner who had immigrated to the United States in 1979, as a consequence of the same negotiations that had also resulted in the family reunification visits that allowed my mother to visit Cuba that same year. The man had owned Tres Monitas only for about a year, opening it to supplement the money he made in his other business, operating jukebox and amusement machine concessions in bars. He was doing well. Business was booming, and at sixty-three, he had been a US citizen for seven years. His wife was thirty-eight years old. Once a week, he took his youngest daughter to her ballet class. He played chess and was thinking of signing up for a French class. He was healthy and fit, regularly lifting weights and running. He had even set records in some local races.

Danny knew my brother as Polo, the same nickname Poly's father had always used. Two or three months before that beautiful January evening, Poly had gotten into a fight at the bar and broken the front window. The bar owner had told him to stay away. But now here he was ordering a drink at the bar. Danny considered Poly "a very problematic person," a man with a "bad aspect about him."

Danny breathed a sigh of relief when my brother left that night even before finishing his first beer. Maybe he got hungry, because when he left, he went only as far as the McDonald's next door. In the parking lot, he ran into some acquaintances having trouble with their car. Poly wanted to come to their rescue, so he went back to the bar to ask Danny for a tire iron to fix the problem.

Danny said he didn't have one. Poly didn't believe him. They argued, and Poly stormed off. Sitting with his back to the front door, Danny didn't see Poly come back just a minute or two later. All he sensed was an unusual coldness and then a horrible pain. Other patrons at the bar saw my brother reach behind his waistband, pull out a knife, and drive it into Danny's back once, twice, three times. Then Poly ran away, dropping the knife as he raced home across the McDonald's parking lot.

Some customers in the bar fled in fear; others hid or held up furniture as shields to protect themselves in case my brother came back. "Oh my God; oh my God, I am going to die," cried Danny on the floor, as everything started to go black. A Salvadoran man, who had migrated to the United States during the worst violence of the civil war in that country, called 911 and then helped move Danny to a table, face down to put pressure on the wounds and slow the bleeding. That was the scene that the police and rescue workers found when they arrived three or four minutes after the call. Someone phoned Danny's son, too, and he arrived in a panic shortly after. Danny was still conscious enough to tell him that Polo had done it.

The police had a description of my brother given at the bar: a short, stocky man, "more or less white," unshaven and with hair that was starting to gray. He'd been wearing an NYPD baseball cap, jeans, a T-shirt or tank top. Five days after the attack in the bar, the police appeared at Poly's doorstep. At the station, after receiving his Miranda notice, Poly confessed to the stabbing. In that moment, the detective thought he sensed Poly's shame and repentance. "Defendant appeared to be remorseful," he wrote.

The line leaps up at me from the arrest record. I can picture Poly: He knows he has lost control; he wishes he could take it back; he thinks of my mother. I can sense his regret as a feeling in my chest.


Poly was taken to the Miami-Dade Pre-Trial Detention Center, also known as the Miami-Dade County Jail, the largest prison in the fourth-largest carceral system in the United States. Built in 1960, it sat on Thirteenth Avenue and Thirteenth Street, "twice unlucky," in the words of one journalist. It had beds for over seventeen hundred souls, but overcrowding was legion, and sometimes people slept on mattresses on the floor. Poly was now prisoner number 028500 there.

At his arraignment on February 19, 2002, my parents and my sister heard the charge against him: attempted murder. Fortunately, Danny had not died. He credited the running and the weightlifting for his easy recovery. Poly's public defender entered a plea of not guilty.

Perhaps it was in preparation for the arraignment that my parents penned the document I found in the same envelope where my mother saved his arrest record. The document is in my father's handwriting with my mother's signature at the bottom. Nothing in the document indicates an addressee, only a fax number and a record of transmission dated February 12, 2002, 5:23 p.m. That means my father walked to the

Kinko's a block and a half from their apartment, between his afternoon coffee and his evening shower. The page consists of two lists. The heading for the first says "Names of the psychiatrist [*sic*] doctors who have seen my son Hipólito." Four doctors are listed. I have encountered their names elsewhere: in medical claims, in loose business cards among my mother's papers, in other records of the court. The second list on the page reads "Some medicines he has taken." It lists just four, an incomplete accounting based on other papers in my mother's possession. It omits, for example, the antipsychotic Haldol, which he'd been prescribed multiple times. At the bottom of the page just above my mother's signature is a spare notation: "August 4, 1997, in Jackson [Memorial Hospital] for attempted suicide." It takes my breath away.

Did I know that before? I wonder. Had my mother kept it from me? Or had she told me and then I just put it out of my mind so successfully that I have no memory of it all?

In September 2002, still awaiting trial at the Miami-Dade County Jail, Poly was transported to Southern Winds Psychiatric Hospital in a "grossly psychotic" state, "verbally and physically aggressive." I don't know what he did, all I know is what the case file reveals: that the question of Poly's mental health became a matter for the court. The judge appointed five doctors to conduct psychiatric evaluations to help determine Poly's capacity to stand trial.

The reports are, like so many archival records, replete with inconsistencies. In one, Poly says he has a third-grade education, in another a ninth-grade one. Sometimes he appeared well groomed; sometimes he didn't. He attested to drug abuse in one session, denied it in the next. He claims never to have been in the bar called Tres Monitas, but in another session says that he had two beers there, though he didn't know the man he was accused of stabbing.

He narrated his life history for the doctors: He was raised by his grand-mother and aunt in Cuba, while his mother and sisters were in the United States. He explained that he rarely saw his father while he was growing up. He mentioned Tía Tatá in Mazorra, a cousin with epilepsy, another who had once set herself on fire. He explained that he dropped out of school "to be in the streets," that he came to the United States during the Mariel Boatlift. He admitted abusing cocaine and marijuana until the late 1990s; if he had had the money, he would have done drugs every day, he confessed. He had started drinking in Cuba when he was fifteen. In the United States, he often used to drink one or two six-packs of beer a day. He had been homeless at different points. Ever since he'd been beaten with a pipe, he suffered from memory problems. He fell often. He said he had attempted suicide by slashing his veins, though one doctor noted that there were no scars on his wrists. He sometimes had seizures. And just a few days prior to one of the psychiatric evaluations, he had been admitted to Westchester General Hospital for Dilantin intoxication, the drug he had been prescribed to treat the seizures.

He told the psychiatrists that he was often sad and depressed. That had started in his early twenties, he explained. (I note that that was when his letters to my mother grew very intense.) He had hallucinations, too. He often saw animals running past him at high speed. Sometimes, they were not animals but "quickly moving shadows." He heard people laughing at him. He described himself as "fearful." At night at home, "a lot of time," he blocked his door. He heard voices call to him, but when he looked there was no one there.

It is hard to know the truth of all that, whether he was being honest or embellishing in the hopes of avoiding a guilty verdict. One of the psy-chiatrists who evaluated him for competency concluded, "It seems that some degree of malingering was present, but his mental state was rather poor." His conclusion for the judge: "Mr. Cabrera is deemed incompetent to stand trial at the present time. His mental condition is fragile, although he likely exaggerated some of his symptoms." Another doctor agreed with that assessment. But three others (a majority) determined that he was fit for trial, and the judge agreed.

Reading the court documents, I am struck by the fact that other psychiatrists—not appointed by the court—also became involved in Poly's case. One of them (whose name was on the list of doctors that my parents had prepared) wrote to the judge explaining that he had been treating Poly for five years for "major mental illness, diagnosis of Schizophrenia, Chronic Paranoid Type." The letter, however, was not written in support of an argument for acquittal or to weigh in on the question of my brother's competency. It was written instead to recommend that Poly be placed in an assisted-living facility (ALF) "for stabilization and ongoing psychiatric care."

It was a growing trend in Miami, where ALFs had first emerged as dumping grounds for former patients at state psychiatric facilities shuttered by deinstitutionalization. But by 2002, the ALFs were also housing people with mental health issues who were either awaiting trial or serving a sentence. In theory, the ALFs were a more humane alternative to prison for mentally ill offenders. Residents were supervised and attended a rehabilitation program every day, while living in a group house in most cases indistinguishable from the ones around it. They could not leave the ALFs, but they could make and receive phone calls, as well as visitors. In most cases, it was a substantial improvement from the Miami-Dade County Jail.

But there was also significant abuse in the system. The county had just two inspectors to oversee almost 650 ALFs. "I wouldn't leave a dog in most of these ALFs," said one Miami police officer to a journalist.

Another person who addressed the court to recommend an ALF placement for Poly was neither a psychiatrist nor a lawyer. His name was Sam Konell, and he was Miami's most successful patient broker. A regular fixture at the courthouse and prison, he looked for mentally ill patients with insurance, often Medicaid, to transfer into the ALF system. Konell would convince lawyers and judges to reduce sentences in exchange for getting the accused into a program that would provide treatment. The rehabilitation programs and ALFs then paid Konell a commission. He also received payment from Southern Winds Psychiatric Hospital and Greater Miami Behavioral Health Care Center, two institutions that had sent their own letters to the court recommending that Poly serve his time in an ALF. In 2018, Sam Konell was found guilty of a $63 million health-care fraud scheme.

On November 4, 2002, while still awaiting trial, Poly was released from prison into an ALF. Then on January 5, 2004, almost two years after the night Poly entered the bar in search of a tire iron to fix a car, the trial judge entered a judgment of guilt on the count of attempted first-degree murder. There was no trial, because Poly pleaded guilty in exchange for being able to serve his time in an ALF. The judge sentenced Poly to twelve years. He had already done two; the remaining ten would also be served at an ALF.

My mother was relieved to know he would not be going to prison. She could call him every night after *Wheel of Fortune*; she could get Aixa to take her to see him in person. When she had open-heart surgery in December 2003, a guard in a suit accompanied Poly to visit her at the hospital. When Tía Niña and later my mother's brother Herminio visited Miami, they both went to see Poly at the ALF.

. . .

The assisted-living facility actually did Poly some good. He stopped drinking, a major achievement by any measure. He began a relationship with a woman named Rosa who used to clean there. Rosa was Cuban, Black, sweet, a little shy, and a few years older than him. In 2007, sober for about five years, he took Rosa to my parents' place for Christmas Eve dinner. I was spending the year in Spain with Gregg and the girls, but the girls made a Christmas video greeting and included regards for Poly and Rosa. My mother was happy.

I don't know when he began seeing another woman: Carmen, also Cuban, younger than Rosa, a woman whom he always called "my *mulatica.*" Carmen was living with the father of her two sons, though she insisted that they were separated and that they were sharing a home only because she had no financial alternative. Poly was obsessed with her.

I can't remember whether it was when he was still with Rosa or later with Carmen that Poly decided that he no longer needed to be at the ALF. To make that happen, he didn't abscond. He just started writing. On March 12, 2008, he wrote to his "Dear Legal Team," detailing the

Tía Niña and my mother visiting Poly at his ALF, 2005. The woman visible in the kitchen may be Poly's girlfriend.

commendations he had received for attendance and participation at the rehabilitation program. He drafted the letter as if one of his sisters had written it: "my brother has changed quite a lot," it reads. "That is why we ask for your effort to get him out of the ALF . . . He will have the supervision of all his family, the support of his partner, and all the moral support of all his family who love him very much." Did he believe that, or was he just saying something he thought might help him get out of his situation?

Poly also drafted letters to the judge. Appeals to courts and judges have a long history. Whether petitions for pardon directed to a king in sixteenth-century France or appeals for freedom made by enslaved people to monarchs and courts, reading such appeals is bread-and-butter stuff for many historians. Sometimes, a petition to a court might be the only opportunity for an ordinary person to tell their story.

Because Poly's case never went to trial, he never offered sworn testimony before a judge or jury. So, the letter he wrote to the judge on October 1, 2008, is the only time we can hear him present his own version of the story. The letter is muddled and long, a 959-word harangue against the world. The first story he tells is about himself as a member "of a decent Catholic family, my family is U.S. citizens." He describes himself as already addicted to alcohol on his arrival in the country in 1980 and as "diagnosed clinically depressed." But there follows one rebuke after another. At the bar, he was the prey before he became the predator, the wounded before the wounder. In the prison and psychiatric hospital, lawyers and case workers tricked him into pleading guilty by scaring him about a sure sentence of seventeen years; at the ALF he was subject to abuse and theft. Everywhere and always, others wronged him. To sum up, Poly's letter sounds just like Poly.

Poly urgently wanted out of the ALF, but no one was listening. When no one listened, Poly seethed. And when no one gave him what he wanted,

Poly became impossible. On January 9, 2009, the ALF gave him forty-five days to vacate the facility. The institution's justification was clearly stated in the record: "Resident has been verbally abusive and aggressive to staff and administrator. A police report was filed on resident on December 22, 2008." At the bottom of the notice to vacate is Poly's signature acknowledging receipt.

Fellowship House, the rehabilitation center that he attended every weekday, was more positive in its evaluation of Poly. His attendance was excellent; he participated in daily group sessions, and he was six years sober and clean. But there was a caveat, a big one. "It is the treatment team's opinion that even though Hipolito attends program every day, he demonstrates poor insight into his mental illness. In the past, he has [had] numerous verbal outbursts. He is manipulative and very demanding. He continues to demonstrate poor impulse control and ruminates about the idea of living independently despite his legal obligations." The team's recommendation was that the issue be addressed in court. Given that the ALF was evicting him, there was really no other choice. On February 10, 2009, Poly appeared before a judge who found him in violation of his parole and sent him again to the twice unlucky Miami-Dade County Jail on the corner of Thirteenth Avenue and Thirteenth Street.

Back in prison, Poly sensed no point in writing to the judge anymore, so he wrote to our mother instead. Over the course of six months in 2009, from three different detention facilities, Poly sent her fifteen letters. I found them in the same plastic box in which she had saved, tied with gold curling ribbon, all the letters Poly had written to her as a boy in Cuba.

I think of my parents, both in their eighties, both receiving letters from sons they had abandoned in Cuba decades earlier. My father stoops to open the squeaky mailbox, the name Ferrer faded to invisible, and pulls out everything inside. I picture his excitement at seeing an envelope from Juan José. I know the feeling in the pit of his stomach at seeing one from Poly.

Poly's first prison letter to my mother was dated April 19, 2009. As he had done in the 1970s in his letters from Cuba, he added a title to the year. In 1979, thinking his reunification with my mother was imminent, he had used the title "Year of My Happiness." Now from prison in Miami, he invented a new header: *Año de mi felicidad o mi desdicha para siempre.* Year of My Happiness or My Misery for Always.

In the letter, Poly admitted to making many mistakes; he said that he prayed every night asking for God's forgiveness. He wanted reconciliation with our family; he wanted, he said, a frank conversation in which all parties participated and owned up to their faults and mistakes. But that was impossible, he said, not because of him, but because of us. We never admitted to having done anything wrong. Most of his mistakes had been induced by alcohol; ours were worse, because they were sober, unfeeling ones. He said we thought ourselves always perfect. My father scorned him, he said, and Aixa preferred to go to an opera or dinner with friends than to go see him or do him a favor. I, meanwhile, had always been on the sidelines, never caring anything at all about him.

As to my mother, he wrote, "How can we speak of reconciliation when ever since I arrived in this country, I have felt your indifference and rejection." He narrated how when he arrived in the United States and tried to put his head on my mother's lap, for example, she would shoo him away, saying he weighed too much. But he used to sit on Tía Niña's lap all the time; she stroked his head, kissed him on the cheek. (I think about my visits to him with my mother, how I always told her not to hug me or put her arms around me. I always sensed that it set him off when he saw her do that. Now I know why.) Even when he did stupid things,

Poly continued, Tía Niña never criticized him or humiliated him. "I tell myself what a coward and fool I was to abandon her . . . because I was and am her son."

He had tried hard to forgive us, he insisted, but how could he, when my mother had never really asked for forgiveness. "You have never opened your mouth to acknowledge your guilt and to let me hear the words, 'Son, forgive me for my wrongs.'"

That was Poly's truth. And it was brutal. My mother did not cry easily. She took antidepressants. One time, I heard her respond to a doctor who asked how she was feeling with a breezy "Me? Delighted by life," a line from an old Benny Moré song with the same title, "Encantado de la vida." She quoted the line without attribution, her voice a little singsong; then she paused for effect and added, "I take Paxil." How much it must have hurt her to read Poly's words.

I once asked my mother if she had ever begged Poly's forgiveness. It might have been that time we were together in the Havana airport in 1991. She said yes. She had said something to him like, "If I had known the damage it would do to you, I would have never left you." But was that a true enough apology, a vulnerable enough plea for forgiveness? The fault, she implied without realizing it, lay at his feet for reacting badly when she left Cuba without him.

When Poly wrote again the following day, his tone had changed completely. He wrote not about my mother, but about his girlfriend, Carmen. She was driving him mad. One day, she said she loved him, the next day she would barely talk to him. Carmen was the subject of another letter the next day. They had been fighting on the phone, and he needed my mother's advice, mother to son. "I am like crazy; I know that I'm too old to torment you with my problems. . . . But you are my mother with whom I unburden myself. Oh, ma, how unlucky I am." Then his tone grew menacing:

Truly, I am very sorry, because I love her with all the strength of my heart. I told her that my love for her was from another era, a love of total devotion in the style of Romeo and Juliet . . . Samson and Delilah, or Odysseus and Helen of Troy. Those were eternal loves of total devotion. Life without [Carmen] is worthless, I don't know what I'm going to do, but I'm not going to resign myself. Maybe we'll both go to the afterlife together.

He sounds like a man capable of what people once euphemistically called a crime of passion and today more aptly name as femicide. The letters continued, though without that specific threat: April 30, May 5, May 6, May 10, two on May 20, and so on. He couldn't stop.

Poly was also making phone calls. He called my mother to ask her for things: to buy him this or that, to pawn a trinket, to visit him at the Miami-Dade County Jail, all things that required a ride from my sister. He called Aixa all the time, too, so that she could patch him through with Carmen on the phone. The first few times, Aixa listened, but soon she would just put the phone down and try to continue with whatever it was she had been doing before the call. If they began arguing too loudly, she might tell them to stop. If it got worse, she disconnected the call. The calls were frequent and endless. On the night of May 3, 2009, she had to turn off her home number to escape his calls. But then he started calling her cell: twenty-eight times between 8 p.m. and 11:50 p.m., until he wore her down, and she answered.

Collect calls from prison are expensive, more than the regular phone rate, more than my mother could afford. Today, when prisoners make collect calls, an automated voice, in addition to providing the caller's name, often urges people receiving calls to report any abuse or harassment by the prisoner. But Florida hadn't started that practice yet, and, in any case, neither my mother nor Aixa would have reported him.

On June 3, 2009, Poly was released from Miami's infamous county jail. But not for the reason or with the outcome he wanted. He did not go to another ALF, nor to my parents' place, much less to an apartment with Carmen. He went instead to the Krome Detention Center. Then at 11:40 p.m. the first night there, someone entered his cell and served him with a notice to appear before an immigration judge in removal proceedings. He was now in the custody of ICE. Like so many others, Poly was caught in the prison-to-deportation pipeline. The attempted murder conviction rendered him an aggravated felon, and that made him deportable under US law.

On June 18, 2009, an immigration judge ordered him removed from the United States. Poly was transferred yet again, this time to Wakulla County Jail, located in the eastern part of the Florida Panhandle, on the way to Eglin Air Force Base, where he had started his American life almost thirty years earlier. Wakulla County Jail expanded in 2004 to more than double its capacity and to open a new section specifically for immigration detainees. Poly's booking sheet indicates that he received the maximum form of supervision given to inmates in the general population there. He was still there on September 3, when prison authorities took him to a nearby medical facility for psychiatric evaluation, because he was displaying "aggressive behaviors." When he returned to the prison, he was separated from the general population but then incorporated once more under a new medication regime.

Despite the order of removal against him, Poly was confident that he would be released and returned to Miami. If he'd been from Mexico or Haiti, say, he would have been deported. But the Cuban government refused to accept the vast majority of Cubans who were ordered removed by the United States. The immigration officer who reviewed his case after the removal order wrote, "The subject is a citizen of Cuba and the issuance of a travel document is NOT likely in the foreseeable future." On September 11, 2009, Poly was released on an order of supervision. Even for someone like Poly, convicted and excludable, Cuban birth still mitigated the effects of the deportation machine.

# TWENTY-EIGHT

# What If

**When Juan José died** in Cuba in November 2009, my father was devastated. I didn't realize at the time just how devastated he was. Now having read their letters, seeing how often they wrote, how much of himself my father poured into them, I understand a little better why he spent so much time staring off into space, why he seemed a little numb. There was no one to write to anymore, no letters to wait for anymore. Recall the letter that Juan José wrote imagining us all together in Miami, enjoying each other's company. It arrived after Juan José died, like a tribute to a future that would never exist, an invitation to too many what-ifs.

My mother stopped receiving letters, too. Poly was back in Miami, having arrived just two months before Juan José's death. He was at a different ALF now. My mother could visit him again, bring him money, do his laundry. She was relieved. I doubt Aixa was; I know I would not have been.

Even in New York, at a safe distance, I had intrusive thoughts: What if he just showed up at my doorstep? I played out conversations in my head: Poly with the girls, home alone after school; Poly with me once I returned from work. I would tell him that I lived in faculty housing, which was like a dorm, and that he couldn't stay with us, because we'd get kicked out. But then I invented a conversation between Poly and a doorman, in which he learned that hardly anyone got kicked out, and that it wouldn't be a problem for him to stay with us. A scene, a fight. He goes to the kitchen for a knife. Then I'd snap myself out of it.

Every year for the holidays and during the summer, Gregg and I made the trip with the girls to Miami—so many visits over the years that they all run together. Part of me couldn't help but be happy. I'd see my parents, Aixa, Nailah. They would get to see the girls and vice versa. At Christmas, we'd open presents together by my mother's small Christmas tree, her favorite ritual on earth. We would eat her cooking, some of the best in the world, we all knew. My parents, my sister, and I would play dominoes. Maybe, if I got lucky before we left for our hotel at night, my father would go to the kitchen for an apple, a bowl, and a knife, and then peel and slice an apple for me, as he had done all through my childhood.

Still on the drive from the airport to my parents' place, my stomach always churned. When the phone rang at my parents' apartment, I would make everyone be quiet in case it was Poly. I did not want him to hear us having fun and get jealous. I would count the days until we could leave and head north to Jensen Beach, to stay with Gregg's parents and lounge in their beautiful lanai with its small kidney-shaped pool.

Sometimes, Poly joined us for Christmas Eve dinner at my parents'.

My mother loved that. Her son was with her on the most important day of the year; her children were all together. No one else shared her enthusiasm. One year, maybe 2010, Poly promised to come to dinner and then backed out. He was angry with our mother, with everyone. He called my mother yelling several times that night. He was threatening to kill himself, Carmen, my parents. Surely, murder would get him deported to Cuba, which is what he said he wanted. Maybe he imagined Tía Niña taking care of him once more. But nothing happened that night.

If Poly didn't come to Christmas Eve dinner, we drove to see him. I would take him presents: Polo cologne, a carton of Marlboros, and some cash. Before going in, as always, I reminded my mother not to put her arms around me. I also always tucked my cell phone in the glove compartment of the car, so that he wouldn't see it and ask for my phone number. One year when he mentioned that he was opening up a Facebook account, I immediately deleted mine. I did not want to give him a glimpse into my life. I was glad when he took in a Chihuahua he called Gordy because the girls could pretend to distract themselves by playing with her. Sometimes Aixa would trim Poly's hair, because he insisted that only she knew how to do it right. At the end of the visit, we'd all hug and kiss, and I'd tuck some cash in his pocket. Gregg would usually insist on taking a few pictures: our daughters with their uncle, Poly with my mother, with his sisters, sometimes all of us together. Gregg would help my mother load Poly's dirty laundry into the trunk. She'd do it at home in the two coin-operated washing machines in their small condo building. I think my mother thought that if we went through these motions enough, Poly would find a way to forgive her.

She had faith; she prayed for Poly all the time. I used to pray, too—mostly that Poly would change. But sometimes, I have to admit—I hate to admit—I wished that he would die. And, somehow, despite everything I've blocked out, trying not to think of his long-ago prophecy that there would be bodies, I know that I am right. I wanted him gone, and I have broken my mother's heart.

Yet there was also a part of me that always wanted to talk to Poly about all of it, about my mother's decision, about his life in Cuba, about his arrival here. But I never dared. The closest we came was on one of his birthdays, December 6. I called him. He answered. I wished him a happy birthday and asked how his day was going. He answered angrily. How could it ever be? And then his rant began: He had never been a part of our family; he was not a Ferrer. Everything was bad, wrong. I could hear my heartbeat in my ears. I finally spoke: I know, I said. But I have my own pains; I suffer, too. (A defensive, guilty, selfish response, I know.) He seemed surprised. It broke the momentum of his rage. I asked him if he was taking antidepressants. He said he refused to take any psychiatric drugs. (I'm not sure if that meant he was not taking the drugs prescribed under the treatment program.) The whole conversation lasted less than ten minutes, maybe even less than five, my heart racing the whole time.

I wonder now what kind of conversation we might have had if I hadn't been so scared. If the woman who began life as the little baby sister he had loved so much as a boy had said something like:

You are right. You have suffered through things that never should have happened to you. I know that the mother who I love as much as anything in this world—the mother who loves me the same way—did that to you. I know I was the chosen one. Please forgive her, forgive me.

But I didn't say any of that. I was too afraid. We just hung up. I wouldn't have mentioned the conversation to Gregg, and certainly not to the girls. I probably just went back to work, grading or writing a letter of recommendation, my mind elsewhere, all the while that familiar anxiety lodging itself in my body, already dreading the next trip at Christmas just about two weeks away.

# PART VI

# The Elders

# TWENTY-NINE

# Tía Tatá

**It was around that time,** in 2008, that Tía Tatá died in Cuba. This was Tatá who had spent most of her adult life in and out of Havana's psychiatric hospital. Mazorra, everyone called it—the place parents used to threaten wayward children with. When people did or said something foolish, silly, crazy, others around them might proclaim *Mazorra pide locos* (Mazorra seeks mad people). I heard my mother say it many times: to me, to herself, even to strangers. Fidel Castro once famously referred to Mazorra before he came along as a veritable Dante's *Inferno*. In 2010, more than fifty years after he took power, it was still shocking. That January, between twenty-six and fifty patients died in the hospital, cold and hungry, as a result of neglect.

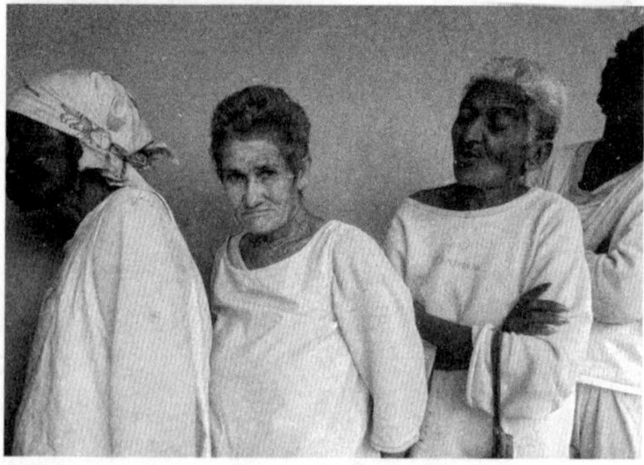

*Top*: Tatá and me at Mazorra, 1990. *Bottom*: Mazorra patients, 1998, photo by Damaris Betancourt.

I don't know exactly when Tatá became ill, or who decided that Mazorra was where she needed to be. When the revolution came to power in 1959, 90 percent of Mazorra patients were deemed chronic, and schizophrenia ailed 68 percent of them. That was what the doctors said my aunt had. As a chronic schizophrenic, she regularly received electroshock therapy. My mother and Tía Niña told me that, and contemporary reports and later histories of the hospital document the prevalence of the practice in the 1950s. Doctors at Mazorra also began performing lobotomies on patients in the late 1940s. Perhaps she underwent that kind of treatment, as well. But I cannot be sure.

Tatá, the darkest child of the twelve siblings, was gorgeous as a young woman, but I'm not sure she saw herself that way. Racism is rampant in Cuba, just as it is in the United States, historically and in the present. An anti-Black language of racial improvement was insidious. People talked of "bettering the race" and "marrying up." That was certainly true in many

mixed-race families such as ours. Sometimes Tatá herself teased our grandmother
by saying that she was going to marry a
Black man. And my grandmother—who
was born a year after the end of slavery,
whose own great-grandmother had been
born in Africa, and who adored her
daughter—would get upset. Tatá was surrounded by that kind of thing all her life.

During my first visit to Cuba, going
through old family photos with Tía Niña,

Tía Tatá as a young woman.

I noticed that in some of the group pictures, Tatá's face had been blotted
out with ink. I asked about it. Tía Niña shook her head sadly. "Tatá did
that." I don't know why she erased her own face in the pictures. I cannot
ask her, and I don't think anyone—maybe not even her doctors—ever did.

From the time she was first admitted almost to the time she died, Tatá
would stay in Mazorra for months or years at a time. But the family
would take her home for weekends or for longer periods when she was
doing better. They brought her home for holidays, or if Tía Niña was on
vacation and could take care of her for a while. Occasionally when she
was home, Tatá would decide on her own that she needed to go back to
the hospital; she could feel something coming on.

Even with her absences in the hospital, Tatá had been a constant
presence in Poly's life in Cuba. When she was home and Poly was still a
boy, she shared a room with him and her own son, Carlitos. She tended
to Poly after school. He went to the store to buy her cigarettes. She loved
the church, and when she was home and well, she would go often to

attend Mass or just to pray for a bit. She used to pray that Poly would be reunited with us; he needed his mother, she used to say, especially in those awful years when he was always getting into trouble.

When Tatá died in 2008, Tía Niña called my mother with the news. Before the prevalence of cell phones and WhatsApp, unplanned calls from Cuba were still often the portents of sad news. My mother called me in New York to share the news, and then she would have done the same with Aixa and Poly in Miami.

It is interesting that with everything that was going on with Poly— his instability, his attempted suicide, his bouts of depression, his threats against us, his claims to see things and hear voices, his diagnoses of schizophrenia—my mother never (as far as I know) compared Poly's struggles to Tatá's illness. For her—as for me—they were fundamentally different.

And another what-if comes to mind. What if Poly had come with us—if my mother had boarded that ship way back in December 1962 with both of us in tow, or if Poly's father had relented and let him leave with us or soon after? Would he still have gotten into trouble? Was my mother's abandonment not the only issue at play? And from that rumination, yet another what-if follows: what if he had come with us and swept us all along with his troubles, made our family a different kind of family, made me a different person?

# THIRTY

# A Family Trip

**It took a lot of doing** to get my father to Cuba. He had always said that he would never visit Cuba while a Castro was in power. Yet, the older he got, the more he thought about returning. Sometimes, he even talked about moving there. He wrote to government officials in the United States, asking that he be allowed to collect his Social Security wages there. There's an economic embargo, I would say. And he would insist that that was why he was writing, so that they would make an exception in his case. To the US State Department, he wrote "I am ninety-two years old, and I long with all my heart to return to my country, Cuba, and spend there the last years of my life." When he requested that his pension be sent to Cuba as my parents' only means of subsistence, he added, "I recognize that these kind of relations don't currently exist between our two countries, but I also understand that in all human matters, there is always a first time." My father was so insistent that I finally composed a later version of the letter in English.

He also drafted letters to Cuban authorities asking for permission to move there with no restrictions at all on his speech and movement. There is no freedom of speech in Cuba, I would say. And his response would be the same. Maybe he would be the exception. I think part of his motivation was to get away from Poly, but he wouldn't go without my mother, and my mother would never leave without Poly again.

I always wanted my father to return to Cuba for a visit. When he talked to me about wanting to move there, I would say, "Go for a little while, see how you feel there and then decide." I knew he wouldn't want to stay once he saw it firsthand. At one point, he and my mother actually applied and received entry permits from the Cuban government and the required licenses from the US Treasury Department. But then my mother fell, stumbling over her rocking chair as she walked to her sewing machine. She suffered a head injury that kept her from traveling, and their travel documents expired. So my father penned more letters, asking for their permissions to be extended or renewed. He was an old man, he wrote, and wanted to see his island of birth before he died. Above all, he wanted to meet his grandchildren and great-grandchildren, referring of course to Juan José's family. He never received a reply.

I urged him to reapply for permission, but by then he was always finding excuses. There was always the old fear: of being arrested, or even executed. Why did he think that still? I would ask. Did you do something? I didn't do anything, he would say. Then why should you be afraid? Because. That was always the course of the conversation.

He had a new excuse now, too: that at his age something would happen to his health in Cuba. His brother Jesús, living in New Jersey, had visited the island a few years earlier and suffered a bad fall. He felt ill for months after the trip. My father would always say things like, "I have to wait for my knee pain to go away," or "my stomach is acting up." Then he ended always with a version of "Let me wait until I feel better." To which I tended to reply something like, "Papi, you're ninety, you may never feel as good as you do now." He didn't like it when I said that. He really, really hated acknowledging his own mortality. So I surprised myself one day when I told him that he needed to decide what was preferable, getting some indigestion in Cuba or dying without ever going back. Apply for the visa, I said. I'll pay for the application. When it comes, if you're feeling okay, you go; if you're not, you don't.

Eventually, I just prepared my parents' visa applications myself, and when they arrived, my parents decided that they did want to make the trip after all. My mother was worried about how Poly would take it: my parents and me going to Cuba when he couldn't go. To ease any potential friction, she scheduled an appointment with a new immigration lawyer to see if there was a way to adjust Poly's status so that he could become a legal permanent resident. He had been found guilty of attempted murder in the first degree; he was an aggravated felon; he had been ordered removed from the country. What she wanted would never happen, the lawyer told her. But Poly surprised her by saying that he thought the trip was a good idea; it made sense for my father to go back before he died and meet his son's family.

We made the trip in March 2016. There was never any question that I would travel with my parents. That was always the assumption. Aixa, who was born in Brooklyn and had never been to Cuba, decided to join us. The trip overlapped with Alina's spring break, so she came, too. The three of us stayed in Vedado, my neighborhood of choice. I reveled in showing

Havana to my sister. The place had been an enormous, inescapable presence in her life, so she was hungry to see it.

My parents stayed with Tía Niña, in the house where they had met and lived together (with Poly) before leaving Cuba. Sometimes, my father sat on the porch, gently rocking in the wood and wicker *sillón*, watching everything before him. He looked so stern and handsome sitting there, his face a face for a sculptor. One day, he insisted on going to seek out an old lover who lived in the neighborhood. My mother had the good sense to accompany him. They walked, him with his elegant wooden cane, but they never found the woman. Chances are she had already died, whether in Cuba or elsewhere. The walk was longer than they had anticipated, and on the way back, they had to stop at a bench to rest for a while. A man came up to them and anxiously asked, "Are you Ada's relatives?," referring not to me but to my aunt, Tía Niña. He was the president of the local Committee for the Defense of the Revolution, and he was looking for them because everyone back at the house was worried that they'd gotten lost. After we returned, I teased my father that he had been right all along: He went back to Cuba, and the communists had come looking for him.

Another day we paid a neighbor with an old American car to take us all to the cemetery in La Lisa, adjacent to Marianao, where my mother's people are buried in one crypt. My mother prayed the rosary, the rest of us, including Tía Niña, trying to rush through the prayers, because it was hot and there was no shade. My father waited in the car. After that, we drove around central and Old Havana. Everywhere, workers were readying the streets and buildings for the arrival of Barack Obama in a matter of days. My father looked out the car window but kept saying that nothing looked familiar. I said we should go to where he used to sell sandals by Fraternity Park after the revolution, and he gave directions to the driver, as if he had needed to. Still, he kept coming back to the same point: Everything looks different. My mother ignored him, insisting on getting out of the car to pose for a photograph in the Plaza de Armas, near the statue of Carlos Manuel de Céspedes, the leader of Cuba's first independence war, the slaveholder with whom I opened the first chapter of my first book.

I think it was the next day that we traveled to Juan José's house in the interior. By 2016, Juan José had been gone for years. But my father got to see the house he had built with his own hands. More importantly, my father got to meet his grandchildren, Aymara and Alain. He could not stop hugging Aymara. He met his great-grandchildren: Amalia, José Alain, and Jesuito. He played ball with them, walked with them to the center of the tiny town, and sat on a bench in the shadow of a monument to the revolutionary, Camilo Cienfuegos. We snapped a photograph, then we walked a little more. But he was confused: Where's the main street? he asked. We were on it. Where's the hotel? he asked. It hadn't existed for a lifetime or two.

While we were staying with Juan José's family, some of my father's family came to visit. By then, his two brothers there had died, but one of their widows, children, and grandchildren came. Orelia, his only surviving sibling, came too. People around him cried, but he didn't. He didn't talk much, doing as he often did and entrusting most of the conversation to my mother. My father had wanted to see the farm where he had grown up and which the family still owned. But the road was impassible by car, and my father, at ninety-four, could not have traveled in a spartan wooden buggy pulled by an old skinny horse. Someone else went and made a video of some of the land and of the house. They did not show him the corner of the house that had recently crumbled and lay in ruins. I don't know what, if anything, my father recognized in the small cell-phone screen before him. But I took a photo of him watching the video.

We returned to Havana, and my parents had one more night with my mother's family. I went with my mother to visit Estela, the old woman who had once been a little girl raised by my grandmother, the one who served as a decoy chaperone for my parents' early dates. Then we went back to Tía Niña's and all had a final dinner. In their generation, only Tía Niña and my mother remained, the two youngest of twelve children, the first of whom had been born 113 years earlier.

Of all my many trips to Cuba, this one was among the most special. I took my parents with me. I helped my father realize one of his dying dreams. After they left, I stayed in Havana to await the arrival of Barack Obama. As a historian, as someone who'd been traveling to Cuba for twenty-six years at that point, I could not miss the historic visit. That, too, made this particular trip especially exciting. All Havana was astir. It really felt like something new was on the horizon; the mood was hopeful in a way that I had never seen there before.

I went to Tía Niña's house to watch Obama's speech, the highlight of his visit. She sat right in front of the television, the poster of Fidel that had once hung there now long gone, a shawl around her shoulders because her bones always hurt in the cool of March. One of the most surprising moments in the speech came early, when North America's first Black president began outlining the commonalities between the two countries. "We share the same blood," he affirmed. I held my breath, unsure if he meant what I thought he did. He then said something obvious but unprecedented in the mouth of an American president: Slavery helped build the United States. That history, moreover, accounted for a fundamental parallel between

Cuba and the United States. "We both live in a new world, colonized by Europeans. Cuba, like the United States, was built in part by slaves brought here from Africa. Like the United States, the Cuban people can trace their heritage to both slaves and slave owners." I felt something like recognition.

I left Havana the same day as Obama. The first thing I did on getting home was to call my parents. I wanted desperately to know what my father had said about his trip to Cuba. But, according to my mother, all he had done since the trip was sit in his armchair in the living room and stare off into space, not bothering even to turn on the television. Let me talk to him, I said. Catching up with him was different than catching up with my mother. He volunteered little, and the pace of the conversation was slower. When I asked him what he thought of Cuba, he didn't say much. I told him a bit about what it was like being there during Obama's visit. He perked up a little. He was not Obama's fan. He had written dozens of letters to Juan José during the long 2008 election season detailing everything he found objectionable about him: He called for change without ever saying what it meant. He was a communist. Still, my father had liked Obama's speech. *Se la comió*, he said, chuckling with approval. "He killed it!" Having loosened him up, I asked again what it had felt like for him to be back in Cuba finally. He grew quiet and then surprised me by responding, "I think I'd like to spend a year there." Perhaps he had my own sabbaticals in mind, the times I'd moved with my family to Spain for a year and then returned. It was an interesting proposition. I ventured, surprised, that if he wanted to go back, he must have felt good being there, he must have liked it. "Nah," he scoffed. "Cuba's a total disaster!" Then he added, "But it's my disaster."

My parents in June 2016, at the ages of ninety-five and almost ninety, having recently returned from their trip to Cuba. To quote Edwidge Danticat, "There are loves that outlive lovers."

# THIRTY-ONE

# A Cuban Funeral

**Gregg and I had been married** about twenty-seven years when he gave me ballroom dancing lessons as a gift. Every Monday night over a couple of months, we walked a few blocks south to a dance studio in SoHo and tried to strike the poses, follow the steps, and look at each other rather than our feet. On April 17, 2017, having a light dinner before we left, I suddenly felt ill. My chest hurt, and I felt overcome by nausea. I put my spoon back in my soup and moved to the couch. I thought of all the heart disease in my family—my mother, Poly, Juan José, and others. But the feeling passed, and we were only a little late to our lesson.

Asleep later that night, I was awakened by a call a little after midnight, never good news. My parents, I thought immediately, assuming it had to be the call I had been dreading for years. My father was soon to turn ninety-six, my mother almost ninety-one. But it wasn't Aixa calling about our parents that night. It was my Cuban cousin Leanet—Carlitos's daughter, Tía Tatá's granddaughter. Leanet and her husband had moved in with Tía Niña shortly after her longtime partner, Onelio, left her. They both worked the evening shift at Havana airport, so they hired a woman named Lucy to help my aunt. She would make dinner at night and then stay and watch soap operas with her until Leanet came back from work. The night of the phone call, my aunt told Lucy to leave early; I'm not sure why. Tía Niña warmed up her own soup and sat down at the table to eat. But she must have felt something strange. She put her spoon back in her soup, walked to the couch, and sat down.

When Leanet and her husband came back a few hours later, they found her there with no pulse, her body leaning just a little to the left. On the dining table sat the cold bowl of soup with the spoon still inside. It wasn't until the next day that I realized that Tía Niña's final actions that night had mirrored my own. Or vice versa.

My aunt always prayed to Saint Jude the Apostle, whose image she kept atop her dresser. She spoke to him a little every night before going to bed. One night when Leanet saw her doing that, she asked what her prayer was. "To die peacefully at home," my aunt responded. She was almost eighty-seven; she felt old and tired, and she was ready. Tía Niña had gotten her wish. She died peacefully in the house where she had lived for some sixty-five years, the house where I had lived for the first ten months of my life, where Poly had grown up after we left.

We had a lot of relatives die in Cuba after we left: three grandparents and most of my parents' many siblings. Before, those middle-of-the-night calls had always gone to my parents. This one had come to me. I would have to tell my mother that her closest and last sibling had passed. I waited until morning to tell her. She didn't say much. I remember a long gasp, a pained "no." But she wasn't really able to talk. I was grateful, though, when she said she would call Poly to let him know.

I knew that Poly would be devastated. All my mother's shortcomings he measured against Tía Niña's love. Our aunt was selfless and had loved him unconditionally. She was his other mother, in his eyes perhaps a truer one than our own. In his little apartment in Hialeah (the working-class Cuban enclave adjacent to Miami), he kept a picture of Tía Niña, not of our mother, on his bedside table. While I did not want to be the one to break the news to him, it didn't take me long to realize that I needed, wanted even, to talk to him. I knew how much he must have been hurting, how could I not. To my relief, he did not pick up when I called. But I left him a message, sending my condolences and my love. And it was sincere. Later he told me how much that call had meant to him. But he hadn't wanted to talk. It hurt too much. He was scared of all the emotion that talking about her death might bring forth.

I seemed to want to seek it out and decided that I needed to go to Havana to be close to her somehow. I did wonder how Poly would feel about my trip. Will he get mad? I asked my mother. After all, Tía Niña had raised him, not me. But as a person deemed deportable, undocumented after the fact, he could not go to Cuba. But I—the one who had always had my mother, the one who'd been given all the opportunities, bearer of both a US and a Cuban passport—could go almost whenever I needed to. Again, Poly surprised us. He was glad I was going, glad that one of us could be there to show our love and respect. I noticed that when my mother told me, she said *us*—one of us—and I wondered if he had used that pronoun, too.

Before traveling, I got a haircut, impulsively deciding to cut my then long hair short. It was not lost on me that it was Tía Niña who had taken me to get my first haircut ever, a baby pixie cut that she had shown off to everyone in the neighborhood. By the time I arrived in Havana, there was no funeral to attend; Tía Niña's ashes were already in the family crypt. I bought some flowers and went to the cemetery, where a little over a year earlier my mother and Tía Niña had prayed together over their dead, knowing that it would soon be their turn.

It was right before my trip that my mother asked me to find and bring back the little book of names, the book in which as a little girl she had recorded details of the births of her siblings. It took a while to find, tucked in a small purse of Tía Niña's hanging in a closet stuffed with clothes and shoes that my mother had sent to her over almost a lifetime. Standing there, thumbing through its little pages for the first time, I began to cry. By then, I had spent almost thirty years traveling to Cuba, digging up old documents in archives. It was always obvious that my initial interest in Cuba had everything to do with my family. Yet I rarely saw them reflected in the histories I read, or in the documents I pored over to tell new stories about the past. Now here before me was a document; it looked like something I might encounter in an archive, yet it was in my mother's hand, written to leave a record of my grandmother and the large family she had created. And that moved me.

But mostly, I cried because I was mourning— mourning my aunt and, in anticipation, my mother. I was mourning all the loss that had come before, all the loss still to come,

Tía Niña and my mother as young women, the two youngest and last living of their generation.

thinking of a time when no one living would remember any of the people named in our family's little book.

I took the book back to my mother, as was her wish. We studied it together, going over all the names. But she seemed tired and a little sad. After a while, my mother looked up at me and said, "You take it." I asked her if she was sure. "Yes, you keep it, take care of it," she said with finality. With that, she designated me the keeper of our kin, of its archive, and of all the memories and stories I might assemble from it. At home in New York, I photographed the book and saved the images as one PDF file, which I shared with other members of our extended family. I titled it the "Book of Siblings."

# THIRTY-TWO

# Very Old Parents

**My mother was in her early nineties** when it occurred to her that she might have been wrong all along. She tried to explain it to me one day standing in her kitchen. "The knife I used to see at night when I woke up and went to the kitchen for water . . ." She looked at me for recognition. "Now I realize that Poly hadn't left it out for me to see. He wasn't threatening me or warning me about what he might do. He wasn't," she repeated for effect, or to convince herself. "It was just your father. He left the knife on the table after peeling your apple."

For decades, my mother had hidden knives in fear. Now she seemed to be saying that one of the reasons that she grew so frightened of Poly after he came to live with us in 1980 had not really happened. Had it begun as a mistaken assumption turned the most tragic of misunderstandings?

That couldn't have been all of it, of course. After all, soon after arriving, Poly told her that he was there to ruin her life. He got into fights, stabbed people, beat me, slapped Aixa, threatened to kill the whole family, his girlfriend, and then himself. My mother's fear as she had stared at the knife on the kitchen table was a product of much more than her imagination. But still, I wonder. We all made mistakes; everyone misunderstood and misinterpreted. And all those missteps piled one on top of another, until it all seemed inescapable and insurmountable, the whole tale as dark and bleak as a Hardy novel.

As an old woman, my mother had a newfound confidence in Poly. Poly would never do anything to us, she said. He had changed. Perhaps it was the change in her outlook toward him that began to produce a change in him. Maybe Tía Niña's death had something to do with it, too. He saw my mother differently after that, as an imperfect mother who at ninety-one was necessarily approaching death. He noted her ailments: hypertension, diabetes, heart disease. He noted her appearance: her fingers a little crooked with arthritis; her usually skinny feet now always swollen and purple, as he had seen our grandmother's feet grow before her death, as I imagine mine will be at some point in the future.

My mother had been thinking about her own death for years. On April 20, 2014, three years before Tía Niña died, my mother wrote a letter that she never mailed. She knew her daughters would find it when the time came. For the sake of readability, I've added punctuation.

I write you this for when I am absent. I want you to take $50 [of what] you give me every month and send it to Tía Niña. Send her $150 four times a year, in Dec-March-June-Sept. You send it to

Mr. [x], his phone [x], his address [x] in Hialeah. He charges $15 per $100 for shipping, so it's $172 each time, and they will bring it to her house. Regarding Poly, as always, don't ever abandon him. Make sure he always has a place to sleep (I'm not saying with you, no). You and La Baby [Aixa] are all that he has, and I feel responsible for the fact that he is the way he is. That's why I ask you to help him, thinking of me (even in death, I keep bothering you). About Papy, if I go first, I won't say anything, because I know that you love him very much and will take care of him as he deserves, that he won't be alone. [I ask] that you and La Baby remain united and in touch, at the very least at Christmas. Play dominoes with Nailah and the girls, and I will be happy in Heaven; keep eating the kind of food I cook. I thank God for the children he gave me and the Ramoncito that he gave me. I love you all so much.

Kisses [for] Papy, Poly, Adita, Baby, Gregg, Adrian, Nailah, Alina, and Lucía.

I am waiting for you in Heaven.

In March 2018, almost a year after Tía Niña died, my mother got up to get water in the middle of the night and fell. My father couldn't get her up. Aixa called an ambulance and then called me on the drive over. She phoned me again at around 4 a.m. from the hospital to confirm what we had assumed. My mother had broken her hip. I flew down the next day, heading to the airport straight from my class.

By the time I arrived in the hospital, my mother had made it out of surgery without any problem. But she was not herself. She would not believe us or the doctors when we told her that she couldn't walk yet. She kept trying to get up, but, of course, was unable to. She was hallucinating, talking loudly to a woman she said was standing right in front of her, feeding a little boy, her son. "Give him more spaghetti! That boy is dying of hunger." *Ese niño está muerto de hambre.* Later, she thought she was in line for voting, and the line was too long and moving too slowly. She spat in my face once. A couple of days later when she was riding with me in the medical transport from the hospital to the rehabilitation center, she got ahold of a loose seat belt and tried to hit my head with the buckle. As the drivers wheeled her into the rehab center and waited for the staff to handle the paperwork, she would not stop screaming. All I could do was assure them that she was a very nice person, that she was not usually like this. I spent the night with her in the room sleeping in a chair, and by morning, she had settled down and proven me right.

My mother was at the rehab center for three weeks but would not spend the night alone there. It was a matter of custom and culture. Most of the staff did not speak Spanish. It is a lonely thing to be ill and vulnerable and have to communicate in a language that is not your own. My sister stayed with her most nights. I had to go back to teaching in New York but would fly down after my last class of the week and fly up right before my first to give her a break. The night before giving a public lecture at a university in Miami, I slept in the rehab center with my mother, rushing to check into the hotel in time to iron my blouse and skirt before the event.

To everyone's astonishment, as my mother recovered and learned to walk again, Poly visited three or four times a week, sitting by her side for hours: a stocky, sixty-four-year-old man, a new tremor in his hands, his voice still loud, but maybe a little less angry in timbre. He would bring her sweet snacks and sometimes a scratch-off lottery ticket. One time we were there at the same time, and he agreed to stay a little longer so I could see an old friend for lunch. I thanked him. "No need to thank me," he said. "Of course, I'll help." He realized that he could not take our mother for granted. "Look what had happened to Tía Niña," he added.

When my mother came home from the rehabilitation center, we faced a new problem. My father, about to turn ninety-seven, didn't do anything around the house. My mother, we knew, would still insist on making three meals a day, with dinner as always consisting of at least five separate items: rice, beans, meat, fried plantains, salad. She was walking well again, more or less, but she was not up to resuming her old routines. We also knew that she would never concede that; she would keep doing it until she fell and hurt herself again.

They needed in-home help, lots of it. My parents were poor enough to qualify for Medicaid, and we applied. But approval took ages, and that only covered about sixty hours a week. In the meantime, we scrambled and made do. My sister bore most of the burden: She stayed with them nights and three full weekends a month, sleeping on the couch. Once a month, I would fly in for a few days to give her a short break—it was much less than she needed, but all I could swing while teaching. I regressed when I was there, playing online card games under the blanket, eating peanut M&Ms and gummy bears until my jaw ached.

All that time, I was working on a new book about Cuba, my third. I had started writing it shortly after I took my parents to Cuba in March 2016. When I was with them in Miami, I talked to them in the evenings and weekends about what I was writing, asking them questions as I had done almost my whole life. When caregivers were with them, I took my laptop to work in different coffee shops. One day, I was walking out the door when my father called me back to tell me that I shouldn't wear tops like the one I was wearing that day. It had horizontal stripes. The stripes make you look shorter, he said authoritatively. "I learned that when I used to work at El

Encanto," referring to Havana's once luxurious department store. Never in my life had I heard that he worked there. My mother looked at me as if to signal that he was talking nonsense. But he insisted, adding that he worked in security. As I tried to find out more, his answers became more muddled. Was it before or after Fidel? I asked. After, he said. Was it before or after you met Mami? Before. But he was already with my mother when Castro arrived in Havana, so both of those answers could not be true at once.

The Encanto had been Havana's most iconic department store since its founding in 1888. On April 14, 1961, in the lead-up to the Bay of Pigs invasion, anti-government saboteurs exploded a bomb in the store that destroyed the building, wounded eighteen, and killed one. I reminded my father of that event. Was he there when it happened? I asked. He looked at me, and I could see him trying to read my face, trying, I think, to figure out how to answer. It wasn't a look of cunning or calculation. It was instead the very familiar look of my father wanting to please me, wondering what answer I most wanted to hear. "No," he said, "I wasn't there." "Are you sure?" I pressed. No, was his final answer. He looked so old, so vulnerable. But he was still handsome.

About six months after her hip surgery, my mother had heart surgery, and soon after, a pleurodesis procedure on her left lung. I remember one time, right after a difficult hospital stay, saying to her something like, "It's not easy getting old, is it?" "You have no idea," she responded, before adding that she didn't want to live long enough to get old. *Yo no quiero llegar a vieja.* When I looked at her incredulously, she just said, "You know what I mean, *really* old." Though she bounced back each time, her overall decline was palpable.

Poly came to visit her regularly now, rather than the other way around. He brought her groceries once a month. I think he may have purchased

Mother's Day, 2019.

them with food stamps, and then our mother gave him some cash. He was affectionate and eager to surprise her with the perfect pineapple, a Cuban tamal, a sweet white cake on her birthday. She loved it when he brought his little dog with him. He did that on Mother's Day 2019, and she told me it was her best Mother's Day ever. She continued to call him every night right after *Wheel of Fortune*, which he watched, too. And now he didn't hang up on her. I imagine that when she nagged (she seemed unable not to with any of her children), rather than lash out, he might simply say *Sí, Mima*, roll his eyes, and hold the phone away from his ear, as Aixa and I might have done.

On December 23, 2019, I was in Miami sleeping on my parents' couch when I heard my father go to the kitchen for water. I watched as he walked back to the bedroom, holding on to the wall for stability, his upper back stooped to watch where he stepped. He is so frail, I thought to myself with a little surprise and a lot of sadness. He was almost at his bed when he fell. I called my sister and then 911. My sister came to stay with my mother, and I went with him to the hospital. Doctors confirmed that his hip was broken and insisted that even though he was ninety-eight, he was strong enough for surgery.

That turned out to be true. But he wasn't strong enough for what came after. His mind could not assimilate what had happened. He refused to cooperate with the physical therapists. He spent only two weeks at the rehabilitation center, because he was making no progress at all. My father never walked again. He was such a proud man that I hesitate to write about that period. As anyone who's ever watched a loved one die a slow death knows, many small deaths precede the final one. I tried to be disciplined, matter-of-fact, not to tear up when I saw the sadness in his eyes as I did things for him. I'd smile, then I'd smooth down the wisps of hair on the top of his head and just kiss his forehead.

In the wake of my father's fall and his lack of recovery, my mother declined further, too. Soon, we were having to feed her in her rented hospital bed, the back raised up almost vertical. Every night after dinner, someone—a caregiver or my sister or me, if I was there—would wheel my father to her bed. He would take her hand and hold it, like they were young lovers courting again. This was the same man, after all, who even in his eighties and nineties used to write her notes if he left the house while she was napping. "I love you more than life itself, my love, my life," read one. Maybe my mother had put her lips to the paper before she tucked it into her bible, where I later found it. One night while he was sitting by her bed, he began to cry. My sister found him that way when she entered the room. "What did you say to him?" she asked our mother. She had just told him that he could not remarry after she died. It wasn't her prohibition that had brought him to tears, but the mention of her death with so much certainty. My sister was incredulous—he's almost a hundred years old; he can't walk. Who's going to marry him? But my mother was indignant. Old women would be lining up to marry him, he was so handsome and good. After all those years, he was still her catch. My sister called to tell me about it.

Then COVID came, and everything became more difficult. I was no longer able to fly down to give my sister her short monthly break. As New York City went into lockdown in March 2020, Poly called to check on me. I missed the call, but he ended his voicemail message as he had signed his letters to me when I was a girl: *Tu hermano que siempre te quiere.* Your brother who always loves you. I sent him a picture of myself masked and heading out to walk our dog, Maddy. He gave me a thumbs-up.

My mother's heart failure was worsening, her lungs kept filling with fluid. We didn't want to take her into a hospital in the midst of COVID. She was too vulnerable, and we wouldn't be able to visit her there. If you take her to the hospital, the cardiologist told my sister, you will never see her again. So we arranged in-home hospice care. In the middle of May, my mother took a turn for the worse, and the nurse advised me to get there quickly if I wanted to see her before she passed.

Gregg and I decided that we would rent a car, a place to stay, and all four of us would spend a month there to help and be with my mother. We found a three-bedroom rental in a neighborhood that real estate agents refer to as the Upper East Side. With COVID, it was renting for a fraction of its usual price. I was sitting on a lounge chair by the pool, reading Valeria Luiselli's novel *Lost Children Archive*, when Poly texted that part of the roof of his Hialeah studio apartment had caved in. He sent a photo.

My mother meanwhile revived. The hospice nurse who had summoned me could not believe her turnaround. We were all so grateful. My daughters, Alina and Lucía, painted her nails and combed her hair. If my mother was feeling up to it, Alina or Nailah's boyfriend, Chip, would transfer her from the bed to the wheelchair and bring her to the table for dinner. She would talk the girls into sharing their Coke with her. With her first sip, she would sigh with loud and thorough satisfaction, like a character in a commercial, like one of us should have exclaimed, "Look, Mami likes it!" Once or twice, we played dominoes after dinner, my sister and I on one team, my parents on the other, each of them playing in their respective wheelchairs. Despite her intermittent confusion, my mother seemed happy and light. Sometimes I lay down next to her in bed, my head on her shoulder as if I was still a young girl. Over and over, we listened to her new favorite song, Mercedes Sosa's rendition of "Gracias a la Vida." *Gracias a la vida que me ha dado tanto.* Thank you to life, which has given me so much. Sometimes when the song ended, she would say, *otra vez.* Again. I watched her eyes as she listened, feeling like I could see through them. I had always wanted to do that; maybe I became a historian in order to do that. I sat there looking at her eyes, picturing what the song's words conjured in her mind, knowing with absolutely certainty that when the lyrics mentioned the depths of a lover's light eyes, my mother saw the depths of my father's. And in that moment, she had no regrets at all.

Every night, when I asked her if she wanted to talk to Poly, she perked up and said *¡Claro!* Of course! I would dial the number, chat with him, and then hold the phone to her ear. It was hard for her to hold it on her own. She wanted to know how he was, what he had for dinner, if he'd watched *Wheel of Fortune.* He called her *Mamita linda,* encouraging her to eat well, so that she would regain her strength. He sounded like he had in his long-ago letters, when he told her she looked too skinny in the pictures and that she needed to eat and gain weight.

One day during our long visit, a hospice nurse, a Cuban woman, told me that my mother wasn't letting go because of us. "She clings to you so dearly," she observed. After a month in Miami, I returned home to New York with Gregg and the girls. My mother had not died, despite her care team's initially urgent prediction. I called her almost every night, but she was often too sleepy to talk. Sometimes, I found it too depressing to call. Occasionally, I rang Poly for no reason. We joked about our mother's new loopiness. One time, he complained of chest pain, attributing it to his new diabetes medicine, and I told him to get it checked out. I sent him money without his asking. It felt a little like love.

# THIRTY-THREE

# Final Journey

**He died alone, as he always feared** he would.

On August 4, 2020, Aixa received a call from a Hialeah detective asking whether she was Poly's sister. The detective was on his way to her office. Aixa called me, worried that something had happened to Poly, or that he had reverted to his old ways. At her office, the detective told her that Poly had been found dead in his apartment, sitting on the toilet. He had been there for days before a neighbor reported the smell. His body was so bloated that the medical examiner could not lift prints from his fingers. It was the metal plate in his skull, placed there after the beating he had suffered on the streets in the early 1990s, that helped the forensics team confirm his identity. The medical examiner ruled out suicide and murder, recording hypertensive crisis as the cause of death. It was a horrible end, seeming almost designed to validate Poly's accusations against us: We had never been there for him. He had never been one of us. He was all alone.

Aixa and I discussed how best to break the news to our mother. I offered to be there via Zoom or FaceTime, but my mother's medical team thought it best not to tell her. She was confused and sleeping most of the time anyway. When she asked to call Poly, which was no longer every night, she was not usually lucid enough to notice when my sister or a caregiver changed the subject. So, we postponed the decision, giving ourselves time to deal with the logistics of his death, navigating the long COVID delays as we tried to figure out what to do with his mortal remains, all the while dreading having to give our mother the news.

Then her hospice nurse summoned me again. If I wanted to see my mother, now was the time. On the afternoon of August 16, I flew to Miami, wearing blue rubber gloves and two masks beneath a face shield. I recall scolding a woman on the plane for wearing her mask under her nose. It was nightfall when I arrived at the apartment. My father and a caregiver were watching television in the living room. My mother was asleep in the bedroom, a male nurse seated by her side, the portrait of Poly as a boy on the dresser.

In the morning, she was worse, her breathing more labored. The hospice nurse gave me instructions on when and how to administer morphine, how to count the rise and fall of her belly, now smooth and large under her pajama top, almost as if she was leaving this earth carrying a child once more.

Late the next afternoon, August 17, her hospice nurse knew that this time it was real. I was downstairs dealing with a telephone repairman. My sister called me to come up. We all gathered around my mother: my sister, Nailah, my mother's caregiver, and me. My father lay on the other twin bed in the room, his eyes open and staring at the ceiling. I held my mother's left hand, Aixa her right. I bent down to her ear and told her what she had always told me, that everything would be all right. I promised to keep sending money to her people in Cuba, those who remained. I said we would take care of our father. I told her she was the best mother in the world, that I adored her. My sister, holding her other hand, said the same things. Then, as I stroked her hair, I told her a lie. "We will take care of Poly," I said. "We won't abandon him."

Did her brow furrow when I said that? Did her eyes seek something from under their lids? Was it anxiety? Guilt? Or did I just imagine it?

She died a few minutes later. Everyone cried except for me. I just went and sat in the bathroom alone for a while, until the telephone repairman called to remind me that he was still waiting downstairs. I'm sorry, I said, my mother just died.

On this journey, my mother and my brother went together. How they struggled, she and him. As for me, I am the one left behind to remember and to wonder if he ever forgave us.

# THIRTY-FOUR

# Mysteries of a Silence

**Deep inside the wooden cabinet** of my mother's sewing machine, Aixa found our inheritance. It consisted of three small white envelopes, each one sealed tight, marked with a name, and followed by a short message. *Para Adita de Mami. Te quiero.* Another: *Para Aixa de Mami. Te quiero.* I can't remember if on Poly's she wrote Poly or Polito, but the message was the same: *Te quiero.* I love you. My mother had stacked the three envelopes one atop the other, then wrapped them all together using invisible packing tape, which she decorated with shiny Christmas stickers. Aixa and I laughed a little over how the whole thing was just so her. Inside each envelope was $3,000 in cash. We divided Poly's money equally among each of the granddaughters: Aixa's Nailah, my Alina and Lucía.

I went back to New York, and eleven days after my mother died, I began writing. August 28, 2020, 8:14 a.m. is the date and time I created a Word document titled "mami poly short memoir." In the mornings that followed, I woke up, set my coffee down next to my computer, and wrote. It was all I felt motivated to do. I wrote without revising, doing a little research as I went. I looked at a map of Marianao to describe our family house's physical proximity to the military hospital, even though I knew it by heart. I looked on ancestry.com for a record of my mother's entry into this country, but I found only my father's. Online, I happened on a collection of photographs from Eglin Air Force Base, where Poly had begun his American life in 1980, and I scoured them for traces of him. I did online criminal background checks to reconstruct some of his arrests, printing out what I found on single sheets and organizing them chronologically so that I could write about them accurately. The essay I speed-wrote in the immediate wake of my brother's and mother's deaths, I eventually published in *The New Yorker*. I asked my father's permission after the fact. I told him that I was writing a story of our family and that I would get paid for it. "Was that okay?" I knew he would say yes. If I had asked him again the next day, he would not have remembered the conversation. It was what happened when I won a Pulitzer for my book on Cuba and the United States. I was heartbroken not to be able to share the news with my mother. My sister joked that I could tell my father every day, and he would congratulate me like he'd never heard it before, because in his mind, he hadn't. I felt too sad to do it for more than two or three days.

·   ·   ·

After my mother died, my father could not stop crying. His dementia made him forget that she was gone. At night, sometimes he'd call for her or talk to her as if she was still in a bed next to his. His voice got louder and louder. When the caregiver asked him what was wrong, he said, "I was talking to Adela, but she wasn't answering." Sometimes at night he said "hello" over and over. It was more like he sang it, turning the *o* at the end into two syllables, his voice going up a few notes on the second. At night when I was visiting and lying on the couch trying to sleep to the soundtrack of his strange chant, I always ignored it for a while, hoping he'd just fall asleep. But inevitably, I would get up, worried that something was wrong, and peek into his bedroom to ask if he was okay. He would respond, "Yes, why?" Nothing, I always said.

One weekday while a caregiver was with him, I went to the archives, the Cuban Heritage Collection at the University of Miami. They had a collection related to the Encanto department store, the one that was destroyed in 1961 and where my father had recently and mysteriously announced that he had once worked. My mother had said it wasn't true. I wanted proof one way or another. But it eluded me: there was no sign of my father in the records. Back at his bedside, I told him some of what I'd found and showed him some photos I'd taken. He added a few things to his story—that he had worked in the men's department, the shirts section, he said. (I had just shown him a photograph of that department.) He also mentioned that he had taken a friend from his home province to the store and that they had been hired together, but he couldn't remember the man's name. I told him that a few of the documents I had read mentioned sabotage, that after Castro's government nationalized the store in October 1960, some employees showed their displeasure by scratching the silver and taking scissors to the Christian Dior dresses in the French salon. He said he remembered that. I asked him if he participated. "No, I wasn't into that," he responded.

I think it was on that same trip that I began sorting the papers he kept behind his recliner. What a surprise it was to discover not only how *much* he had written, but also how many different kinds of things he had written—the poems and the prayer, the letters to Fidel and the people of Cuba, or of Miami. It was also only then, on seeing how much he and Juan José had written to each other over the years, that it dawned on me how much my father would have missed him.

Among the papers I found was a notebook that my daughters had given him for Christmas in 2004. On its first page he wrote, "In this notebook that I have just received from my two beautiful granddaughters Alina and Lucía, I propose to write the diary of my life, which I will baptize with the name 'Mysteries of a Silence,' mystery, because I have never been able to understand the scope of the secret that produced it, and silence because for many years action to reveal the mystery in question has been blocked." I have no idea what he was talking about. He left the pages that followed mostly blank.

Every time I visited, I tried giving him the notebook to see if he would write again. My sister sometimes did the same thing. "I'll write it down," she begged, "you can just dictate." One day, he recited a poem of his own invention, and she transcribed it just as he said it, in Spanish. I reproduce part of it here in my own translation. But I didn't have to translate the word *beautiful*, because that one for some reason my father said in English.

I have before me

A pretty vase of flowers

With white, red, green, and yellow petals.

They are *beautiful*

They asked me to write more
But frankly, what I want to do
Is tell my daughter
To go to hell.

He and Aixa would have laughed together. The rest of the notebook is completely empty.

Whenever I visited, I spent time sitting in a recliner next to his rented hospital bed. I'd extend my hand and take his, and we'd just be quiet together. One day I asked him about his letters to Fidel Castro. How did you get Fidel's address? I asked. He told me he had just figured it out. I asked if Fidel ever replied. He said he couldn't remember ever having received a response. I asked him what he had said to Fidel in the letters. He paused, then said sheepishly *cualquiera se equivoca*. Anyone can make a mistake. But I don't know if he meant that the mistake had been his (in writing to Castro at all) or Fidel's (in making the revolution as he had).

Another day, sitting in the same manner, our hands linked together on the edge of his bed, I thanked him for bringing me to the United States. I have never quite felt one with this country, but I know with absolute certainty that I have made a life here that would have been inaccessible to me in Cuba. That day, I pondered aloud with my father what might have happened if he hadn't brought me to the United States when he did. Maybe I would have left later as an adult; maybe I'd be trying to leave now, I said, across the US-Mexico border, as so many Cubans were then doing. Maybe, I added, I wouldn't have made it; who knows what might have happened? So, I thanked him again, and he looked pleased. It was more intense than pleasure. He looked into my eyes like I was the proof of something.

A little while later, my father resumed the conversation unprompted.

"I wonder what would have happened if I hadn't left when I did?" he wondered aloud. "Maybe Fidel's people would have killed me." The statement didn't surprise me exactly; I had heard milder versions of it before. I asked him what he had done to make anyone want to kill him. He looked at me, his eyes unsettled, confused. "I'm not saying they would have killed me, maybe not, I don't know." Was it the paranoia of a very old man? Or was it provoked by the memory of something real? And will I ever know?

My father died on September 8, 2022, the feast day of La Caridad del Cobre, and the same day that Queen Elizabeth died. I think he would have liked that. He had received his COVID vaccine exactly one day before she got hers, and we all used to joke how he had beaten a queen to it. I was there when he died, so was Aixa, as we had both been when our mother passed. We were standing by his bed talking to a priest from the hospice service who had just arrived. We introduced him to our father, who looked up at the stranger and smiled. A minute or two later, I glanced away from the priest and noticed that my father's chest was no longer rising and falling. It was all very peaceful, no distress, no need for morphine, not even a whispered goodbye. He just stopped breathing and was gone. He was a hundred and one.

# History's Remains

**In 2024, my younger daughter,** Lucía, went to Havana for about three weeks as part of a January-term course at NYU. It was her idea, but it pleased me, just as it would have pleased my parents. Most mornings, Lucía went for a walk by herself along the Malecón. A few times, she saw a man dressed in scuba gear, and she smiled at him. On the way back to the residence where the students were all staying, she used to stop by a little park where a group of older women always exercised. Lucía chatted with them, joined them for a few stretches sometimes. While she was in Cuba, she made a present for me: a handmade book written in Spanish. It wasn't as fancy as the ones she made in New York, because she didn't have access to many materials in Havana. In her Cuban book, there is a story about the exercising women she befriended and another about the man in the scuba suit. She titled that one "Wizard" (*Mago*). Another chapter in the book, she tells me, is nonfiction. In it, Lucía is on the plane from Miami to Havana, and she feels the presence of my parents so strongly that it is almost as if they were occupying the two empty seats next to her, keeping her company, occasionally grabbing her knee, enjoying her adventure, protecting her.

Meanwhile, my older daughter, Alina, who is a photographer, is working on a project she calls "The Box." The box is an archival box, an invented box that a researcher might find in an archive. (I can't help but love the idea. She is, after all, the same girl who once played hide-and-seek among the document bundles of a provincial archive while I worked.) In Alina's box are old press photos that she purchased on eBay mixed in with her own photographs, staged to look like historical ones. Many of the photos have something to do with Cuba. One shows men in suits gathered around maps—US leaders during the Bay of Pigs or the Missile Crisis. It might be a real photo or a staged one. There are real and staged photos of family reunifications, of Cuban mothers hugging their sons, wives kissing their husbands, a daughter embracing an aging mother, all after long separations. Another photo, historical, depicts Tatá's hero Arnaldo Tamayo, the Cuban cosmonaut who in 1980 became the first Latin American and the first Black person in space. Alina hopes to go to Cuba for the project someday to take photos, to talk to people, maybe even to find the now elderly Cuban man who in space preferred to take photographs out the spacecraft's window than to sleep.

It surprises me, my daughters' connection to a place where they have never lived. Despite sometimes taking them to Cuba, I don't think I've forced it on them. But maybe because it is so much with me and they love me, they let themselves feel its pull.

. . .

After my parents died, I found it harder to travel to Cuba. I felt as nervous about the prospect as I had decades earlier, when I first started going. On those earlier occasions, I had often felt like I was recording the place with my eyes to show my parents the imaginary film on my return. It had felt as if they were a little with me, like two figures accidentally caught in the reflection of a mirror, looking at me, watching me flourish, watching me struggle. What would it feel like now to be in Cuba without my parents anywhere in this world?

As of this writing, I have been back to Cuba only twice since their passing. On the first of those trips, I flew directly to Santa Clara where Juan José's son, Alain, picked me up at the airport. All of Juan José's family was waiting for me at Alain's house in Remedios—everyone except Juan José, of course, who had been gone already for over ten years. Also absent was Juan José's only granddaughter, Amalia, who as a little girl used to catch him reading and writing in the bathroom in the middle of the night. Today a young woman of twenty-six, she is in the United States. Amalia made the excruciating decision that so many from around the world feel forced to make everyday: to leave the people they love most in the world and launch themselves into a future that is as uncertain as the one back home feels hopeless.

Amalia was in Miami when I stopped there on my way to Cuba that trip. I sent her money ahead of time, and she went out and bought gifts for everyone back home. Maybe she bought more for her mother, Aymara, whom she adored. In Remedios, I sat on the bed with Aymara and Hildita, Juan José's widow, as I took things out of my suitcase. They held up this and that; they peeked inside the pockets of Aymara's new purse to see what treat Amalia might have hidden there. At everything, they oohed with delight, remarking on her taste, her thoughtfulness, her instinct for knowing just what to send. And they reached out to touch me as they did that, as if for a moment it was Amalia sitting before them and not me. It was a familiar ritual. I had done it many times, except now I was the bridge not between my mother and Tía Niña, but between other family members still early into their separation.

That visit with Juan José's family felt magical; it felt a little like my first trip to meet them in the summer of 1990. We stayed up late, talked, laughed, played dominoes, went for walks. I taught them how to fry eggs without so much oil; they introduced me to smoked *jutía*, technically a rodent, I suppose. But it was what Cuban soldiers in the independence wars I'd written about had eaten in their rebel camps, what my grandmother, Rita, might have eaten as an orphan in wartime. So I tried it. Aymara gave me some of Juan José's things: a bag of letters that my father had sent him, his badge and pin from his time in the Literacy Campaign. I am their keeper for now.

We missed Amalia; I know they did even more than me. Amalia, Juan José's granddaughter, cannot visit Cuba. She aches to see her mother, her grandmother, her father, her uncle, cousins. She doesn't have any close friends to visit there, because, like her, they are in the United States now, or in Spain. She uses WhatsApp to see and talk to her family in Cuba every day, sometimes several times a day. It is much easier now than when my parents left, and letters were the principal means of communication. But if Amalia ever has a daughter, that daughter will never be able to retrieve the exchanges across the hollow of family separation.

From Remedios, I went to Havana. I cannot imagine visiting Cuba and not going to Havana. I love Havana, even though it hurts to see so much of it in ruins, so much worse even than when I started going there in 1990. This was my first time going to Havana without visiting the old house by the military hospital. Leanet, Carlitos's daughter who stayed there after Tía Niña died, had left the country in 2020. She sold the house to help finance her relocation to Spain. The house where our family had lived for about seventy years was now a house full of strangers. I didn't even bother to make a trip there.

One place I did go on that trip was my other anchor in Havana: the National Archives. Truly, I don't know how to be in Havana without going there. I didn't find much by way of documents that time, but I did notice how much more crowded the reading room was. Most of the visitors were there looking for evidence of Spanish grandparents so they could take advantage of Spain's Law of Memory, which provides Spanish residency for people with Spanish parents or grandparents. People were there, in other words, looking for a way out.

I think it was my loneliest trip to Havana ever. Two good friends were traveling out of the country. Someone else was sick. A few had died; more had left permanently. One thing that is hard about going to Havana over so many decades is that you keep having to make connections and friends in waves. The people who were my friends during my earliest trips are almost all gone; the ones who haven't died are mostly in the United States and Spain. The friends I made in the next stage of my travels there are now gone, too, with the same destinations. I've heard it before from people who live or lived there; I've read it in documents in the archives. "One gets tired of always saying goodbye." On this trip, I did a book presentation on my then most recent book, *Cuba: An American History*, a book, like me, always between two places. Someone in the audience rose to ask a question. But it was more of a comment. She wished that her grandson, who had recently left the country, might return, as I had.

One day during that trip, after a morning in the archives, I went back to Vedado, still and always my favorite neighborhood in Havana. I was on my own for lunch, something that very rarely happened in all my many trips there. I ate at a place with tables on a second-floor terrace facing the Malecón. I could eat looking out to sea, watching spray from the waves skim the surface of the famed sea wall. Sitting there contemplating the view, I suddenly asked myself, "What am I still doing here? Have I not given enough to this place? Must I always come back?" And as I posed those questions, I truly did not know the answer.

Before the end of the year, however, I was back. I had to steel myself to do it, but I had a purpose that helped me do that: to find more material for this book. I traveled to my mother's home province, to the provincial archive in the city of Pinar del Río. They had not had water in twenty-one days, but I found a few things there, hints to my grandmother's life as an orphan in wartime. I went to San Cristóbal and Chirigota, where I photographed the ruins of a house that once belonged to the family who owned the land on which my grandparents raised my mother and her siblings. I want to go back to the province again, this time farther west to see the place where my grandmother was born, to see if it is true, as I wrote here, that when she looked north, she might have seen the mountains.

But really, what I most wanted to do on that trip was to find more family archives. I had recently read some of my old notes from my first trip to Cuba in 1990. And in them, I found confirmation of a vague memory: I had seen piles of my mother's letters to Poly in Tía Niña's closet in the old house by the military hospital. What had happened to those letters and to all the other papers Tía Niña had stored in that closet when Leanet migrated and sold the house?

Leanet assured me that she had packed them all up and left them with a friend in Havana for safekeeping. I made arrangements to visit that friend. I was so nervous, excited to find this piece of my mother, to read what she had written about her early life in the United States, to know what she told Poly in those first years of their separation.

Leanet's friend was lovely: funny, smart, gracious. She had great Cuban art on her walls and a poster from a film her son had directed. We chatted easily. But we needed help to get to the stuff Leanet had left with her. It was all stored in a large enclosed loft that made use of the apartment's extra-tall ceilings for storage. There were two entrances to it, both reachable only with a ladder. She called a friend who had one; he was tall and skinny and also willing to climb it. One of the ladder's hinges or spreaders was missing, replaced with a fraying bungee cord. I spotted the man as he stood at the top and wrenched open the door to the strange closet. Inside were dozens of overstuffed garbage bags and a smaller number of cardboard boxes.

"My cousin left you all that?" I asked her friend. No, she explained, the stuff belonged to many friends, all people who'd left the country and deposited their things with her for safekeeping in case life abroad didn't work, in case they had to return for some reason.

It wasn't new, the drive to do this: the reluctance to discard a present that was not yet past, this uneasy hedging of bets on an unknown future. Cubans had been doing it for generations. At the beginning of the revolution, people who fled sometimes left their possessions with neighbors and friends so the government would not confiscate them. They deposited them also with a certainty that they would be back, that Fidel Castro and his revolution would not last, that this place they knew so well would be theirs once more. I had seen a place like that once, the home of someone long ago designated as a custodian for the valuables of others: French china, Portuguese linens, nineteenth-century women's fans, oil paintings of people descended from Spanish nobility, of people who had made their fortunes in sugar and slavery. Eerie as Miss Havisham's house, the home was a dusty monument to a world long ago abandoned and disappeared.

The only treasure I expected to find in my new friend's closet in a ceiling was my mother's letters, perhaps some old photographs, maybe some of Tía Niña's papers, as well. One by one, the man on the ladder began handing everything down, all these objects that Cubans leaving today deemed worth saving. He passed down the large bags first; they were easier to reach than the boxes. I opened the first bag and found used clothing. The next one had a stack of towels, the top one frayed at the edge. Then came a bag stuffed with wire hangers. Two, three, four bags full of hangers. Looking at everything gathering around me, I understood that these were the ruins of a revolution, the remains of history.

I left the house feeling a terrible sadness, feeling the burden of knowing that history and loss were irreversible. My mother's old letters, our family's old photographs might still turn up somewhere. But I doubt it. Leanet left a few things with a different friend, but that friend, too—a man of his time—has left the island for good.

So many people have left that it is hard to say exactly how many. The last Cuban census, conducted in 2012, put the country's population at 11.2 million. Everyone agrees that the number has dropped considerably. A recent estimate from the Cuban government puts the figure at 9.7 million. One demographer says the number is even lower, 8.6 million. If true, that would suggest a population loss of 23 percent, a staggering statistic. But without a census—which keeps getting postponed for lack of resources—it is impossible to know.

Data publicly available from the US Customs and Border Patrol, meanwhile, shows that almost 650,000 Cubans arrived at the US-Mexico border in just three years (2022–2024). That number does not count all those Cubans who arrived in the United States by other means, by sea or aboard planes with visas or parole documents in hand. Neither, obviously, does it count the very significant number of Cubans who have moved to Spain or the smaller numbers turning up in Brazil, Italy, Uruguay, Russia, Turkey, and beyond. Whatever the exact number of people who have left the island in recent years, it is—by far—the largest exodus in Cuban history.

If the press in Cuba was free, it would be material for front page news. Eventually, it will be the stuff of history. All I know for certain is that when I'm in Cuba now, the Malecón feels empty.

I think of my new friend's closet, the overstuffed bags full of bent hangers and old towels belonging to people who have scattered to the winds. I picture the travelers getting ready for their journeys, packing up those same bags, some saying goodbye to their loved ones, others not daring to. Everyone who departs leaves a wake of separation. But wake is not the right word. It describes something behind you. The separation, though, is everywhere. It is your present. You fear it is your future. And as the years pass, you realize that it is all the unshared days in either direction.

Juan José's granddaughter, Amalia, sent me a song late last year: "Ilegal" by Grupo Recluta, which tells the story of a young man, a boy really, who makes the trek across the border and the desert. *Un abrazo de mamá deseé mil veces*, he sings. A hug from Mamá I wished for a thousand times. How could Amalia not feel that, video-calling home, seeing in her mother's eyes the toll of her own decision, even though she does not regret it?

And I know when I talk to her, or to her mother in Cuba, that my parents' story of migration and separation finds an echo in theirs. With countless variations, versions of our story belong also to the million and more Cubans who have left the island over the last few years. It belongs to people from countless other places who trek across borders, climb onto perilous rafts, or simply board a plane to leave places that they call home.

As I write this, I think of all of them: the ones today, the ones earlier, in Poly's time and in my parents', and long before that, in the time of Encarnación, the woman wrenched from her people and marched onto a ship to cross the Atlantic in chains. This story is for them—for us—before, now, always. It is my declaration of love to all those who have had to abandon their homes for whatever reason, my plea for forgiveness from all the loved ones left behind and hurt by our leaving. This is me: an American woman, ever the immigrant daughter, clamoring to the wind that we were here, that we still are, that we will always be.

# Acknowledgments

This has not been an easy one for me to write. I am eternally grateful that I did not always have to do it alone. Several friends and colleagues read all or parts of earlier drafts: Martha Jones, Sara Johnson, Ana Dopico, Kate Tuttle, and Marisa Silver. For their feedback, for telling me to keep going, for assuring me that it was okay for me to write this—that it was good that I was writing this—I am deeply and forever thankful. For years, decades even, I have been talking about family, history, and writing with Martha Hodes, Martha Jones, and Sara Johnson. Stéphane Gerson, Leslie Harris, and Kendra Fields graciously extended invitations to participate in broader conversations about historians and their families. What a privilege it has been to share this project with them, to share the intellectual and personal anxieties that come with the territory.

I am grateful for the many conversations I've had about this project with an enviable group of friends and colleagues: Kerri Arsenault,

Carmen Barcia, Monique Bedasse, Yarimar Bonilla, Odette Casamayor, Nathan Connolly, Ava Chin, Arlene Davila, Lillian Guerra, Aleksandar Hemon, Jennifer Morgan, Debora Munczek, Ladane Nasseri, Miriam Pensack, Lisandro Pérez, Julia Rodas, Romy Sánchez, Sarah Schulman, Rebecca Scott, Martín Sivak, Alexander Stephens, Emily Stokes, and Natasha Trethewey. For help fact-checking and more, I thank the wonderful Elina San Blas.

Several institutions have been enormously helpful to me in this endeavor. I started drafting this book at the Oxford Centre for Life-Writing at Wolfson College, Oxford University. It was the perfect place and the perfect company. Very special writing time at MacDowell in New Hampshire, The Writers Room in New York City, and Easton's Nook in Newark were all invaluable at different stages of the process. At NYU, the work of the Asylum H-Lab, directed by Sibylle Fischer and Ellen Noonan, first let me see the potential of Alien Files for this project. My thanks to them, as well as to Benjamin Schmidt and Bita Mousavi for their guidance.

My team at Scribner has been fantastic: Emily Polson, Kathy Belden, Nan Graham, Jason Chappell, and especially my editor, Colin Harrison. I wasn't always happy when Colin asked me to dig deeper but I now know that he was right, and for that I thank him. My agent, Gail Ross, was there from proposal to publication, always ready with sage advice, support, and humor. My thanks to them, and to my publicists Whitney Peeling and Kate Lloyd at Broadside and Paul Samuelson and Mark Galarrita at Scribner, for all their work on this book's behalf.

I have never met Luis Cabrera, the distant relative who found me on 23andMe. But his knowledge of family history and of ancestors we share in common led me to discoveries I would have never made otherwise. I am endlessly grateful to him, as well as to genealogist extraordinaire

Lourdes Del Pino, who should be a national treasure here and in Cuba. Thanks to Marial Iglesias and Skip Gates for leading me to her.

Many relatives have put up with my seemingly random questions. I thank and love all of them: Adrian, Gladys, Miriam, Carlitos, Eladio, Rachel, María Elena, Madelyn, Jesús Alberto, Isabel, and Leanet. Juan José's family—especially Amalia, Alain, Aymara, and Hildita—have become a more important part of my life as I've written this book, and for that I am thankful. I know it would have made Juan José happy. Nailah, my niece and goddaughter, has long been one of my favorite people on earth. She has answered my questions, given me advice, and just listened. I love imagining her beautiful son, Herbert Lee Polite III, someday reading this book and learning about his Cuban ancestors. My mother would have adored him. Gregg's parents, Lani and David, have always been a source of support and calm; whether in Maine or Florida, their home is a haven. There are many other family members who are now gone: my grandmother Rita Blanco and her ancestors, my other grandparents, a score of aunts and uncles. And, of course, there are my two brothers: Poly and Juan José. I don't know how they would feel about my writing this book. But it is a testament of my love for them.

The thing I have absolutely loved about writing this book—the thing I will most miss when I'm finished with it—is that it has become a strange sanctuary where every morning I get to spend a few hours with my departed parents. To them I owe everything. I hope I have done them justice here; I hope I have not offended their memory. Here I write what I say to them almost every day in my head, "Thank you. I love you always."

I may have been the keeper of the family in terms of papers and stories, but my sister Aixa was the family's keeper in the truest sense. She lived near my parents, near Poly. She was the one who always had to do everything: drive them places, show up when someone felt ill, talk to law-yers and social workers, sleep on my parents' couch and take care of them in the final years of their lives. It was material labor and hard emotional labor. I know that dealing with my insistent, sometimes unwelcome ques-tions was emotional labor, too. I thank her with all my heart. If there is one silver lining to the passing of our parents, it is that she and I can now travel the world—or parts of it anyway—together.

My husband, Gregg, and my daughters, Alina and Lucía, have lived with this book more intensely than with any I have written before. They also appear in its pages, another new experience. They have listened and read, built me up when I needed, and brought me back to the present when I most needed that. They make me possible. All my love to them always and forever.

# Notes

**Abbreviations Used in Notes**

A-File: Alien File

AC: Author's Collection

ANC: Archivo Nacional de Cuba

CHC: Cuban Heritage Collection, University of Miami

EAFB, CRR: Eglin Air Force Base, Historian Background Files Concerning
Cuban Refugee Resettlement

FOIA: Freedom of Information Act

L.: Libro

NARA: National Archives and Records Administration (US)

NS: Nailah Summers

NYPL: New York Public Library

NYT: *New York Times*

RG: Record Group

USCIS: United States Citizenship and Immigration Services

v.: verso

## Prologue: In My Mother's Arms

2 **$5 and thirty pounds of luggage:** María Cristina García, *Havana, USA: Cuban Exiles and Cuban Americans in South Florida, 1959–1994* (University of California Press, 1996), 17–18.

3 **Painful heels, no money:** My mother told me these stories all the time. On April 20, 2012, she sat down for a recorded oral history interview with my niece Nailah Summers, then a student at the University of Florida. The interview became part of the Samuel Proctor Oral History Program Collection at the University of Florida. (Hereafter NS interview with my mother.)

4 **limestone fountains:** This description borrows from Cristina Rivera Garza, *Liliana's Invincible Summer: A Sister's Search for Justice* (Hogarth, 2023), 7.

4 **Every week my father sent money:** NS interview with my mother; Letter from Concepción to my mother, September 20, 1966, AC.

4 **earning $48 a week:** Nat Manley to Whom it May Concern, May 14, 1963, in my mother's A-File, USCIS, FOIA Request.

4 **$60 weekly:** Victor [illeg] to US Consular Service, May 3, 1963, in my mother's A-File, USCIS, FOIA Request.

4 **the US Consulate issued:** Immigrant Visa and Registration, June 28, 1963, in my mother's A-File, USCIS, FOIA.

4 **Then on July 1:** Our naturalization certificates give July 1, 1963, as our date of entry.

5 **my mother ran into an old acquaintance:** I heard this story many times; she repeated it in NS interview with my mother. José (Bebo) Zamora appears in several photos in the Cuban Refugee Center Archives housed at the CHC.

8 **published an essay about it:** "My Brother's Keeper," *The New Yorker*, March 1, 2021, 26–31.

13 **because I can and they can't:** Edwidge Danticat, *Brother, I'm Dying* (Vintage, 2008), 26.

## 1. Rita, Mother of Our Mother

18 **to reflect the sun's light:** Padre Joaquín Gaiga, *No sólo de tabaco: apuntes para la historia de San Luis de Occidente* (Ediciones Vital, 2006), 29.

19 **"mantles of emerald":** Antonio María de Paula Arias, *El veguero de Vuelta Abajo: Apuntes sobre el cultivo de tabaco* (Vives, 1887), 57.

19 **The word *pardo*:** Esteban Pichardo, *Diccionario provincial casi razonado de vozes cubanas*, 3rd edition (La Antilla, 1862), 200.

19   **The brief handwritten entry:** Parroquía San Joaquín, San Luis, Pinar del Río, Libro 4 de Bautismos de Pardos y Morenos, f. 14, n. 35.

19   **a cobbler, who merely repaired shoes:** The Spanish term in the record for Juan's profession is *obra prima*, rather than *zapatero*.

20   **(father unknown):** Juan Blanco's birth year comes from his baptismal record. Parroquía de San Rosendo, Pinar del Río, Libro 10, Bautismos de Pardos y Morenos, n. 2704.

20   **Secundina Blanco, a *parda ingenua*:** Parroquía de San Rosendo, Pinar del Río, Libro 10, Bautismos de Pardos y Morenos, n. 2704.

21   **the matriarch of the clan:** ANC, Gobierno General, Leg. 278, exp. 13716. Padrón General de habitantes del Término Municipal de San Luis, 1886.

21   **Encarnación Carabalí:** Parroquía de San Joaquín, *Libro de Entierros de Pardos y Morenos*, L. 1, f. 189v, n. 879.

21   **a boy she named Epifanio:** Epifanio's birth record has not turned up, but he appears as the father to more than a dozen children. Lourdes Del Pino Report, February 17, 2025.

21   **all of them born into slavery:** I calculated Inés's birth year by using her age at the time of the censuses of 1861 (ANC, Fondo Gobierno General, Leg. 263, exp. 13475) and 1886 (ANC, Gobierno General, Leg. 278, exp. 13716). For the births of the children: Parroquía de San Joaquín, *Libro de Bautismos de Pardos y Morenos*, L. 1, f. 22, n. 155 (Matilde), f. 33v, n. 202 (Lucía), f. 61, n. 314 (María del Pilar), f. 75, n. 368 (Raimundo Enrique).

21   **In 1851, Encarnación buried:** Parroquía de San Joaquín, *Libro de Defunciones de Pardos y Morenos*, L. 1, f. 22v, n. 156.

21   **Inés among them—also now free:** 1861 Census, ANC, Fondo Gobierno General, Leg. 263, exp. 13475.

22   **the priest added a single word:** Parroquía de San Joaquín, *Libro de Entierros de Pardos y Morenos*, L. 1, f. 189v, n. 879.

22   ***Pobre.* Poor:** Parroquía de San Joaquín, Libro 1, Defunciones de Pardos y Morenos, no. 90. The marginal comment indicates that he was twenty-three years old, but he was in fact twenty, having been born in 1868, according to his baptismal record Parroquía de San Rosendo, Pinar del Río, L. 10 de Bautismos de Pardos y Morenos, n. 2704.

26   **old books of the church:** *Provincia de Pinar del Río* (Editorial Santiago, 1978), 17, 168; Goltrán Pérez, *San Juan y Martínez: Pequeña historia de un pueblo grande* (New York, 1974), 6, 11, 17–18, 31.

26   **reconcentration:** Guadalupe García, "Urban *Guajiros*: Colonial Reconcentration, Rural Displacement, and Criminalization in Western Cuba, 1895–1902," *Journal of Latin American Studies* 43 (2011): 216.

26 **smallpox and yellow fever:** Emeterio Santovenia, *Pinar del Río* (Fondo de Cultura Económica, 1946), 187.

26 **fifteen thousand died:** Francisco Pérez Guzmán, *La herida profunda* (Ediciones Unión, 1998), 96.

26 **no space to bury the dead:** Pérez Guzmán, *La herida*, 101.

27 **many reconcentrated children:** Archivo Provincial de Pinar del Río, Gobierno Civil de la Provincia, Secretaría de Guerra. Leg. 80, exp. 553. *Expediente que contiene comunicación sobre los niños huérfanos afectados por la reconcentración.* See also Pérez Guzmán, *La herida*, 105.

27 **one local historian:** Luis Osvaldo Escobar, *Ensayo histórico de San Luis de Occidente* (Miami, 1979), 76.

27 **She was so hungry:** Conversation with my cousin Carlitos, Havana, December 2, 2023.

27 **tobacco and sugar cane:** Gaiga, *No sólo de tabaco*, 157.

27 **aunt to Rita:** I have pieced this together through correspondence with Luis Cabrera, the great-grandson of Isidoro and Águeda, November 3, December 15, and December 18, 2024.

28 **songs to them:** The fact that my grandmother used to sing in French and indications that there was a population of people from the French colony of Saint-Domingue who arrived in San Luis/San Juan y Martínez during the Haitian Revolution once led me to believe that my grandmother might have been descended from those refugees. The new research for this book has revealed that her family goes back generations in Cuba.

28 **started vomiting and died:** Luis Cabrera, personal communication, May 26, 2025.

28 ***niños regalados*—children given as gifts:** Rachel Nolan, *Until I Find You: Disappeared Children and Coercive Adoptions in Guatemala* (Harvard University Press, 2024), 30.

## 2. Children of Rita Blanco

30 **over nine hundred people:** *Military Notes on Cuba, 1909* (Washington, DC), 171–74.

31 **cockfights lasted for days:** Adolfo Dollero, *Cultura Cuban: la Provincia de Pinar del Río y su evolución* (Seoane y Fernández, 1921), 392.

31 **joined the rebel army:** Carlos Roloff, *Índice alfabéticoy defunciones del Ejército Libertador de Cuba, Guerra de Independencia* (Havana, 1901), 601.

31 **in exchange for $75:** NARA, RG 140, Records of the Military Government of Cuba, Records Relating to the Payment of the Liberating Army of Cuba,

Book 4, "Liberating Army of Cuba, 6th Corp, 1st Division, 1st Brigade, Infantry Regiment Maceo," 13.

31    **"because she was Black":** Communication with Lola's granddaughter, Rachel, February 24, 2020.

33    **a terrible hurricane:** "Hurricane Killed Hundreds in Cuba," *NYT*, October 22, 1926, 1.

34    *una niña blanca*: Adela Fernández Blanco, Acta de Bautismo, Parroquía de San Cristóbal, Diócesis de Pinar del Río, L. 33, f. 357, n. 713.

35    **books on the history of Cuba:** My mother and Tía Niña both told me this story. I mentioned them in *Insurgent Cuba*, 68, and in *Cuba*, 138.

36    **thirty-seven children in one go:** NS interview with my mother.

36    **anyone courting her:** NS interview with my mother.

36    **six people could ride on his back:** NS interview with my mother.

37    **favors in exchange for votes:** NS interview with my mother.

37    **lovely framed painting:** *Diario de la Marina*: Año XCV, Número 74 - de mañana (March 15, 1927), 22.

38    **burned to the ground:** Ecured entry for Chirigota, https://www.ecured.cu /Chirigota_(San_Cristóbal).

38    **She died of a heart attack:** Conversation with my cousin Rachel, Lola's granddaughter, May 11, 2024.

## 3. A Home Behind the Military Hospital

41    **her feet bloody and swollen:** NS interview with my mother.

42    **in the summer of 1954:** NS interview with my mother. Dates of their marriage and divorce also appear in my own A-File, USCIS, FOIA.

43    **in one decade alone:** Joseph Scarpaci, Roberto Segre, and Mario Coyula, *Havana: Two Faces of the Antillean Metropolis* (UNC Press, 2002), 120.

43    **50 pesos a month:** Rent receipt, AC; my mother's stories.

43    **75 percent of Havana's residents:** Susan Schroeder, *Cuba: A Handbook of Historical Statistics* (G.K. Hall & Co., 1982), indicates that the daily minimum wage in Havana and Marianao in 1958 was $3.30/day or $85/month (p. 180).

44    **moved back into the family home:** Conversation with Carlitos, Havana, December 1, 2023.

44    **everyone just made room:** NS interview with my mother; author interviews with Gladys, Union City, New Jersey, November 27, 2022, and with Carlitos, Havana, April 3, 2023.

44   **The family ran a little restaurant:** NS interview with my mother. I also heard many parts of this story over the years.

45   **the third *r* for his name Ramón:** Archives of the Instituto de Historia de Cuba, Fondo Ejército. 24/3.14/1:1.2/190-364.

46   **"he is just what the doctor ordered":** NS interview with my mother.

46   **New York or Paris:** Carolina Sandretto, *Cines de Cuba* (Skira, 2019).

46   **he did not like being left behind:** NS interview with my mother.

47   **the sweetest pickup line:** My father to Juan José, January 27, 2006, AC.

47   **"But he was so beautiful":** NS interview with my mother.

## 4. This Love of a Man

48   **May 2, 1921, at 11:23 a.m.:** "En una bella mañana" and "En una bella y radiante mañana," both undated; "Día de los Padres," May 18, 2006, all in AC.

48   **the hour at six p.m.:** My father's birth certificate, in his A-File, USCIS, FOIA.

49   **who put no stock in demons:** Fernando Ortiz, *Historia de una pelea cubana contra los demonios* (Santa Clara, 1959).

49   **some twenty-five years her senior:** Their approximate ages come from my mother's notations in our family bible.

49   **adjacent to La Rosa:** "En una bella mañana," AC.

50   **the dance of the millions:** Ferrer, *Cuba*, 217.

50   **US-owned companies:** Ferrer, *Cuba*, 217–18.

50   **Bank of Canada:** Leonel Pérez, *Desarrollo industrial de Cuba* (Instituto del Libro Cubano), 2024.

50   **crossed through their farmland:** My father, January 1, 2000 (in navy-blue-lined bound journal), AC; NS interview with my father, April 21, 2012.

52   **the story those scraps of writing tell:** My father wrote this scene at least four times, with minor variations. Undated, spiral notebook paper, numbered 3-5; undated, loose-leaf paper, numbered 3-4; loose-leaf single sheet, numbered 55, undated; undated draft to Juan José, undated to Sra. E., all in AC. He shares some basic details of the story also in NS interview with my father.

54   **he ventured at the age of ninety-one:** NS interview with my father.

54   **His oldest brother, Gregorio:** Conversation with my cousin Eladio, Miami, December 10, 2023.

## 5. A Revolution Story

56  **"secret location in the liberated territory of Cuba":** Princeton University Library, Carlos Franqui Papers, Box 9, Folder 3, Radio Broadcasts, December 1958.

57  **early in the morning of January 1, 1959:** NS interview with my mother.

**Cubans poured into the streets:** Ferrer, *Cuba*, 318–20.

58  **search for hidden weapons:** NS interview with my mother.

59  **Without a job or a uniform:** My father's stories; conversation with Eladio, December 10, 2023.

59  **Tía Niña in the last room:** Gladys interview, November 27, 2022.

59  **give him a few coins:** Conversation with Poly, c. 2019.

60  **beef had become almost impossible to come by:** The Cuban Economic Research Project, *A Study on Cuba* (University of Miami, 1965), 743–44.

60  **fifty-three people and killed seven:** Ferrer, *Cuba*, 366.

61  **"We have made a socialist revolution":** Fidel Castro speech, April 16, 1961.

61  **temporary detention centers:** Ferrer, *Cuba*, 366.

61  **an acquaintance to whom he owed money:** My father's stories.

61  **killing one worker and injuring eighteen:** FBIS Latin America Daily Report on Cuba Committee, Deposition of Phillip Agee, Mary Ferrell Foundation, Online Digital Archive, Doc. ID 56844; R. Hart Phillips, "Fire Wrecks Big Havana Store," *NYT*, April 15, 1961, 1.

61  **revolutionary tribunals and firing squads:** R. Hart Phillips, "Cuban Sugar Workers Granted Authority to Execute Saboteurs," *NYT*, April 13, 1961, 6.

62  **"In order to keep the prisoners quiet":** US Department of Justice, FBI, June 6, 1961, Memo on "Cuban Situation" in Mary Ferrell Foundation, Doc. ID 146680.

63  **applying for entry to the United States:** Ferrer, *Cuba*, 401.

63  **On April 24, 1962:** Visa Waiver issued to my father, Miami 4/24/1962, AC.

63  **applauded in unison:** "Flight of Cubans Puts Pan Am in the Red," *Desert Sun* (Palm Springs, CA), April 16, 1962.

64  *patria potestad*: Certificación de Sentencia de Divorcio, June 12, 1962, AC.

64  **telegram at the Sagamore:** Telegram to my father, June 18, 1962, AC.

64  **my mother's divorce:** Certificación de Sentencia de Divorcio, June 12, 1962, AC.

65  **"Today I got angry with Mamá":** Poly to my father, July 18, 1962, AC.

66  **I can no longer live without you:** Audio recording by my mother, c. 1973.

66  **she would add a million kisses:** My mother to me, May 6, 1992.

67  **"against the Western Hemisphere":** JFK, Address to Nation, October 22, 1962; Ferrer, *Cuba*, 369–70.

67  **"trapped in Cuba.":** My father to Juan José, November 30, 2007.

69  **not overthinking things:** My father to Juan José, November 30, 2007.

69  **the US-bound ship:** US House of Representatives, 88th Congress, Committee on the Judiciary, *Study of Population and Immigration Problems* (Washington, DC: GPO, 1963), 62, 94–97, 104.

69  **clamored for passage:** "Man Pulled Off Vessel as It Sails," *Baltimore Sun*, December 27, 1962; "Crowds Trying to Leave Cuba," *Baltimore Sun*, December 28, 1962.

## 6. Letters to Our Mother

73  **grandmother and aunts told him:** Conversation with my mother in the hospital, Miami Beach, 2019.

73  **my mother's housedress and cried:** Conversation with my aunt Ada (Tía Niña), Havana, early 1990s.

73  **People took turns taking him to school:** Carlitos to my mother, undated [1963]; Poly to my mother, September 3, 1963, November 22, 1963, February 7, 1964, March 13, 1964, November 12, 1965, AC.

74  **would probably not have gone otherwise:** Poly to my mother, January 10, 1964, March 13, 1964, July 10, 1964, December 6, 1964, AC.

74  **roast pork and sweets:** Poly to my mother, January 10, 1964, July 2, 1964, December 6, 1964, AC.

74  **"how to indulge him":** Carlito to my mother, undated [1963], AC.

74  **a nervous tic:** Conversation with Gladys, November 22, 2022.

74  **a letter to my mother, to our mother:** Poly to my mother, May 4, 1963, AC.

74  **"without help, I can't write":** Poly to my mother, October 8, 1963, AC.

74  **The first lines of Poly's first missive:** Poly to my mother, May 4, 1963, AC.

76  **"I beg you not to hit her":** Poly to my mother, May 6, 1963, AC.

76  **"on behalf of both of us":** Poly to my mother, May 27, 1963, AC.

76  **"I couldn't give it to you":** Poly to my mother, July 27, 1963, AC.

77  **"I am behaving well":** Poly to my mother, undated [1963], AC.

77  **"send me presents":** Poly to my mother, undated [1963], AC.

77  **"to go on a trip":** Poly to my mother [between July 4 and 26] 1963, AC.

77    "I really want to be with Adita": Poly to my mother, July 27, 1963, AC.

77    "Mima, if you only knew": Poly to my mother, September 30, 1963, AC.

79    my mother and I left in 1963: Poly to my mother, May 6, 1963, AC.

80    crawl into bed with her: Carlitos to my mother, undated [1963], AC.

## 7. A World of Dusk and Iron

83    if the baby was a girl: Poly to my mother, May 1 and May 10, 1964, AC.

83    a pink *mosquitero*: Poly to my mother, August 7, 1964, AC.

83    "we will be together and happy": Poly to my mother, July 2, 1964, AC.

83    "God willing": Poly to my mother, September 18, 1964, AC.

84    not to ignore me: Poly to my mother, October 9, 1964, AC.

84    to make him comply: Poly to my mother, May 7, 1965, AC.

84    "Pipo says that he will *not* sign": Poly to my mother, December 13, 1965, AC. Emphasis mine.

85    drapes on windows: On East New York's Jewish community, Richard Rabinowitz, *Objects of Love and Regret: A Brooklyn Story* (Harvard University Press, 2022).

85    snowstorms every few days: "Snow Emergency Is Declared," *NYT*, January 11, 1965; 1, "East Harassed by Driving Snow," *NYT*, January 18, 1965, 1.

85    howled through the city: "Blizzard Brings 7-Inch Snow," *NYT*, January 31, 1966, 1; "Blizzard Cripples East Coast," *NYT*, February 8, 1967, 1.

86    misdeeds real and perceived: Rabinowitz, *Objects*, 240–41.

87    "buy me a pair of shoes": Poly to my mother, May 27, 1963, AC.

88    next to his bed at night: Poly to my mother, July 10, 1964, October 9, 1964, January 15, 1965; Poly to Papi, January 15, 1965, AC.

88    sell it for twenty pesos: Poly to my mother, June 12, 1965, AC.

89    "it hurts my feelings": Poly to my mother, November 12, [1965], AC.

90    drops me off at Bay Reyna: Poly to my mother, February 5, 1967, March 4, 1967, AC.

90    the nation's transition to communism: Ferrer, *Cuba*, 386.

90    the barbershop, Bar Reyna: Poly to my mother, March 21, 1968, AC.

91    it felt like a miracle to them: Interview with Miriam, July 4, 2024.

92    Black and Puerto Rican: Walter Thabit, *How East New York Became a Ghetto* (NYU Press, 2003), 7, 13–14; Rabinowitz, *Objects*, 258.

92    **"pocket of poverty and racial tension"**: "Progress Is Mixed in Brooklyn Slums,"
*NYT,* June 15, 1967, 41.

92    **"rained down from rooftops at the police"**: Vincent Cannato, *The Ungovernable
City: John Lindsay and His Struggle to Save New York* (Basic Books, 2019), 120–25.
See also "Brooklyn Sniper Kills Negro Boy in Race Disorder," *NYT,* July 22, 1966, 1.

93    **"fork in the road where all American lives cross"**: Alfred Kazin, *A Walker in
the City* (Harcourt Books, 1951), 171.

93    **Gilma's Fashions:** My parents' tax returns, 1969, AC.

## 8. Across the Skyline

96    **Cuban humorist Álvarez Guedes:** *El Día Que Cayó Fidel Castro* was released
in 1967. But this episode happened shortly after our move to New Jersey in
1969.

99    **places such as West New York:** Ferrer, *Cuba,* 406.

99    **unable to speak the language:** Eleanor Meyer Rogg, *The Assimilation of Cuban
Exiles* (Aberdeen Press, 1974), 52.

99    **born in Cuba:** Alfonso Narvaez, "50,000 Cubans Add Prosperity and Problems
to Jersey," *NYT,* November 24, 1970, 43.

100    **until 1965:** Ferrer, *Cuba,* 404.

100    **turned fifty a few months earlier:** Certificates of Naturalization, AC.

100    **jacket and tie:** Immigration and Naturalization Service to my mother, re.
Petition Number 116716, October 28, 1971, in her A-File, USCIS, FOIA.

100    **those were the Americans:** This is a common theme in immigrant memoirs.
See, for example, Viet Thanh Nguyen, *Man of Two Faces: A Memoir, A History,
A Memorial* (Grove Press, 2023).

101    **Miller as a Jewish name:** Phillip Roth, "The Conversion of the Jews," in
*Goodbye, Columbus,* 142.

101    **not one child:** *¿Qué Pasa, U.S.A?* was a bilingual show about a Cuban family
living in Miami that aired on PBS between 1977 and 1980, but it does not
appear to have aired on our local PBS station (13-WNET), according to copies
of the New York Metro edition of *TV Guide* that I've been able to locate for
those years.

102    **thought of herself as Cuban:** This was my impression, and I confirmed it with
her. Phone conversation, July 4, 2024.

102    **"straight shot of Spanish"**: Junot Díaz, *The Brief and Wondrous Life of Oscar
Wao* (Penguin, 2008), 12.

103 **Alpha 66 and Omega-7**: Ferrer, *Cuba*, 408.

105 **"An absent presence"**: Ferrer, *Cuba*, 2.

107 **All those scenes my mother read:** Poly to my mother, July 14, 1967 (tamales); September 4, 1968 (porch); December 11, 1966 (feet); February 4, 1971 (handkerchief); October 31, 1967 (Murine); June 6, 1973 (chick).

## 9. Mother Hunger

110 **with a graffiti tag:** Poly to my mother, September 4, 1968, AC. He continues to sign most of his letters that way, with some minor modifications.

110 **he shaved now:** Poly to my mother, February 26, 1967, March 4, 1967, March 2, 1969, March 29, 1970, February 24, 1971, June 6, 1973, May 17, 1977, AC.

110 **no longer a boy's news:** Poly to my mother, May 13, 1967, August 7, 1967, March 21, 1968, April 18, 1968, October 17, 1969, December 9, 1969, February 24, 1971, AC.

110 **to buy a wristwatch:** Poly to my mother, June 14, 1969, AC.

111 **"a good girl who liked school":** Poly to my mother, October 16, 1968, AC.

111 **beer, rum, and cigarettes:** Poly to my mother, December 11, 1966, September 4, 1968, and October 16, 1968, AC.

112 **"students who come to this school":** NYU, Tamiment Archives, Marvin Leiner Papers, Box 4, Folder 10, "Interview with Gladys," p. 1.

112 **didn't mention in what grade:** Poly to my mother, September 30, 1963, AC.

113 **promoted to fourth grade:** Poly to my mother, July 10, 1964, October 9, 1964, AC.

113 **which card was the prettiest:** Poly to my mother, September 20, 1965, November 12, 1965.

113 **was held back every year:** NYU, Tamiment Archives, Marvin Leiner Papers, Box 4, Folder 10, "Interview with Gladys," p. 16.

113 **"without going to school":** NYU, Tamiment Archives, Marvin Leiner Papers, Box 4, Folder 10, "Interview with Gladys," p. 4.

113 **"How come you're in this class":** NYU, Tamiment Archives, Marvin Leiner Papers, Box 4, Folder 10, "Interview with Gladys," p. 4.

113 **everyone called *la beca*:** Poly to my mother, February 5, 1967, AC.

114 **the collective good:** Lillian Guerra, *Patriots and Traitors in Revolutionary Cuba, 1961–1981* (University of Pittsburgh Press, 2023), 225–48; Denise Blum, *Cuban Youth and Revolutionary Values: Educating the New Socialist Citizen* (University of Texas Press, 2011), 55, 60.

114 **to play baseball:** Poly to my mother, February 5, 1967, AC.

114 **without achieving that goal:** Poly to my mother, March 4, 1967, AC.

114 **make my mother happy:** Poly to my mother, March 18, 1967, AC.

114 **"was blown away":** Poly to my mother, March 4, 1967, AC.

114 **promoted to sixth grade or not:** Poly to my mother, August 7, 1967, AC.

114 **whatever else was needed:** Poly to my mother, October 18, 1967, AC.

114 **"I feel very happy with my *compañeros*":** Poly to my mother, undated, AC.

115 **They gave him a test:** Poly to my mother, October 18, 1967, AC.

115 **a note justifying the absence:** Poly to my mother, April 18, 1968, AC.

115 **Tía Niña wrote to my mother:** Niña to my mother, June 17, 1968, AC.

115 **stipend for their labor:** Poly to my mother, August 3, 1968, AC.

116 **"only an animal can think":** Poly to my mother, June 14, 1969, AC.

116 **"love like that of mother and son":** Poly to my mother, October 13, 1969, AC.

117 **play baseball and dominoes:** Poly to my mother, October 26, 1969, AC.

117 **alcohol was suspended:** Guerra, *Patriots and Traitors*, 195.

117 **birthday on December 6, 1969:** Poly to my mother, December 9, 1969, AC.

117 **"dedicate to you, *madrecita*":** Poly to my mother, December 28, 1969, AC.

117 **my sister and me:** Poly to my mother, January 28, 1970, AC.

118 **That's not for me:** Interview, Carlitos, December 2, 2023.

118 **"the name of my absent mother":** Poly to my mother, May 13, 1970, AC.

118 **the textile industry:** Poly to my mother, February 24, 1971, AC.

118 **a full-time worker:** Poly to my mother, May 24, 1971, AC.

118 **unpaid labor on state farms:** Guerra, *Patriots and Traitors*, 225.

118 **apologies for his silences:** Poly to my mother, March 2, 1969, February 24, 1971, 1973 (undated), AC.

118 **He was lazy:** Poly to my mother, December 30, 1973, 1974 (undated), January 28, 1978, AC

119 **happy from a distance:** Poly to my mother, January 28, 1978, AC.

119 **"when I have you at my side":** Poly to my mother, 1973, no date, AC.

120 **"things of this life":** Poly to my mother, 1974, no date, AC.

120 **visit before she died:** My mother always talked about this.

121 **the dictum to heart:** Poly to me, May 17, 1977, AC.

121 **"sending me some clothes"**: Poly to my mother, January 20, 1978, AC.

123 **issued in chronological order**: US Immigration and Naturalization Service, Notice of Approval of Relative Immigrant Visa Petition, March 18, 1978, AC.

123 **"he thinks only about leaving"**: Tía Niña to Mami, undated (but before my grandmother's death in 1975), AC.

## 10. Fidel Castro's Surprise

124 **volunteering for the talks in Havana**: Ferrer, *Cuba*, 408–9.

125 **gifts, cash, and love**: Ferrer, *Cuba*, 409-10.

125 **just for Poly**: Tía Niña to my mother, March 5, 1979 A and B, AC.

126 **Year of My Happiness**: Poly to Mami, March 6, 1979, AC.

126 **just under $14,000**: My parents' 1040A form, 1979, AC.

129 **her head in alarm**: María Elena, WhatsApp message, March 17, 2024.

129 **break the camera lens**: Tía Niña to my mother, December 30, 1974, and June 2, 1979, AC.

130 **two sisters, so long away**: Tía Niña to my mother, June 2, 1979, AC.

130 **Right, Mommy?**: Poly to my mother, May 2, 1979, AC.

130 **"Para Adita, de su hermano"**: Poly postcard to me, undated (1979), AC.

## 11. Exodus

132 **had not yet turned twenty-six**: Poly to my mother, November 1, 1979, AC.

133 **"I understand, though"**: Tía Niña to my mother, September 7, 1979, February 12, 1980, March 5, 1979 A and B, AC.

133 **"doctor says I'm neurotic"**: Tía Niña to my mother, January 28, 1979, AC.

133 **"[I am no longer good for anything]"**: Tía Niña to my mother, January 28, 1979, AC. Emphasis mine.

133 *la poca cosa de la familia*: Tía Niña to my mother, March 5, 1979, AC.

134 *fueron terribles*: Tía Niña to my mother, February 12, 1980, AC.

134 **"He cannot know"**: Tía Niña to my mother, February 12, 1980.

134 **a year after my mother's visit**: Poly, Cuban passport, dated April 13, 1980, reproduced in his A-File, USCIS, FOIA, f. 142. (The page numbers refer to my own numbering system on my printout of the A-File.)

135 **the Cuban government would no longer**: Ferrer, *Cuba*, 411–15.

137 **jail time for vagrancy**: Poly, Request for Asylum, May 17, 1980, in his A-File, USCIS, FOIA, ff. 108–11; Poly to my mother, April 19, 2009.

137 **passage to Florida:** Receipt from Gene Brenner, May 7, 1980, AC.

138 **passengers in prayer:** Phone interview with my mother, May 10, 2019.

138 **floodlights illuminated everything:** A college classmate, Matt Cartsonis, traveled to Cuba aboard the *Sundance II* and provided some of this information. Interview, September 18, 2020.

139 **received the message only later:** Tía Niña to my mother, June 28, 1980, AC.

139 **"since Mother's Day":** Phone interview with my mother, May 10, 2019.

139 **May 6 but not after:** Tía Niña to my mother, June 28, 1980, AC.

139 **But she thanked God:** Tía Niña to my mother, June 28, 1980; phone interview with my mother, May 10, 2019.

140 **never really felt like:** Hospital conversation with my mother, April 2019; phone conversation with my mother, May 10, 2019.

## 12. Camp Liberty

142 **37,000 Cubans had landed in Key West:** "Unfounded Fears Empty Key West Hotels," *NYT,* May 13, 1980, A14.

142 **gone by sea in just a few months:** Miami city population was 346,865, see https://www2.census.gov/prod2/decennial/documents/1980a_flABCs1-01.pdf; Cuba population figures was 9,809,107, see https://countryeconomy.com /demography/population/cuba?year=1980.

142 **remained for many months:** Ferrer, *Cuba,* 416–17.

143 **camp was fully operational:** Project Red White and Blue Briefing, by General Chapman, in Box 6, Folder "Briefing" in NARA, RG 343, EAFB, CRR.

143 **thirty thousand meals a day:** Eglin AFB, Joint Message, May 16, 1980, Box 2, Folder "May: Incoming" in NARA, RG343, EAFB, CRR.

144 **clothing drives for the destitute arrivals:** CHC, Fort Chaffee Collection, Box 5, folder 1, Gastón Fernández, Consolidation, "A Comprehensive Report of 'El Campo de la Libertad,'" Prepared by the Assessment Team sponsored by S.A.L.A.D, Eglin Air Force Base, June 5, 1980.

144 **the ages of twenty-one and forty:** "Palace Mission. General Background," in Box 6, Folder "Cuban Report," in NARA, RG343, EAFB, CRR.

144 **the words of one Eglin general:** Project Red White and Blue Briefing, by General Chapman, in Box 6, Folder "Briefing."

145 **camp on May 13, 1980:** "Report INS 007, Latest Update 13/05/80. Estos Cubanos están en la computadora hasta ahora," in Box 22, Folder: Status Reports, in NARA, RG343, EAFB, CRR.

145 **just as his little card said:** "Report INS 006, Latest Update 13/05/80. Estos Cubanos están en la computadora hasta ahora," in Box 22, Folder: Status Reports, in NARA, RG343, EAFB, CRR.

145 **camp named Liberty:** Box 9, Folder Maps, in NARA, RG343, EAFB, CRR.

146 **sent back to their tent:** May 16, 1980 entries in Folder Security Blotters #2, Box 5, NARA, RG343, EAFB, CRR.

146 **Mia's Pizza Parlor in town:** Security Blotter entries from May 17–22, 1980, Box 5, NARA, RG343, EAFB, CRR.

147 **where Poly was left back:** Form G-325A, May 17, 1980, in A-File, USCIS, FOIA, ff. 205v–206.

147 **"[he] wasn't doing anything":** Request for Asylum, May 17, 1980, in A-File, USCIS, FOIA, ff. 108–11. There seem to be two 1-94 cards in his file for his arrival, one dated May 9, 1980, that states that Poly arrived on the vessel of a Captain McGuinn; the other from Fort Eglin, dated May 30, 1980. The second is the one that assigns him an "alien" number (ff. 190–190v).

147 **half a pack of cigarettes:** Medical Examination of Visa Applicants, A-File, USCIS, FOIA, f. 205.

147 **he smoked there, too:** Cuban Refugee Operation Log, in Box 6, Folder Cuban Report, in NARA, RG343, EAFB, CRR.

148 **two locals tried to crash:** "Cuban Refugee Operation Log," in Box 6, Folder Cuban Report, in NARA, RG343, EAFB, CRR.

148 **KKK banner over the scene:** Operation Red, White, and Blue Briefing by General Chapman, in Box 6, Folder Briefing, in NARA, RG343, EAFB, CRR; Tom Mason Operation Red, White, and Blue: Eglin Air Force Base and the Mariel Boatlift, https://www.afmc.af.mil/News/Article-Display/Article /1703372/operation-red-white-and-blue-eglin-afb-and-the-mariel-boatlift/.

148 **159 refugees had been released:** Eglin Joint Message, May 16, 1980, Box 2, Folder May Incoming, in NARA, RG343, EAFB, CRR.

148 **"internal security of Camp Libertad":** Eglin Joint Message, May 16, 1980, Box 2, Folder May Incoming, in NARA, RG343, EAFB, CRR.

149 **a fight with his boyfriend:** May 24, "Security Police Blotters, #2" in Box 5, NARA, RG343, EAFB, CRR.

149 **"We want to leave":** "Cuban Refugee Operation Log," in Box 6, Folder Cuban Report, in NARA, RG343, EAFB, CRR.

149 **"to save their friend":** May 24, "Security Police Blotters, #2" in Box 5, NARA, RG343, EAFB, CRR.

149 **police and military tents:** "Cuban Refugee Operation Log," in Box 6, Folder Cuban Report, in NARA, RG343, EAFB, CRR.

150 **to jump the fences:** "Cuban Refugee Operation Log," in Box 6, Folder, Cuban Report, in NARA, RG343, EAFB, CRR.

150 **how many people had escaped:** "Security Police Blotters, #2" in Box 5, NARA, RG343, EAFB, CRR.

150 **the pace of out-processing:** Mason, "Operation Red, White, and Blue," https://www.afmc.af.mil/News/Article-Display/Article/1703372/operation-red -white-and-blue-eglin-afb-and-the-mariel-boatlift/.

151 **I found a photograph in the archives:** Box 13, NARA, RG343, EAFB, CRR.

151 **"You remember the rest":** Phone interview with my mother, May 10, 2019.


## 13. Hello, Goodbye


156 **first gift to her in the United States:** Manuela to Poly, August 4, 1980, AC.

156 **company was not around:** Zoom interview with my sister, July 11, 2023.

157 **an "etc." at the end:** Yellow journal, August 20, 1980 entry, AC.

158 **very quiet around this time:** Zoom interview with my sister, July 11, 2023.

158 **happy and excited my mother was:** Georgia Pestana, communication, July 12, 2023.


## 14. Tía Niña


160 **she was shedding pounds:** Tía Niña to Mami, June 28, 1980; Manuela to Poly, June 6, 1980, AC.

160 **Poly had arrived safely:** Tía Niña to Poly, June 3, 1980, AC.

161 **"Goodbyes are sad":** Tía Niña to Poly, undated [June-August 1980], AC.

162 **"like you, and we, so much wanted":** Tía Niña to Poly, June 3, 1980, AC.

162 **the start of our summer:** Tía Niña to Poly, August 7, 1980, AC.

162 **"your mother and your sisters":** Tía Niña to Poly, September 27, 1980, AC.

162 **"*Chico*, seriously":** Tía Niña to Poly, August 7, 1980, AC.

162 **"conversing a little with you":** Tía Niña to Poly, August 28, 1980, AC.

163 **his life with us:** Tía Niña to Poly, September 27, 1980, July 7, 1985, AC.

163 **"I knew you would be":** Tía Niña to Poly, August 28, 1980, AC.

163 **"good luck will keep accompanying you":** Tía Niña to Poly, September 10, 1980, AC.

164 **helped entertain her a little:** Tía Niña to Poly, undated [Summer, 1980]; Manuela to Poly, August 4, 1980, AC.

164 **praying aloud about Poly:** Tía Niña to Poly, undated [Summer, 1980], AC.

164 **a Cuban in outer space:** Tía Niña to Poly, October 12, [1980], AC; María A. Cabrera Arús, "Una plantilla de zapatos y el Vuelo Espacial Conjunto Soviético-Cubano," *Hypermedia Magazine*, January 24, 2019.

164 **"you dedicated it to me, right?":** Tía Niña to Poly, December 20, 1980, AC.

165 **"See why I feel so calm now?":** Tía Niña to Poly, May 27, 1981, AC.

## 15. Exit

167 **Where was I "from from"?:** Monica Youn, *From From* (Graywolf, 2023).

## 16. Vengeance

173 **because of his *hombría*:** I have reconstructed this event from memory, but this detail—that he justified his beating by citing his *hombría*—comes from my diary. Yellow journal, entry for July 18, 1981, AC.

174 **"and I HATE him":** Yellow journal, entry for July 18, 1981, AC.

174 **bark with more than one mouth:** Esther Kinsky, *Rombo*, Translated by Caroline Schmidt (Fitzarraldo, 2022), 11.

## 17. Guns, Knives, and Books

175 **two months of her salary:** "Colony TV & Furniture" receipt, March 2, 1982; my mother's W-2 form for 1981, AC.

176 **across the two towns:** https://www.hobokengirl.com/hudson-county-history-embroidery-capital/.

176 **monitor for thread breaks:** https://www.mrxstitch.com/machine-embroidery-observation/.

176 **he earned $8,650:** Poly W-2 and 1040A forms for 1981, AC.

176 **He had a bank account:** Provident Savings Bank Account Book, AC.

176 **high school graduation photos:** Zoom interview with my sister, July 11, 2023; Tía Niña to Poly, August 10, 1981, AC.

177 **knife hidden in a drawer, too:** Zoom interview with my sister, July 11, 2023.

177 **shut the closet door:** Zoom interview with my sister, July 11, 2023.

179 **she concludes a little later:** Zoom interview with my sister, July 11, 2023, and phone call July 12, 2023.

179 **"It was miserable":** Zoom interview with my sister, July 11, 2023.

180 **I am still surprised:** Untitled paper for Professor Shields, March 28, 1983, AC.

181 **"for your own good":** Tía Niña to Poly, September 13, 1984, AC.

182 **had settled in Miami:** Historian Alexander Stephens has found interesting connections between policing in neighborhoods such as Marianao, patterns of migration during the Mariel Boatlift, and subsequent experiences of detention in the United States. See "Excludable: Race, Policing, and Migration in Cuba and the United States, 1959–1986," (PhD dissertation, University of Michigan, 2025), especially chapter 4.

182 **"he casts a bad shadow":** Tía Niña, October 12, 1980, AC.

183 **summarized their reasons:** Poly, A-File, USCIS, FOIA, ff. 97, 208v.

183 **"I want to get my residency":** Poly, A-File, USCIS, FOIA, ff. 85, 87.

183 **April 1, 1985:** Poly, A-File, USCIS, FOIA, ff. 52, 98v–100v, 103.

184 **$2,500 paid to the lawyer:** Receipts dated January 7 and 8, 1985, AC.

184 **I wrote as if I was Poly:** My brother to Whom It May Concern, June 11, 1985, AC.

185 **"The bad die well":** Tía Niña to Poly, July 18, 1984, AC.

185 **beloved young men now in the United States:** Tía Niña to Poly, August 7, 1980, August 10, 1981, AC.

185 **stuffed into the trunk of a car:** Tía Niña to Poly, December 26, 1984, AC. Both my mother and Tía Niña talked to me about his murder.

## 18. History Moves

190 **"its essential counterpoint":** Carolyn Kay Steedman, *Landscape for a Good Woman: A Story of Two Lives* (Rutgers University Press, 1987), 22.

191 **working off the books:** Unemployment reporting document, AC.

## 19. Long-Lost Brother

196 **fatherless children:** Conversation with Hilda Gómez, March 31, 2023.

196 **she tells me:** Conversation with my sister, October 28, 2022.

197 **Havana because my father was there:** Conversation with Hildita, March 31, 2023.

197 **unfeeling gossip:** Conversations with Hildita and Alain, March 31, 2023.

198 **my father ignored the warnings:** Conversation with Hildita and Aymara, Remedios, March 30, 2023.

198 **over two hundred wounded:** Telegram from Embassy to Dept of State, Havana, March 4, 1960, 8:55pm, in DNSA, http://ezproxy.nypl.org /login?url=https://search-proquest-com.i.ezproxy.nypl.org/docview /1967780739?accountid=35635.

198 **special youth brigades:** Ferrer, *Cuba*, 388–89.

199 **by canoe and pack mule:** Hildita interview, January 22, 2025.

199 **suffered from parasites:** Theron Corse, "Presbyterians in the Revolution: An American Missionary Church and the Challenge of Castro's Cuba, 1959–1970," *Cuban Studies* 31 (2000): 1–33.

199 **badge and pin from the campaign:** Conversation with Hildita, March 31, 2023, and January 22, 2025.

200 **their first meeting, they married:** Hildita interview, January 17, 2025.

200 **born in 1971:** Juan José to me, November 6, 1988, AC.

201 **sustain the rudeness for long:** Conversation with Hildita, March 31, 2023.

201 **"I didn't think you even remembered my name":** Emelanio Ferrer to my father, April 17, 1988, AC.

201 **supported the idea:** Hildita conversation, March 31, 2023; Juan José to my father, July 16, 1988, AC.

201 **my father already knew:** Emelanio Ferrer to my father, April 17, 1988, AC.

202 **just Juan José's response:** Juan José to my father, July 16, 1988, AC.

202 **I tend a white rose:** José Marti, *Versos Sencillos*, XXX. My translation.

203 **"so much love, have merit":** Juan José to my father, July 16, 1988, AC.

203 **"you do not know him," I wrote:** Author to Juan José, August 19, 1988, AC.

204 **I did not know that yet:** Martí published the piece in Spanish in *La America*; it appears in translation as "The Distribution of Diplomas at a College in the United States," in *The Vassar Quarterly*, June 1, 1954, https:// newspaperarchives.vassar.edu/?a=d&d=vq19540601-01.2.11.

204 **and so he hadn't asked:** Juan José to me, November 6, 1988, AC.

205 **"lost for so many years":** Juan José to me, November 6, 1988, AC.

205 **"going with this relationship?":** Juan José to my father, February 17, 1989, AC.

205 **"haven't heard from me":** Juan José to my father, August 31, 1989, AC.

206 **depends on you:** Juan José to my father, August 31, 1989, AC.

206 "I pray it will happen": Juan José to my father, August 31, 1989, AC.

207 "for your decisions": Juan José to my father, October 30, 1989, AC.

207 "Ada intends to come to Cuba": Juan José to my father, October 30, 1989, AC.

## 20. First Return

209 inches above my head: Cuba 1990 trip, undated note on yellow legal paper, AC.

209 8506 from Miami to Havana: Cuba 1990 trip, boarding pass, AC.

210 both groups at the same time: Ada to Gregg, June 30, 1990, AC.

210 they had been impressed: Ada to Gregg, June 30, 1990, AC.

211 inspect all those overstuffed bags: Ada to Gregg, June 30, 1990, AC.

212 assumed I was her: Many years later, traveling in Cuba with my husband, Gregg, and our two daughters (Alina and Lucía), I saw a woman who looked like her in front of a tourist site. I rolled down my window, and called out her name. She looked up immediately. Though she did not remember me, when I told her she was the first person I'd met on my first trip there, that I loved her name, that I'd been back many times, that I wrote books about Cuba, that I named my first daughter Alina, she cried a little. We took a picture together.

213 for only an hour that night: Ada to Gregg, June 30, 1990, AC.

213 renters when we lived there: Ada to Gregg, July 4, 1990, AC.

215 writing in Spanish: Ada, November 17, 1990, AC.

215 one of Fidel Castro: Ada to Gregg, July 4, 1990, AC.

216 "Flies everywhere": Ada to Gregg, July 4. 1990, AC.

## 21. The Milky Way with My Brother

220 a late supper and sleep: Emelanio Ferrer to my father, September 1, 1988, AC.

221 "to see each other again soon": Juan José to my father, undated [July 1990], AC.

## 22. My Cuba

223 a foreign language to me: Jhumpa Lahiri writes brilliantly about this, *In Other Words* (Vintage, 2016), 21.

## 23. Motherhood

228 midthought, midsleep, midgesture: Sarah Knott, *Mother Is a Verb: An Unconventional History* (Farrar, Straus and Giroux, 2019).

229 **motherhood** *is* **eternal interruption:** Author email to Sarah Knott, January 26, 2022.

## 24. Reading an Alien File with My Mother

234 **It looks like a tombstone:** Edwidge Danticat, *The Art of Death, Writing the Final Story* (Graywolf, 2017), 34.

235 **his arrest on the affidavit:** Complaint/Arrest Affidavit, Police Case No. 182-17816R, July 1, 1991. A-File, USCIS, FOIA, ff. 60–66v.

235 **mother trying to take care of him:** Interview with my sister, August 9, 2023.

236 **for the occasion:** My mother to me, May 14, 1992, AC.

236 **third verdict to not guilty:** A-File, USCIS, FOIA, ff. 60–66v.

236 **Nothing happened:** Conversations with Aixa and Adrian, May 22, 2025.

237 **income in three years:** A-File, USCIS, FOIA, f. 71.

237 **she wrote to me:** My mother to me, April 4, [1992].

237 **an alcoholic beverage:** "Complaint/Arrest Record," August 8, 1993, in A-File, USCIS, FOIA, p. 76v.

237 **charges were dismissed:** Criminal Division, Certified Record Search, Date illegible, A-File, USCIS, FOIA, 56v. (A different version of his arrests appears on 128v.)

237 **He never did:** Advocate Program, September 16, 1993; Advocate Program, Notice of Intention to Revoke, November 3, 1993, both in Poly, 1991–1993; Court Oriented Rehabilitation and Education Program Reminder Notice, February 18, 1994, AC.

237 **operating room topped $71,000:** Jackson Memorial Hospital Bill for $71,227.18, AC.

238 **Poly was not fit to work:** Miami-Dade County, Dept. of Human Resources, Office of Community Services, Medical Information Form, February 17, 1994, AC.

238 **the original prescriptions:** Prescriptions from Miami Mental Health Center, November 7, 1994 and June 29, 1994, AC.

238 **Restoril for sleeping:** Illeg. to Whom it May Concern, November 17, 1993, in A-File, USCIS, FOIA, f. 74v.

239 **"To Whom It May Concern":** Illeg. to Whom It May Concern, November 25, 1993, in A-File, USCIS, FOIA, f. 72v.

239 **starting in fall 1994:** Notice of Start of Medicaid Eligibility, March 1, 1994; SSI Authorization Form, March 16, 1994; Social Security Administration, Office of Disability, to Poly, March 18, 1995, AC; OMB 1115-0053.

Application to Register Permanent Residence of Adjust Status, Part 3. Processing Information, in A-File, USCIS, FOIA, f. 34.

239 **biographic information form:** Form G-325A, Biographic Information, January 24, 1996, in A-File, USCIS, FOIA, f. 69v.

239 **"high blood pressure":** Undated, detainee form, A-File, USCIS, FOIA, f. 133.

239 **"into his mental illness":** COMPASS Case Manager, Fellowship House, January 23, 2009, in Poly court file, f. 150v.

240 **dated September 7, 1995:** Record of Action, September 7, 1995, A-File, USCIS, FOIA, f. 94.

240 **accents missing:** My mother to Whom It May Concern, INS, April 11, 1998, in A-File, USCIS, FOIA, f. 67.

## 25. Letters to Fidel

242 **She missed talking:** My mother to me, October 8, 1992, AC.

242 **to Spain with me:** My postcard to my parents, March 2, 1993, AC.

243 **What more could he ask for:** My father to me, March 11, 1993, AC.

243 **how I took them with me:** Daisy Hernández, *A Cup of Water Under My Bed* (Beacon Press, 2014), 147.

243 *tú sabes como tengo la cabeza:* My father to Juan José, December 24, 2004, AC.

244 **"understand the reasons":** My father's notebook, May 18, 2006, AC.

245 **"who surrounded [him] daily":** Papi, three prayers, two undated and one July 11, 1996, AC.

246 **"Free Trade Treaty for the Republic of Cuba":** All the essays listed here are the folders I have numbered 9 and 18 of my father's papers, AC.

246 **Elián González:** "Chess Piece: The Elián González Story," Futuro Media, https://futurostudios.org/podcasts/chess-piece/.

246 **"solution to the Cuban problem":** My father to President Carlos Menem, March 10, 1993; my father to President Carlos Salinas de Gortari, March 18, 1993, AC.

246 **interview with Fidel Castro:** My father to Diane Sawyer, March 12, 1993, AC.

247 **in the margin, "Not sent.":** My father to Fidel Castro, April 19, 1993, AC.

247 **"Cuba to young Cubans":** My father to Fidel Castro, handwritten draft, undated [1999], AC.

247 **"It is time, Dr. Castro":** My father to Fidel Castro, May 13, 2005, AC. Early in the Cuban Revolution, Fidel Castro used the title Dr., referring to his law degree. On June 9, 1960, Arthur H. Sulzberger, then publisher of *The New*

*York Times*, asked a colleague: "Have we ever had a story on what Castro is Dr. of beside invective?" NYPL, Manuscripts Division, New York Times Company Records, Box 149.

247 **"Time does not stand still"**: My father to Fidel Castro, undated [after Fidel gets sick in 2006], AC.

248 **"and with it my life"**: Handwritten note, September 17, 2006, AC.

248 **"when one dies many times too much"**: My father to Sr. Orlando González Esteves, February 28, 2008, AC.

249 **"*morirse muchas veces mucho*"**: Ángel González, "Cumpleaños," *Áspero mundo* (Ediciones Rialp, 1956), 16. Reprinted with the permission of his widow, Susana Rivera. The translation of the poem is my own.

250 **"To write in silence is a marvelous thing"**: My father to Juan José, February 2, 2005, AC.

## 26. Love Letters

252 **anything he could get his hands on**: Interview with Aymara and Alain, March 30, 2023; Juan José to my father, October 13, 1999; May 3, 2009; my father to Juan José, December 24, 2004, AC.

252 **without disturbing anyone**: Multiple conversations with Amalia.

252 **"for the muses to descend"**: Juan José to my father, January 15, 2008, AC.

252 **"at film-strip speed"**: Juan José to my father, February 12, 1996, AC.

253 **"to share them with you?"**: Juan José to my father, April 18, 2009, AC.

253 **from his small hometown**: Juan José to my father, December 2, 2007, AC.

253 **"what cannot be solved is best forgotten"**: Juan José to my father, April 18, 2009, AC.

254 **"ever having uttered the word *papá*"**: Juan José to my father, June 9, 2009, AC.

255 **"a hunger to know everything"**: Juan José to my father, February 12, 1996, AC.

255 **"men are men and nothing more"**: Juan José to my father, November 18, 2008, AC.

255 **"my real father by my side"**: Juan José to my father, June 26, 2007, AC. Emphasis in original.

255 **one of his first letters**: Juan José to my father, August 31, 1989, AC.

255 **"feeling you as my father"**: Juan José to my father, June 3, 2007, AC.

255 **"I assure you, J.J."**: Juan José to my father, April 16, 2008, AC.

255 **"Hey, really, I love you"**: Juan José to my father, April 8, 2009, AC.

256 **"remembering it makes you happy"**: Juan José to my father, August 14, 2007, AC.

256 **it did make him happy:** My father to Juan José, September 5, 2007, AC.

256 **becoming president of the United States:** My father to Juan José, February 2, 2005, February 9, 2007, June 22, 2008, AC.

256 **"exquisite" and "eloquent.":** Juan José to my father, June 3, 2007, AC.

258 **$350 a month for the rest of their lives:** "La fabulosa herencia cubana de Bartolomé Manso de Contreras," February 21, 2017, at https://www .thecubanhistory.com; https://www.thecubanhistory.com/2017/02/la-fabulous -cuban-heritage-of-bartolome-manso-de-contreras-la-fabulosa-herencia-cubana -de-bartolome-manso-de-contreras/#google_vignette.

258 **percent of people owned cars:** Martin Piszczalski, "Cars in Cuba," February 1, 2003, in Gardner Business Media, Manufacturing Marketer Blog, https://www.gardnerweb.com/articles/cars-in-cuba.

258 **equivalent to $11:** Jorge Domínguez, "Cuba's Many Faces: Not Quite the New Millennium," *ReVista: Harvard Review of Latin America*, Winter 2000, https:// revista.drclas.harvard.edu/cubas-many-faces/.

258 **Cuban fortune in a London bank:** Ferrer, *Cuba*, 439–41.

259 **underlining the words:** Juan José to my father, June 26, 2007, AC.

259 **among the hundreds of other ones:** Juan José to my father, October 13, 1999, AC.

259 ***"thought about it and remembered it"***: Juan José to my father, May 5, 2007, AC. Emphasis in original.

259 **"it would be too sad and painful":** My father to Juan José, July 23, 2003, AC.

260 **for now let us leave it:** My father to Juan José, July 15, 2007; Juan José to my father, August 14, 2007.

262 **immigrant visas to become available:** Federal Register, November 21, 2007, https://www.federalregister.gov/documents/2007/11/21/E7-22679/cuban -family-reunification-parole-program.

262 **gifts from abroad:** Juan José's statement brought to mind the work of Carolyn Kay Steedman, who wrote about her mother's desire for a New Look skirt as the stuff of politics. *Landscape for a Good Woman.*

263 **"eat only the whites":** My father to Juan José, June 22, 2008, AC.

263 **"where the Lord will send me":** My father to Juan José, December 19, 2008, AC.

263 **"a tumult of ideas in my mind":** Juan José to my father, November 18, 2008, AC.

263 **Everything he did, he did for them:** Juan José to my father, November 12, 2008, AC.

263 **"deposit my faith in God":** Juan José, September 18, 2009, AC.

264 **"Let us pray to God that they will":** Juan José to Ramón, Adela, Ada, Aixa, Nailah, Alina, and Lucía, November 14, 2009, AC.

## 27. Letters to a Judge, Letters to a Mother

265 **I was a child:** Weather Spark Historical Data: https://weatherspark.com/h/d /18622/2002/1/24/Historical-Weather-on-Thursday-January-24-2002-in -Miami-Florida-United-States#google_vignette.

266 **three little monkeys on the sign outside:** The description of the events that night is taken from the victim's deposition in criminal case F02-002877, State of Florida vs. Hipólito Cabrera. Hereafter I will refer to this case only by the number. The page numbers refer to my pagination of the printout of the court docket.

266 **set records in some local races:** Victim's deposition, criminal case F02-002877, ff. 89v–91, 93, 95, 101.

267 **"bad aspect about him":** Victim's deposition, criminal case F02-002877, court record, f. 94, 96.

267 **finishing his first beer:** Victim's deposition, criminal case F02-002877, court record, f. 96.

267 **then a horrible pain:** Victim's deposition, criminal case F02-002877, court record, ff. 93, 97v.

267 **everything started to go black:** Victim's deposition, criminal case F02-002877, court record, f. 98.

267 **Polo had done it:** Victim's deposition, criminal case F02-002877, court record, f. 78.

268 **"twice unlucky":** Peter Earley, *Crazy: A Father's Search Through America's Mental Health Madness* (Berkley Books, 2006), 39–41.

268 **entered a plea of not guilty:** "Notice of Defendant's Invocation of the Right to Counsel" in State of Florida vs. Hipólito Cabrera, Case No. F02002877, in manila envelope "Reporte del detective Fuetes. Papeles del juicio," AC.

268 **February 12, 2002, 5:23 p.m.:** Handwritten document in manila envelope "Reporte del detective. Papeles del juicio," AC.

269 **"verbally and physically aggressive":** Competency Evaluation, Hipólito Cabrera, October 14, 2002 in Court Case file, f. 165.

269 **Poly's capacity to stand trial:** Competency Evaluations in Court Case file, ff. 157v–67v.

271 **and the judge agreed:** Competency Evaluation in Court Case file, ff. 163–64.

271 **"stabilization and ongoing psychiatric care":** Dr. C. Psychiatrist [to Honorable Judge], November 1, 2002, in manila envelope "Reporte del detective. Papeles del juicio," AC.

272 **almost 650 ALFs:** Earley, *Crazy*, 271.

272 **Miami police officer to a journalist:** Earley, *Crazy*, 301–4.

272 **was Sam Konell:** Letter from Sam Konell to the court, May 19, 2003.

272 **paid Konell a commission:** Earley, *Crazy*, 301–4.

272 **time in an ALF:** Southern Winds to Court, September 9, October 15, November 1, and November 26, 2002.

272 **health-care fraud scheme:** David Ovalle, "He Devoted His Career to Helping Mentally Ill Defendants. Now He's Going to Prison for Fraud," *Miami Herald*, February 23, 2018, 4A; "Miami-Area Man Sentenced to Five Years in Prison for Role in $63 Million Health Care Fraud Scheme," US Department of Justice, Press Release, February 22, 2018.

272 **released from prison into an ALF:** Inmate profile from Miami-Dade County's Department of Corrections.

272 **remaining ten would also be served in an ALF:** Docket, Course Case F-02-002877, Miami-Dade County Clerk of the Courts, Criminal Justice Online System.

274 **"his family who love him very much":** Poly to "Dear Legal Team," March 12, 2008, AC.

275 **Poly's signature acknowledging receipt:** Revival Home, Inc, to Hipolito Cabrera, January 9, 2003, in Poly court file, f. 150.

275 **that the issue be addressed in court:** COMPASS Case Manager, Fellowship House, January 23, 2009, in Poly court file, f. 150v.

276 **My Misery for Always:** Poly to my mother, April 19, 2009, AC.

276 **"your indifference and rejection":** Poly to my mother, April 19, 2009, and undated letter postmarked April 28, 2009, AC.

276 **kissed him on the cheek:** Poly to my mother, April 19, 2009, AC.

277 **"because I was and am her son":** Poly to my mother, April 26, 2009, AC.

277 **"'Son, forgive me for my wrongs'":** Poly to my mother, April 26, 2009, AC.

277 **"Oh, ma, how unlucky I am":** Poly to my mother, April 28, 2009, AC.

278 **"go to the afterlife together":** Poly to my mother, April 28, 2009, AC.

278 **aptly named as femicide:** One of the most powerful and moving treatments I have read of femicide is Rivera Garza, *Liliana's Invincible Summer*.

278 **two on May 20, and so on:** Poly to my mother, April 30, 2009, AC.

278 **wore her down:** Aixa to me, email, May 4, 2009.

279 **would have reported him:** For a poignant discussion of the financial and emotional burdens of collect calls from people in prison, see Reuben Jonathan Miller, *Halfway Home: Race, Punishment, and the Afterlife of Mass Incarceration* (Back Bay Books, 2021).

279 **in the custody of ICE:** Post-Order Custody Review Worksheet, A-File, USCIS, FOIA, 128–128v.

279 **deportable under US law:** US Department of Homeland Security, Notice to Appear, June 3, 2009, A-File, USCIS, FOIA, f. 24v.

279 **removed from the United States:** Order of the Immigration Judge in the Matter of Cabrera, Hipolito, Respondent, June 18, 2009, A-File, USCIS, FOIA file, f. 139.

279 **inmates in the general population there:** Wakulla County Sheriff, Booking Information for Hipolito Cabrera, obtained through Public Records Request.

279 **under a new medication regime:** Institutional/Disciplinary Record, A-File, USCIS, FOIA, f. 130.

279 **released and returned to Miami:** Poly to my mother, August 10, 12, and 26, and September 5, 2009.

280 **"NOT likely in the foreseeable future":** Post Order Custody Review Worksheet, September 9, 2009, p. 7, in A-File, USCIS, FOIA, f. 131.

## 29. Tía Tatá

289 **a veritable Dante's *Inferno*:** Jennifer Lambe, *Madhouse: Psychiatry and Politics in Cuban History* (UNC Press, 2017), 140.

289 **as a result of neglect:** Damaris Betancourt, *Diez días en Mazorra* (Rialta, 2021), 9.

290 **performing lobotomies:** Lambe, *Madhouse*, 124–25, 260.

291 **going to marry a Black man:** Carlitos to my mother, December 11, 1966, AC.

291 **that kind of thing all her life:** Anti-Black racism was (and is) legion in Cuba. Intimate family stories can reveal its presence even among families who acknowledge themselves to be mixed race. It is evident, among other things, in the insidious language of color, in which darker skin color is cast as inferior to lighter ones, as well as in a pervasive language of "improving the race." On anti-Blackness and colorism in Latin America, see Edward Telles, *Pigmentocracies: Ethnicity, Race, and Color in Latin America* (University of

North Carolina Press, 2014), and among Latinos in the United States, Tanya Katerí Hernández, *Racial Innocence: Unmasking Latino Anti-Blackness and the Struggle for Equality* (Beacon Press, 2022).

291 **to buy her cigarettes:** Poly to my mother, February 4, 1971, AC.

292 **just to pray for a bit:** Tía Niña to Poly, September 27, 1980, AC.

292 **needed his mother:** Tía Niña to Poly, undated [June–August, 1980], AC.

## 30. A Family Trip

294 **"there is always a first time":** My father to US Department of State, 2013, draft letter, handwritten with many cross-outs, AC.

294 **version of the letter in English:** My father to US Department of State, January 9, 2014, AC. The letter should have been addressed to the US Treasury Department. But my father insisted it go to State, because he said it was a broader, diplomatic issue. Perhaps he was right. But there was no way either agency was ever going to approve his request.

298 **Obama's speech:** "Remarks by President Obama to the People of Cuba," March 22, 2016, https://obamawhitehouse.archives.gov/the-press -office/2016/03/22/remarks-president-obama-people-cuba.

300 **"There are loves that outlive lovers":** Edwidge Danticat, "Without Inspection," in *Everything Inside* (Alfred A. Knopf, 2019), 219.

## 32. Very Old Parents

308 **"I am waiting for you in Heaven":** My mother to me, April 20, 2014, AC.

## 34. Mysteries of a Silence

321 **Christian Dior dresses:** CHC, El Encanto Collection, Box 1, Folder: Exile Clippings, Associación de Antiguos Empleados de El Encanto, "El Encanto simboliza la magia de la Cuba de ayer."

322 **"No, I wasn't into that,":** Conversation with my father, May 12, 2022.

322 **"the mystery in question has been blocked":** Handwritten note in blank book, December 25, 2004, AC.

323 **To go to hell:** Poem by my father, August 31, 2020, in the same book, AC.

## Epilogue: History's Remains

326 **spacecraft's window than to sleep:** Interview with Aranldo Tamayo Méndez, https://www.youtube.com/watch?v=CQVib6ib1KE&t=1242s.

329 **"tired of always saying goodbye":** Ferrer, *Cuba*, 401–2.

332 **a staggering statistic:** Carla Gloria Colomé, "Cuba Gets Old," *El País*, March 10, 2025, https://english.elpais.com/international/2025-03-10/cuba-gets-older-the-island-reports-its-lowest-birth-rate-since-the-revolution.html; Claudia Gloria Colomé, "From a Population 11 Million to Little More Than 8.5: The Real Toll of Cuba's Migratory Crisis," *El País*, July 23, 2024, https://english.elpais.com/international/2024-07-23/from-a-population-of-11-million-to-little-more-than-85-million-the-real-toll-of-cubas-migratory-crisis.html.

333 **almost 650,000 Cubans:** The total for the calendar (not fiscal years) 2022, 2023, and 2024, is 647,172, https://www.cbp.gov/newsroom/stats/nationwide-encounters.

# Image Credits

**(for items not part of the author's collection)**

20 Sacramental books. Photograph by David LeFevor. Courtesy of David LaFevor, Jane Landers, and the Slave Societies Digital Archive Project, Vanderbilt University.

24 Death record of Juan Blanco. Parroquía de San Joaquín, San Luis. Libro 1, Defunciones de Pardos y Morenos, no. 90.

58 Fidel Castro enters Havana, January 8, 1959. Alamy.

112 Ciudad Libertad School, 1968. NYU, Tamiment Archives, Marvin Leiner Papers, Box 13.

112 Pages from student notebooks, Ciudad Libertad, 1968. NYU, Tamiment Archives, Marvin Leiner Papers, Box 4 and Box 10.

119 Cuban mother and son reunite after a long separation, Miami, 1966. Courtesy of the Cuban Heritage Collection, University of Miami.

138 Mariel Harbor, May 1, 1980. Associated Press.

143 Aerial view of sleeping/tent area of Camp Liberty, Eglin Air Force Base, 1980. NARA, RG343, EAFB, CRR, Box 14.

147 A group of Cuban refugees at Camp Liberty, Eglin Air Force Base, 1980. NARA, RG343, EAFB, CRR, Box 14.

151 Refugee, possibly Poly, looking at national map with volunteers, at Camp Liberty, Eglin Air Force Base, 1980. NARA, RG343, EAFB, CRR, Box 14.

290 Patients at Mazorra. Photograph by Damaris Betancourt, in *Diez días en Mazorra* (Rialta, 2021). Courtesy of Damaris Betancourt.